POSTCARD HISTORY SERIES

Southeastern Berks County

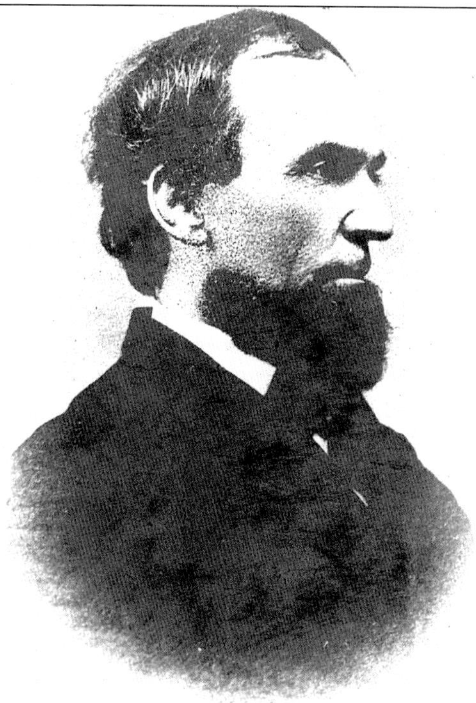

Dr. PETER G. BERTOLET,

—Son of—

Daniel and Mary Griesemer Bertolet,

was a man of unusual intelligence, an eminent physician and writer of "Oley and Vicinity," relating to the early settlers, genealogy of their families, indians and other interesting topics. Born 1822—Died 1865.

Compliments of Harvey M. Bertolet.
10th. Bertolet Family Association Meeting
Oley, Pa., August 27, 1910.

Dr. Peter Bertolet is probably one of Southeastern Berks County's best-known 19th-century Huguenot descendants. He is the embodiment of all the attributes those French ex-patriots brought to the New World. In the 1850s, he compiled a book based on the reminiscences of his grandmother Esther DeTurk Bertolet and the oral histories shared by his many elderly patients. This book, published posthumously from his handwritten notes by the Woman's Club of Oley Valley in 1980, offers people in the 21st century a glimpse of what life was like for those early settlers who learned to live among the hunters and gatherers of the Lenni-Lenape Native Americans, who were here in the early 1700s when the Europeans arrived. The two peoples appeared to live in harmony for a number of years with the Lenapes allowed to retain their custom of yearly burning of much of the lower Oley Valley basin to allow it to become a haven for small game. The settlers took the wooded areas south and north, and for a time a type of central "reservation" existed in the Oley Valley for the Native Americans. But, as is the course of history elsewhere, when the European population increased, the Lenapes were forced to move on.

On the front cover: Please see page 90. (Courtesy of Charles Moyer.)
On the back cover: Please see page 52. (Courtesy of Charles Moyer.)

POSTCARD HISTORY SERIES

Southeastern Berks County

Patricia Wanger Smith

ARCADIA
PUBLISHING

ISBN 978-0-7385-4909-5

Published by Arcadia Publishing
Charleston, South Carolina

Printed in the United States of America

Library of Congress Catalog Card Number: 2006929702

For all general information contact Arcadia Publishing at:
Telephone 843-853-2070
Fax 843-853-0044
E-mail sales@arcadiapublishing.com
For customer service and orders:
Toll-Free 1-888-313-2665

Visit us on the Internet at www.arcadiapublishing.com

Dedicated with respect to the early settlers of Southeastern Berks County who dared to venture into an unknown wilderness, dared to tame it, dared to cultivate the land, and dared to nurture families whose names endure and whose lives have strengthened the heritage of the area covered in this book.

Contents

ACKNOWLEDGMENTS

A most sincere thank-you is extended to Charles Moyer for allowing me to draw upon his extensive collection of postcards of the area. It is a treasure trove of material and comprised the majority of the cards used in this book. His knowledge of the "lore" gained from talking to the "old timers" was much appreciated as well. I wish to thank Kathryn Ballein, my friend, for her help, encouragement, and patience during the writing period, and Erin Vosgien, my editor, for her ongoing assistance in making this book a reality. The photographers of this early time are unsung heroes certainly worthy of gratitude. A thank-you must be extended to the many people of whom I have asked questions and received valuable insight as to locations of things no longer present. The Oley Woman's Club must be acknowledged for its 1980 publication of Peter Bertolet's *Fragments of the Past*. To Philip Pendleton, the late Peter Croll, and countless other unnamed writers of history whose material was absorbed by this author in the creation of this book, it is with a debt of gratitude that I offer my sincerest thanks.

INTRODUCTION

Southeastern Berks County, Pennsylvania, can be described in the following simplistic manner. As students of Berks County schools, namely the Pine Forge Consolidated School (now part of the Boyertown Area Schools), we were told by our teacher to imagine the whole of Berks County as a giant baseball field. By doing this, Reading becomes the pitcher's mound pitching south to Caenarvon Township. The area covered by this book consists of some of the first-base line. Berks County is rich in its farmland, scenic beauty, and industry; but, more importantly, its wealth of peoples and their ethnicity that have combined to create the composite hard-working, baseball-loving, stoic, intelligent individuals who have their ancestral ties to Southeastern Berks County. They hail from the townships of Oley, Exeter, Earl, Amity, Douglass, and Colebrookdale as well as the borough of Boyertown.

Native Americans of the Lenni-Lenape Tribe inhabited and enjoyed this fertile hunting ground and its myriad of fishing streams in the pre-Colonial days. Their words have become the names of many places in the area. Examples of these include Manatawny, place where we drank (liquor); Olenka, bowl, corrupted first by the German settlers to Olich (oil or fertile) and now Oley; and Popadicken, a chief's name, which has lent itself to a location near Boyertown. Of course, as with all the land in Pennsylvania, it was once the property of William Penn, who opened it to Europeans as a haven from religious persecution. Berks County was named by Penn himself after his family home in Berkshire, England. The Berks County seat of Reading was named after the principle town in his native Berkshire.

The earliest settlers to the area were the Swedes, who traveled up the Schuylkill River and who established a settlement at a place they called Morlatton, now present-day Douglassville in Amity Township. The Swedes were followed within a very short time by the French Huguenots to the eastern part of Berks County. After nearly 125 years of massacres, religious persecution, and forced wandering about Europe seeking a welcoming land, the Protestant French Huguenots embraced their newfound religious freedom in Penn's Woods. They, at one time, were the most industrious, most intelligent, and sincerely religious people in all of France. Their native country lost many of its merchants, manufacturers, and skilled artisans who carried their gifts to their places of exile in Germany, Switzerland, and other Rhine countries and from there to the New World. From England came the sons and daughters of landed gentry as well as the common worker. Some of these were Quakers fresh from Newgate Prison. The Welsh joined the mix with laborers for the iron industry. The native Germans and Swiss brought their gifts of farming. What a wonderful blending of cultures to tame the wilderness and make it home! It is that blending that has produced the Berks County folk of today.

Most of these people arrived in the early 1700s to the Berks area in a western movement within Penn's Woods from Philadelphia, specifically the Germantown area. By 1752, the county of Berks was incorporated from portions of Chester, Lancaster, and Philadelphia Counties. Usually when people refer to the Pennsylvania Dutch, Lancaster County comes to mind; however, Berks

Countians for the most part are no less a part of this ethnic root. The Lancaster Countians were primarily from the "plain" religious sects such as Mennonites and Amish, while the settlers of Berks County were from more of the German Reformed and German Lutheran religions.

Small towns and villages sprang up as more people converged in settling the "frontier." These hamlets provided the stores, merchants, and artisans to serve the farmers as they came to trade crops and livestock for goods and services. The creeks of the area, primarily the Manatawny, became the basis for powering the numerous mills—grist, lumber, fulling, and paper. The creeks were also instrumental in the establishment of the numerous iron forges that began in the 1700s. Most notable of these was Pool Forge. Thomas Rutter, an English Quaker friend of William Penn, was encouraged by Penn to venture from Philadelphia to an area 40 miles to the west where iron ore had been found. At the base of Pool Hill, along the Manatawny Creek in Douglass Township near present-day Pine Forge, Rutter and his men built a primitive charcoal iron smelting operation, the first in the colony.

Exeter Township was a part of Oley Township until the mid-1700s, as was Earl Township. The ancestors of two well-known Americans came from the Exeter area. George Boone, grandfather of Daniel Boone, arrived in 1717 in the Exeter area at the urging of William Penn. A little known fact is that Kit Carson, another pioneer, was the grandson of Daniel Boone. Excerpts from P. C. Croll's *Annals of Berks County* say that "Boone led the way across the Appalachians, Crockett across the Mississippi and Carson across the Rockies." Abraham Lincoln's great-great-grandfather was also an early landowner in the area.

It is my most sincere wish that the postcards and narratives in this book will present you, the reader, with a deeper understanding, knowledge, and appreciation of this unique area as it was in earlier days and to seek further knowledge from the Berks County Historical Society as well as the local historical societies and commissions. I am proud to be a descendant of those immigrants who made Eastern Berks County a very special place in which to live.

One

Oley and Exeter

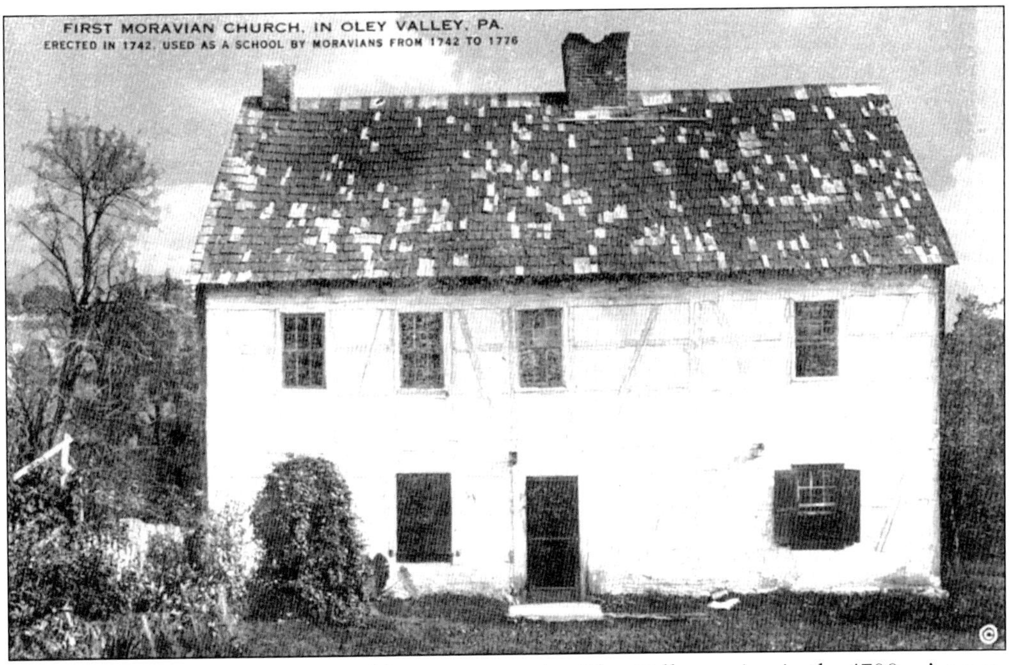

Many religious sects were spawned in or came to the Oley Valley region in the 1700s. Among these were the Moravians, a zealous Protestant group sometimes called United Brethren. The Moravians from Europe were well known for their missions among the so-called "heathens" of the world. Establishing themselves in Bethlehem, Pennsylvania, they founded this church in Oley in 1742 to baptize. They also formed a school to teach the Native Americans and others of the Oley Valley.

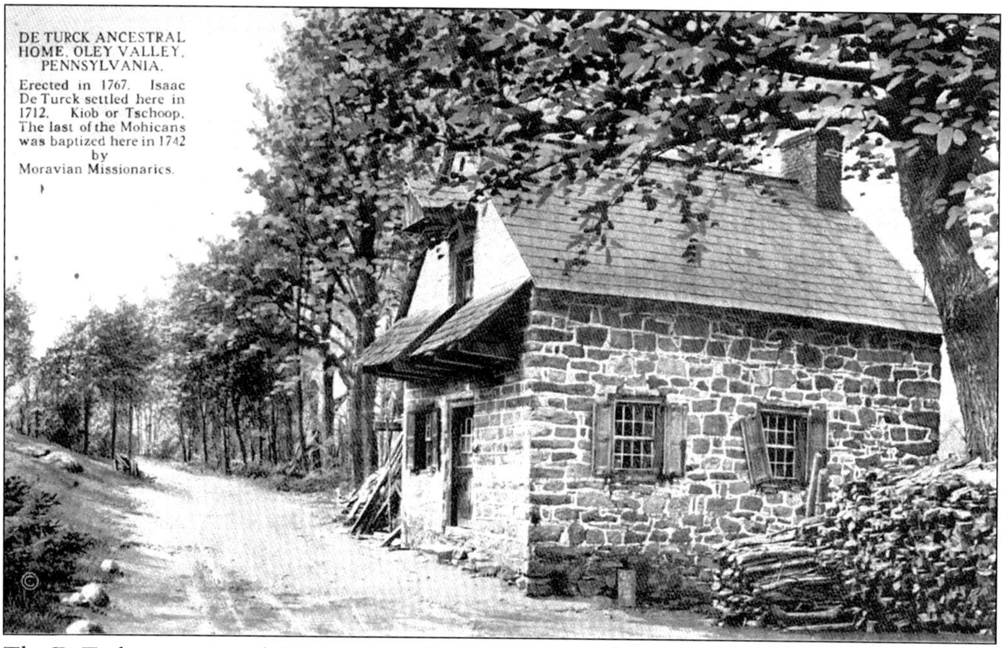

The DeTurks were French Huguenots who aligned themselves with the Moravian church. This ancestral cabin still stands just south of Oley village. A small stream lying just behind it may have been the site of the baptism of Tscoop, the last of the Mohicans to be converted in this area.

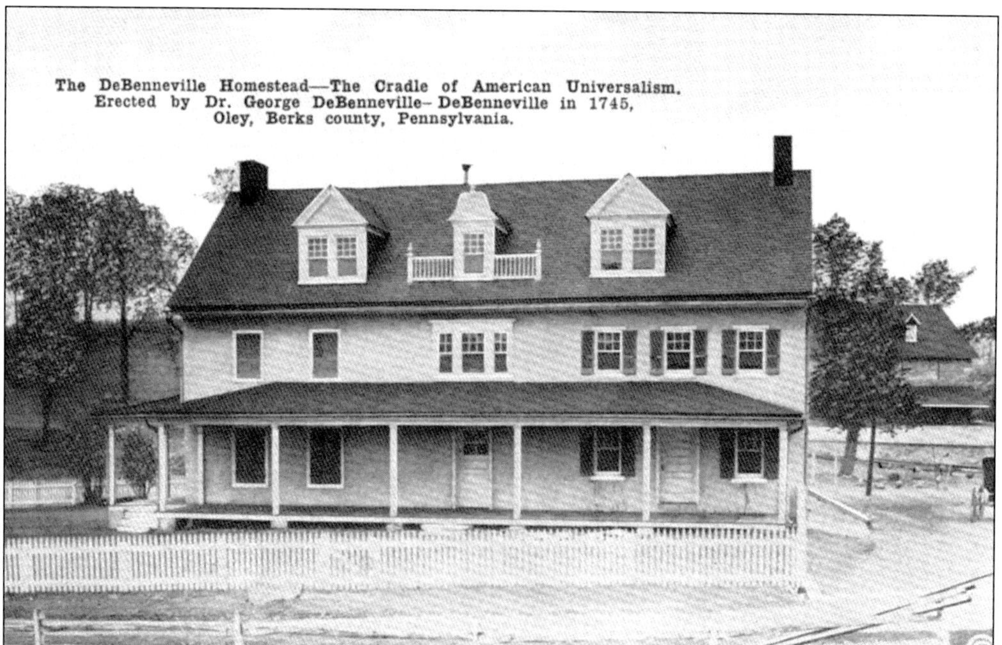

George DeBenneville, another early Huguenot, arrived here in 1743 from Germantown, Pennsylvania. At the invitation of Jean Bertolet, one of the earliest Huguenots in the valley, DeBenneville came to the valley to preach, practice medicine, and teach school. In 1745, he married Bertolet's daughter Esther and built this lovely home that still stands today.

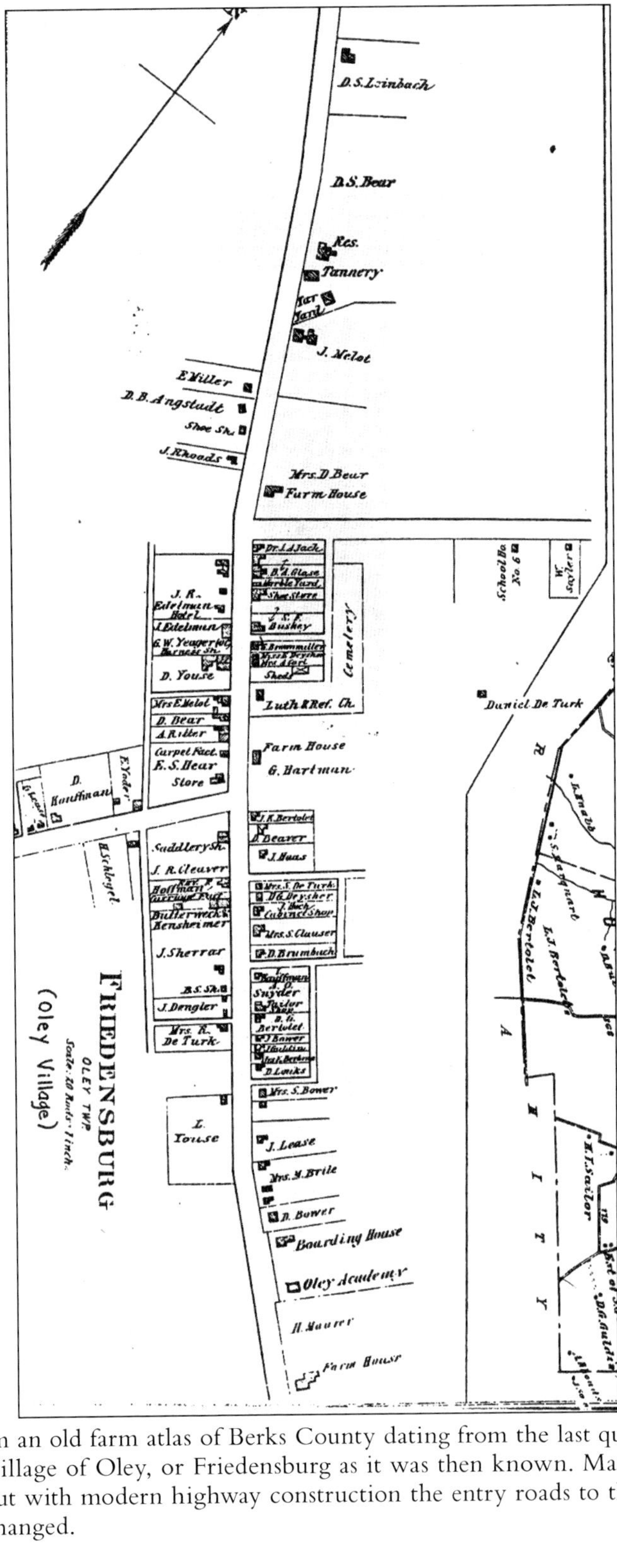

This map is from an old farm atlas of Berks County dating from the last quarter of the 1800s and shows the village of Oley, or Friedensburg as it was then known. Many of these homes remain today, but with modern highway construction the entry roads to the village in some instances have changed.

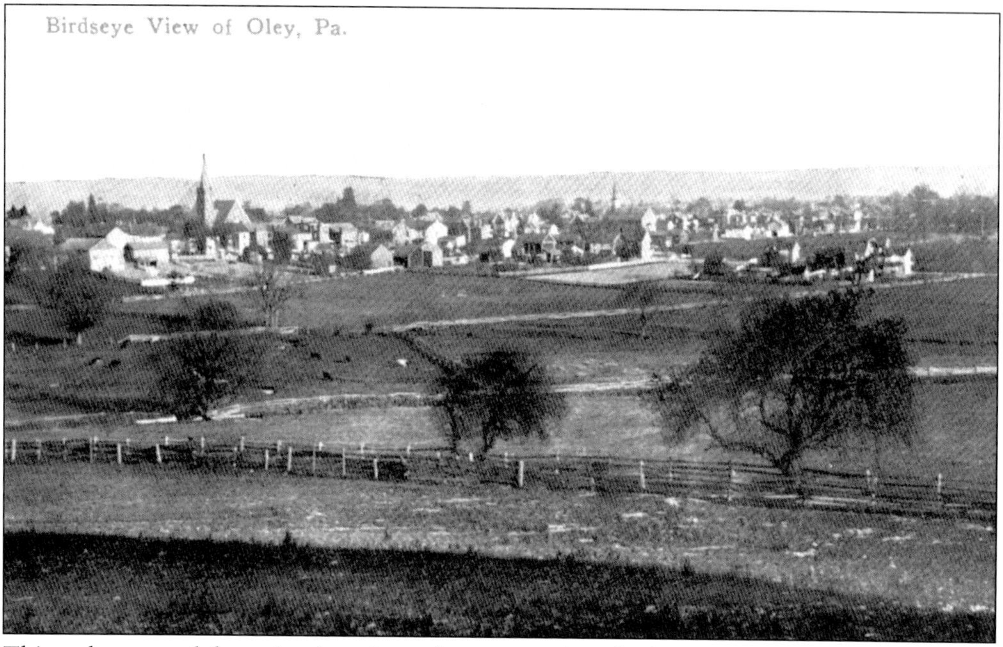

This early postcard shows just how large the community of Oley was in the early 20th century. Yet it is totally surrounded by rolling hills and verdant meadows. The descendants of the early settlers saved much of this rural atmosphere when they had the foresight to preserve Oley Township on the National Historic Register as a National Historic Site. The spire of Freiden's Church is most evident to the left.

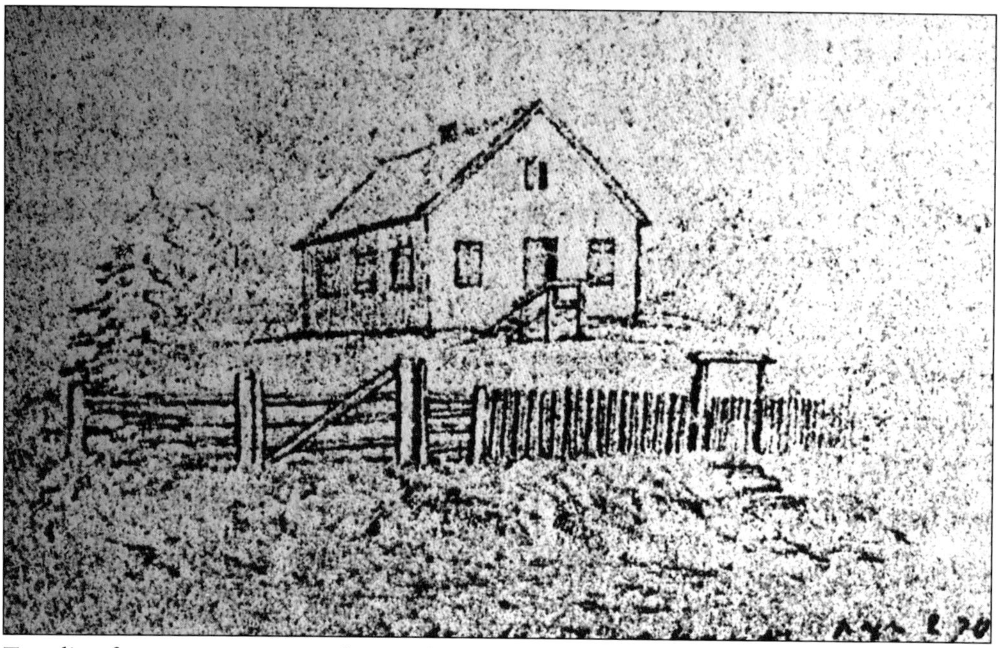

Traveling from east to west on what was known as the Philadelphia-Hamburg Road, seen here is a meetinghouse built by Daniel Bertolet Sr., Jean Bertolet's grandson. Built in the mid-1800s at Daniel's own expense as a nondenominational chapel, it opened its doors to all who preached the gospel. The picture is from Dr. Peter Bertolet's book, *Fragments of History*.

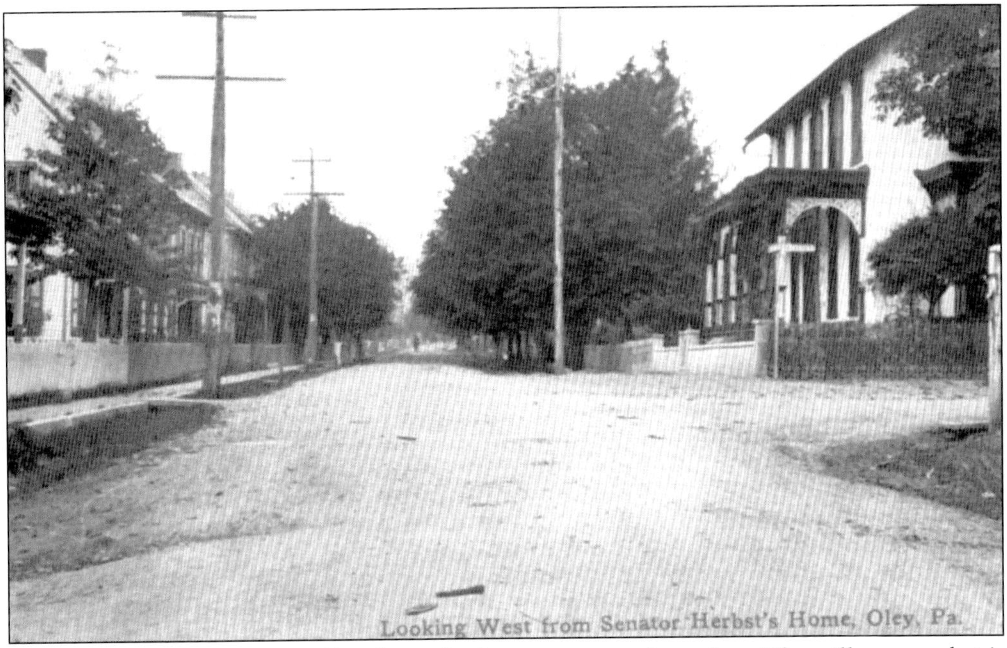

From Daniel Bertolet's sawmill and meetinghouse, one continues into Oley village on what is now Main Street where one finds a commercial establishment. It appears to be the hotel of a Mr. Rhoads, located on the northeast corner of Main and Jefferson Streets. Please note the hitching area for horses and buggies. The postmark on the card reads 1906.

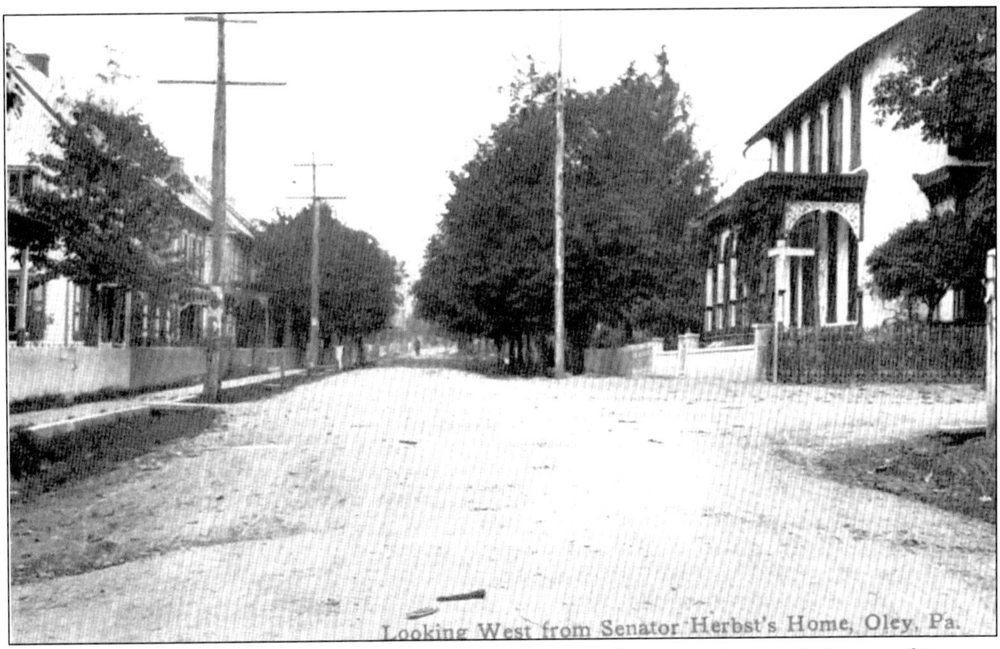

This view places one just west of the previous picture and depicts the stately home of Senator Herbst. The home still stands on the northwest corner of Jefferson and Main Streets.

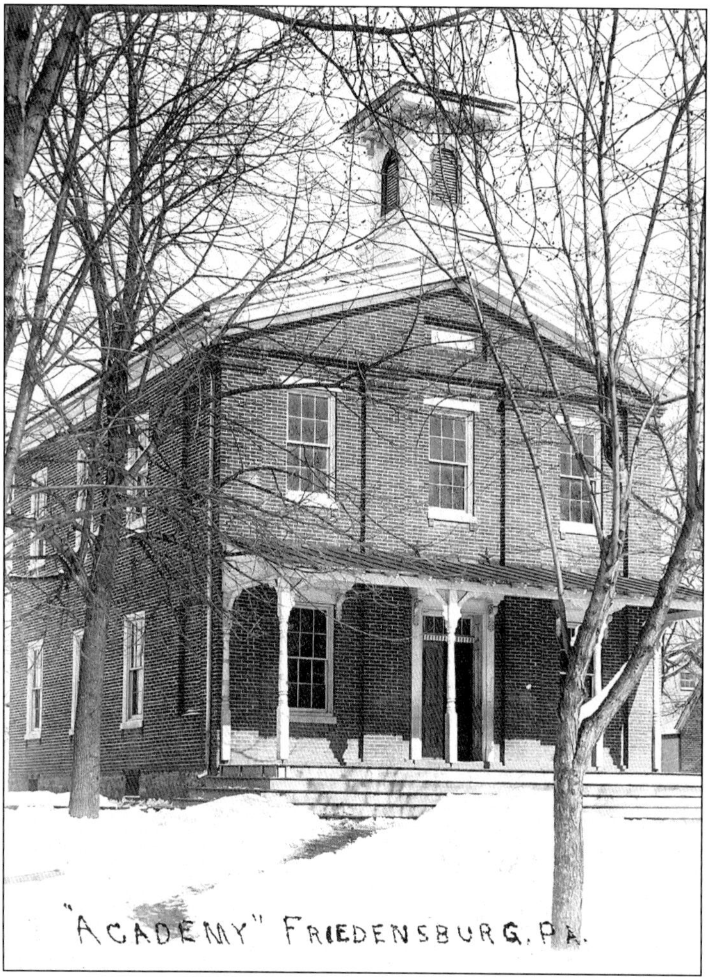

Next on the north side of Main Street was the Oley Academy established as a private school in 1857 to meet the academic needs of a community that would not vote to improve the public schools. Costing about $3,000, it accommodated up to 80 students. Well known for its advanced courses, providing for those wishing to go on to higher education, it remained a viable institution until the establishment of Keystone State Normal School (Kutztown University).

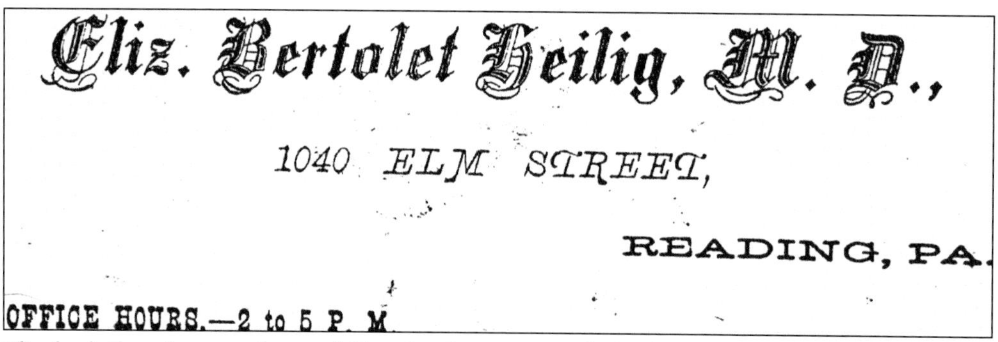
Eliz. Bertolet Heilig, M. D.,

1040 ELM STREET,

READING, PA.

OFFICE HOURS.—2 to 5 P. M.

Elizabeth Bertolet, a graduate of Oley Academy, pursued a higher education at Mount Holyoke Academy in Massachusetts and later at Womens College of Pennsylvania in Philadelphia where she received a medical degree. She became the first female physician in Berks County but left her practice to become a farmer's wife. She and her husband, Francis Heilig, are buried at the Bertolet Meeting House Cemetery.

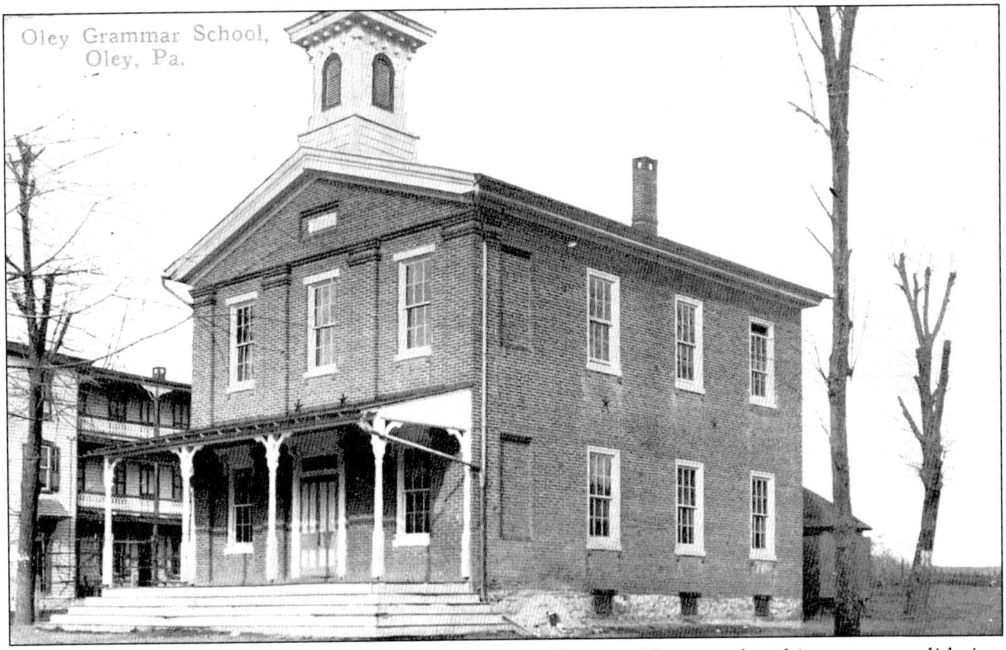

In 1905, the academy became the Oley Grammar School. It would appear that this was a consolidation of several Oley-area grammar schools. The academy had remained in existence for nearly 50 years. With many architectural changes, the academy now houses the local fire company.

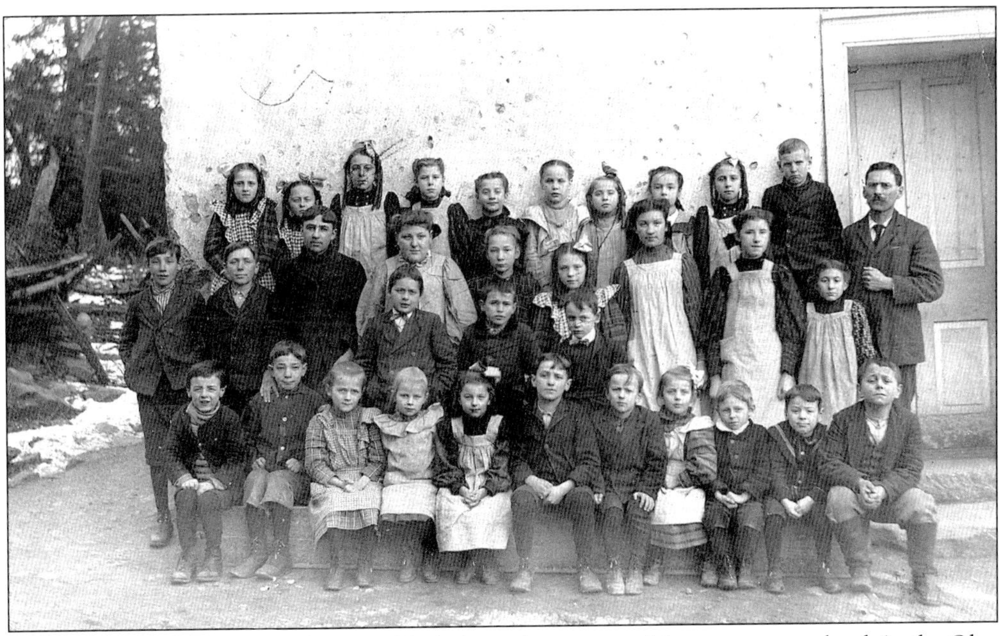

Seen here are some students shown with their teacher at one of the one-room schools in the Oley area. It would appear from their dress that this was taken between 1900 and 1910. The school would have provided education for grades one through eight. Thirty-three pupils are shown here, making the average number in each grade about four.

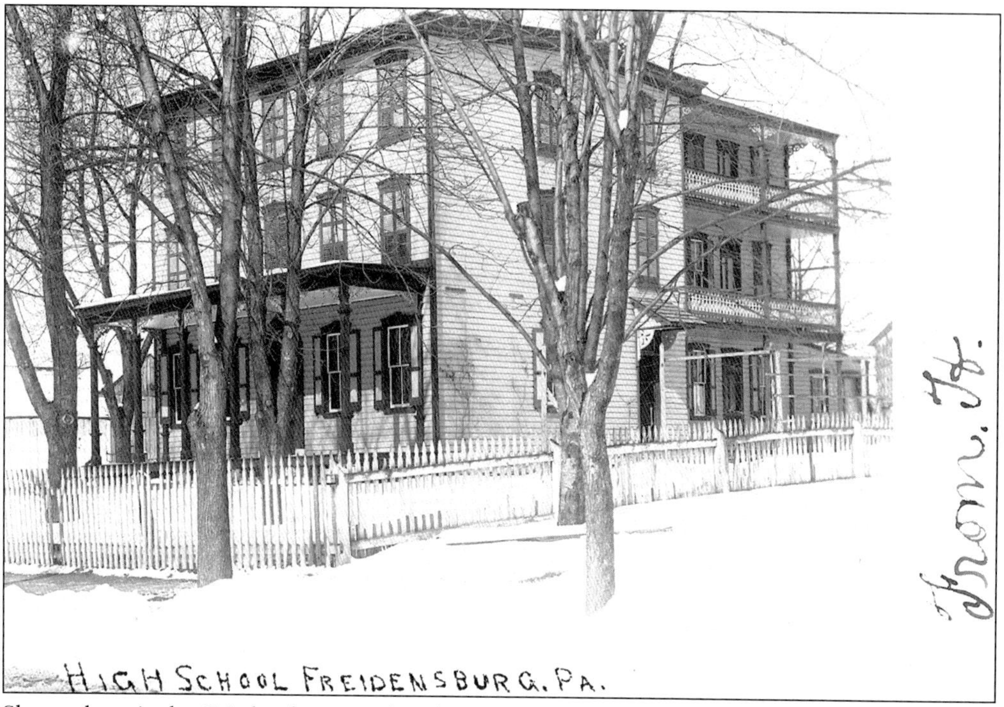

Shown here is the Friedensburg High School, which was on the west side of the academy. A nearby student boarding home was discussed by Dr. Bertolet in his book. It is likely this was the same building. Children could leave school at age 14 or after completion of the eighth grade. Many left to help their parents on the farm.

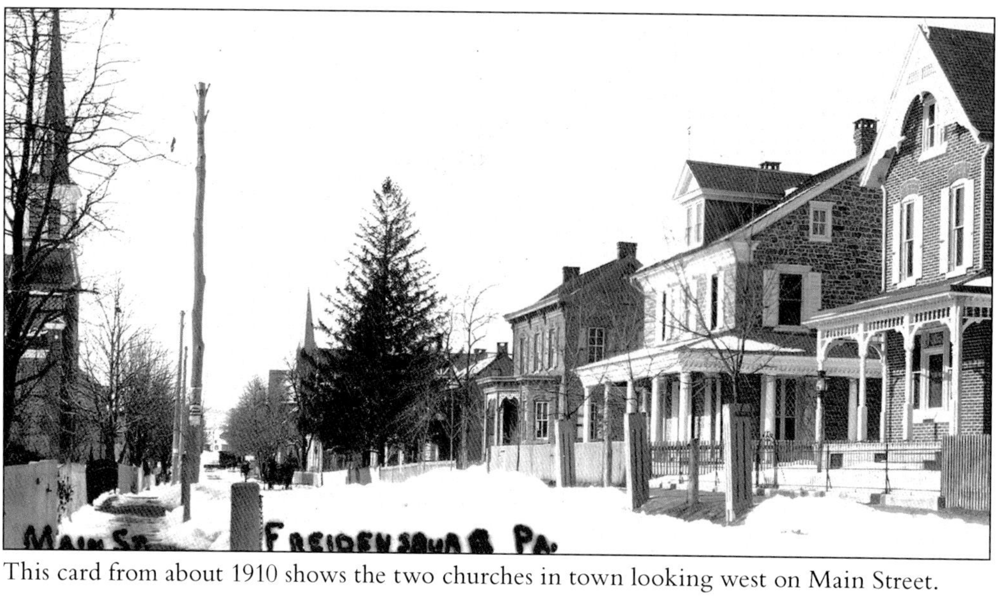

This card from about 1910 shows the two churches in town looking west on Main Street.

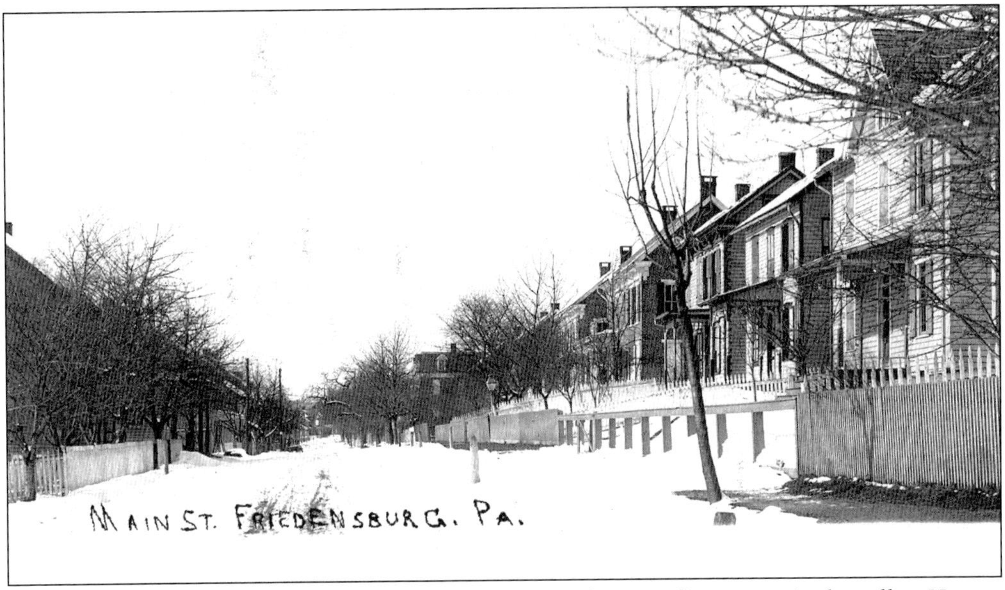

A snow scene brings to mind a story related by Dr. Bertolet regarding snows in the valley. He was told, by a relative, that snows averaging four feet fell in the 1700s, isolating the scattered settlements in the area. The snows eventually settled, crusted over, and became avenues of conveyance via sleds and sleighs. The fences were buried and no longer were impediments to travel.

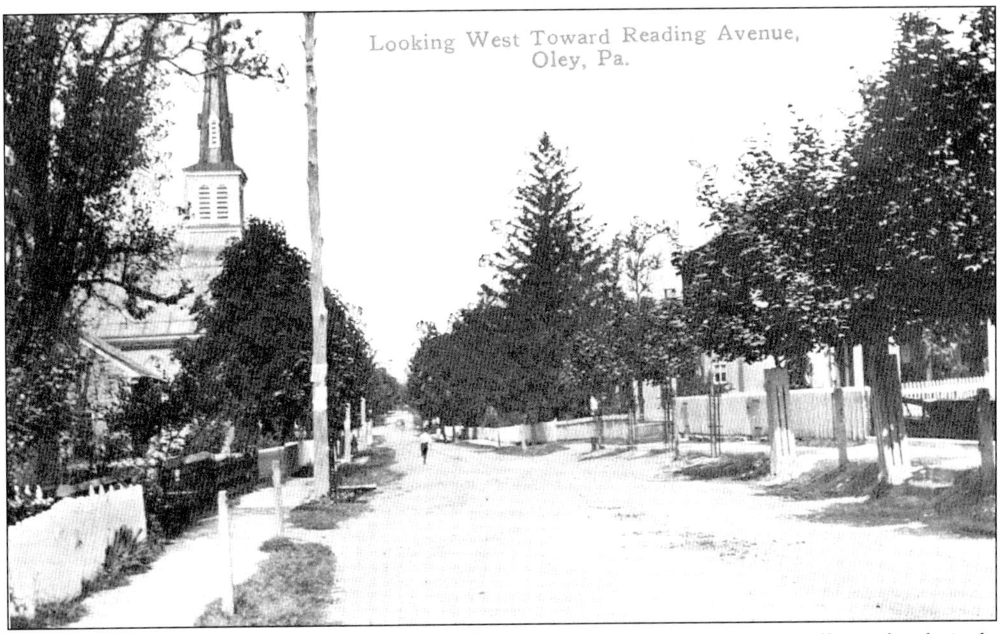

In this scene one is looking west toward Reading Avenue. It appears that sidewalks with relatively young protected trees are evident, although Main Street remains a dirt road.

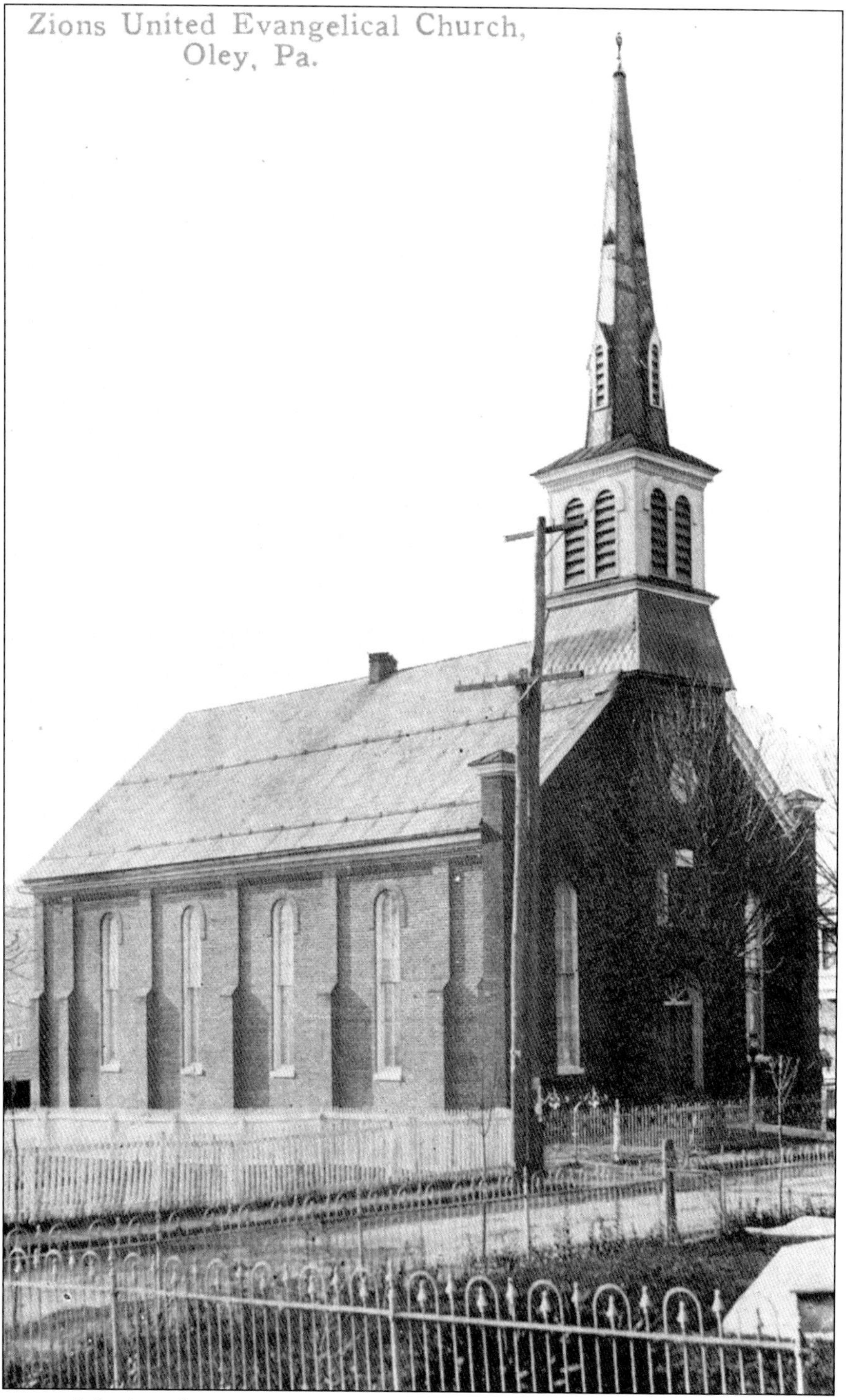

This postcard depicts the Zion United Evangelical Church on Main Street. The original congregation met in a meetinghouse built in 1853 on the north side of Main Street on Meeting House Lane. The congregation of that early church met twice a week with services in both German and English.

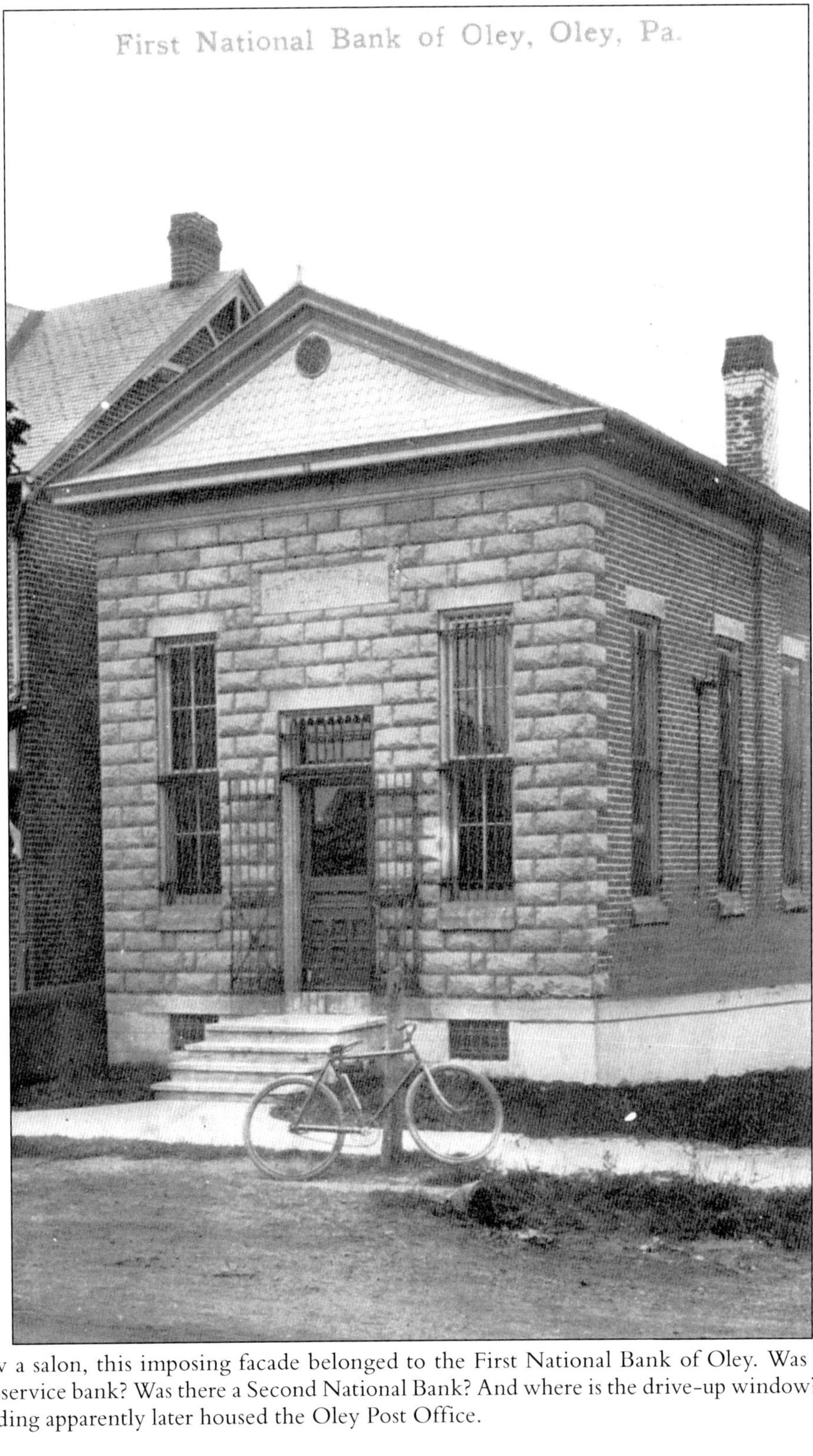

Now a salon, this imposing facade belonged to the First National Bank of Oley. Was this a full-service bank? Was there a Second National Bank? And where is the drive-up window? This building apparently later housed the Oley Post Office.

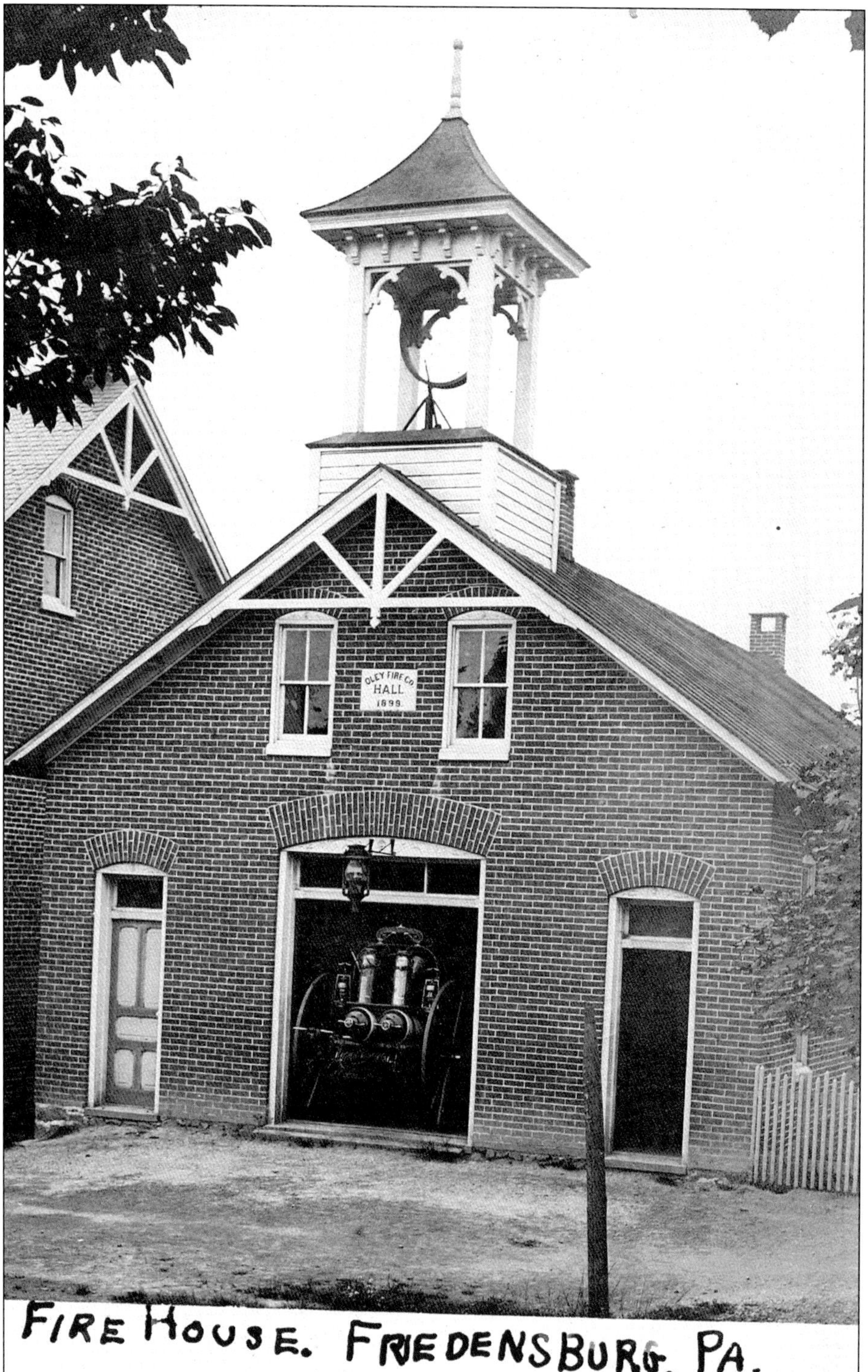

On the south side of Main Street in the 400 block was the firehouse established in 1898. The building remains and is now a youth center. Please note the old fire apparatus and the early lamp above the door.

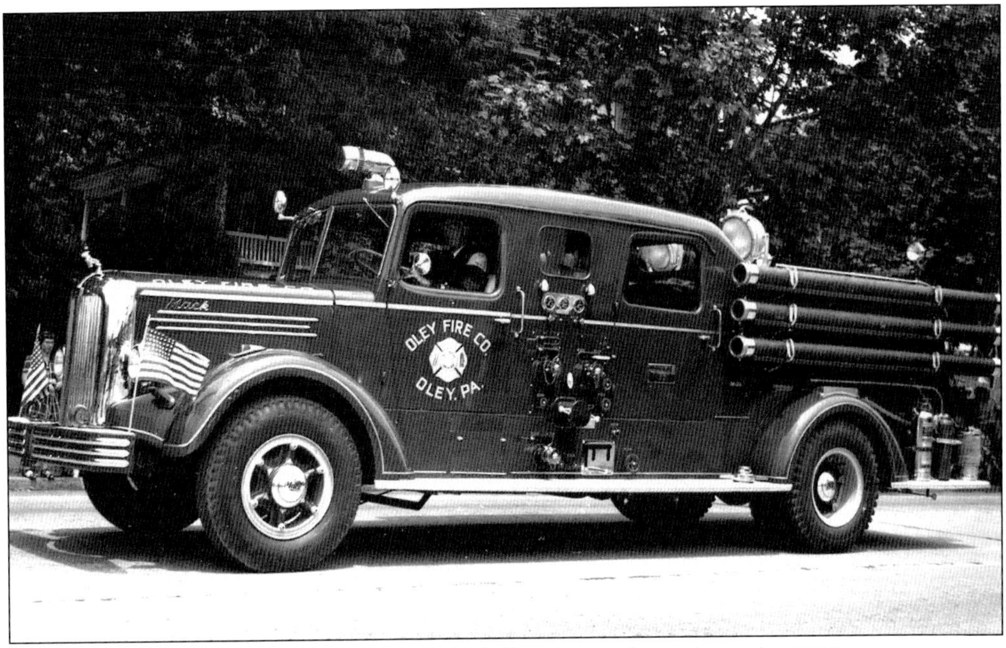

Seen here in a patriotic parade is a great Mack fire engine from about the 1930s.

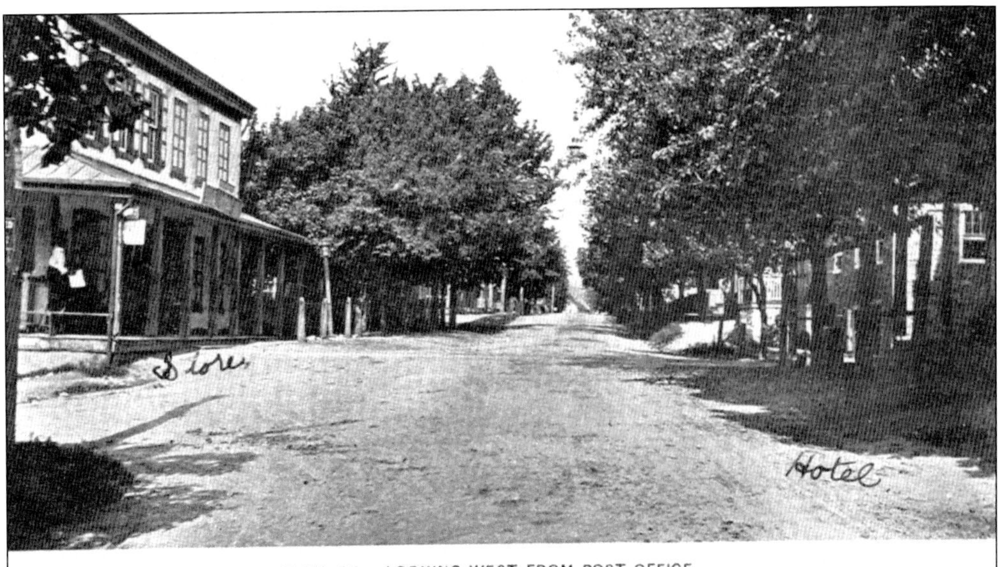

This view is just east of Friedensburg Road looking west. The sender of this card has kindly indicated the store on the south side and the hotel on the north.

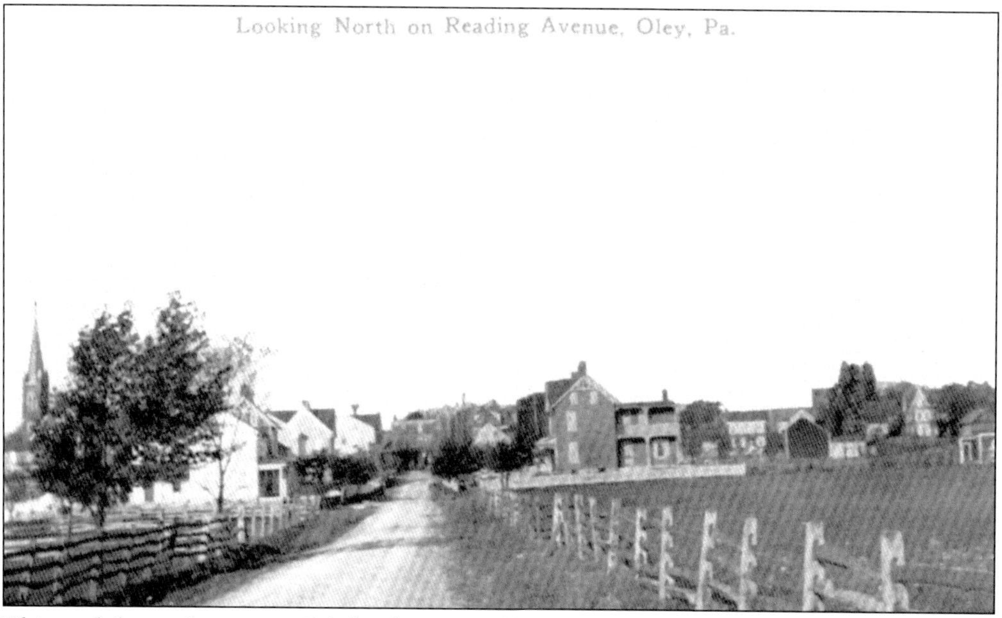

This card shows the current Friedensburg Road leading to the hotel, which can be seen at the far end of the road. Also visible is the Friedens Church spire. Some of these homes remain.

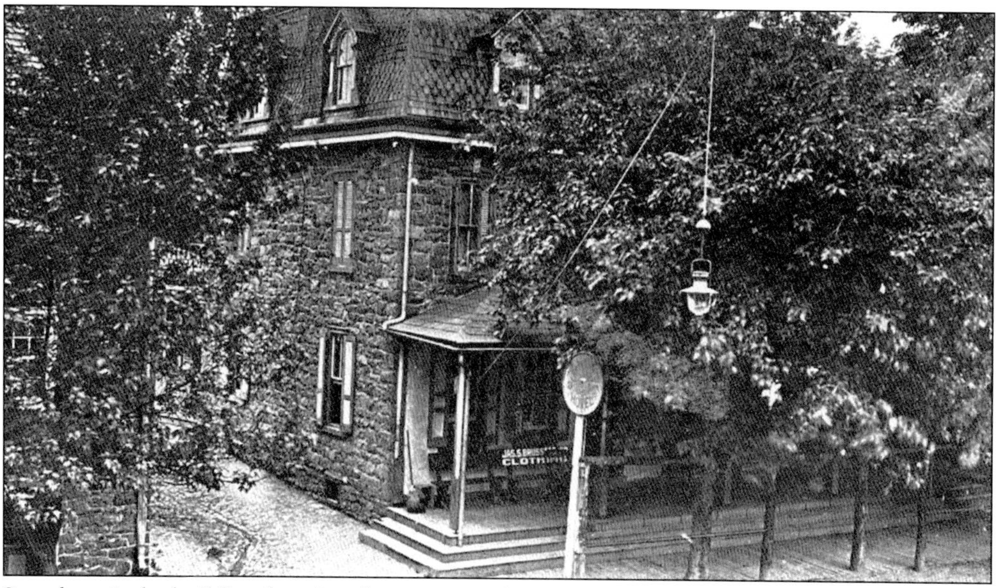

Seen here is the building housing the current Oley Valley Inn, a lovely place in which to dine. In this picture it appears to be a clothing store. Please note the great streetlamp similar to the one at the firehouse.

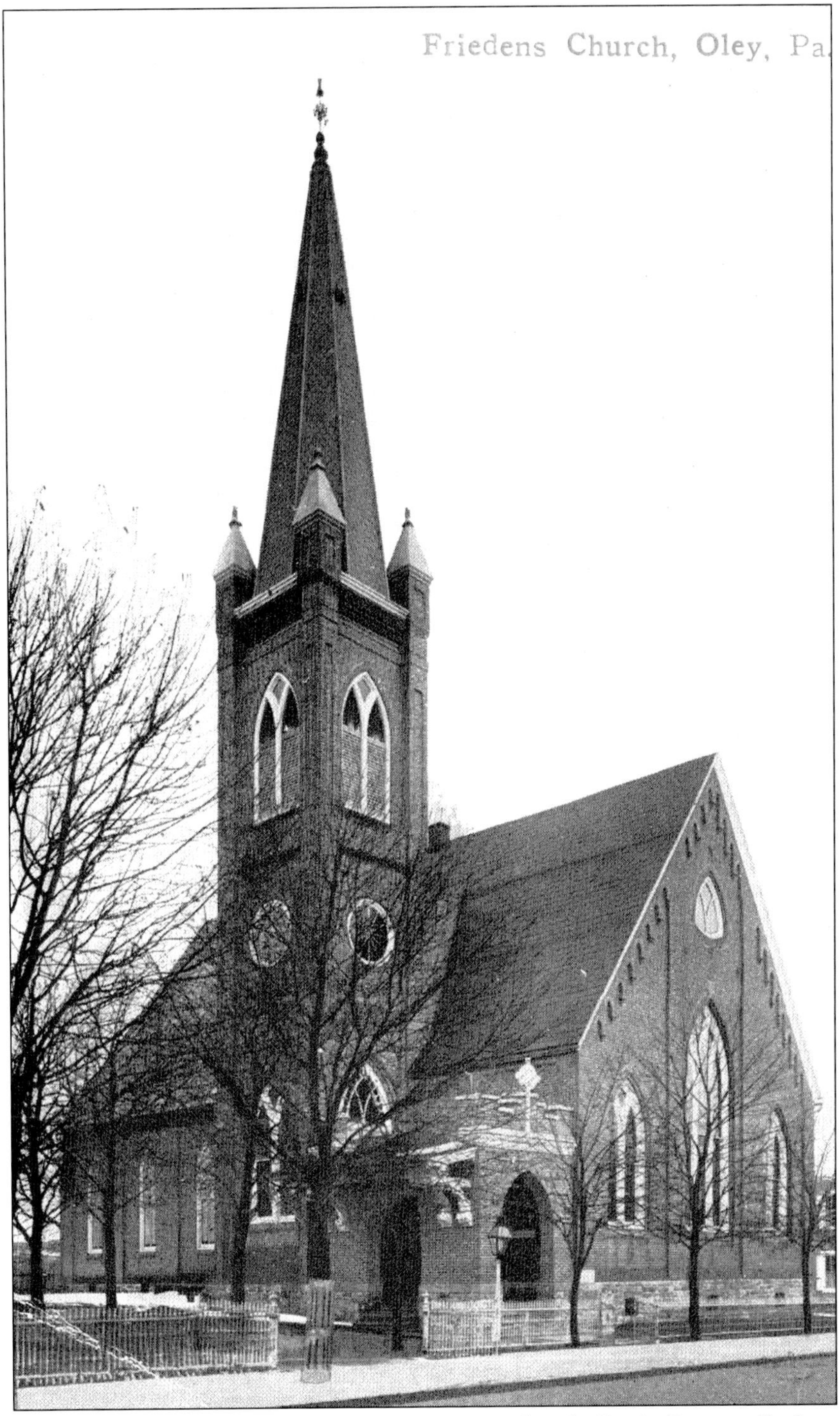

Friedens Church was established in 1832 as a union church. Both German Reformed and Lutheran congregations worshipped here. It has remained a United Church of Christ, while the Lutherans have built a new edifice south of town. A large cemetery north of this church is the final resting place for many of the Oley Valley's early residents.

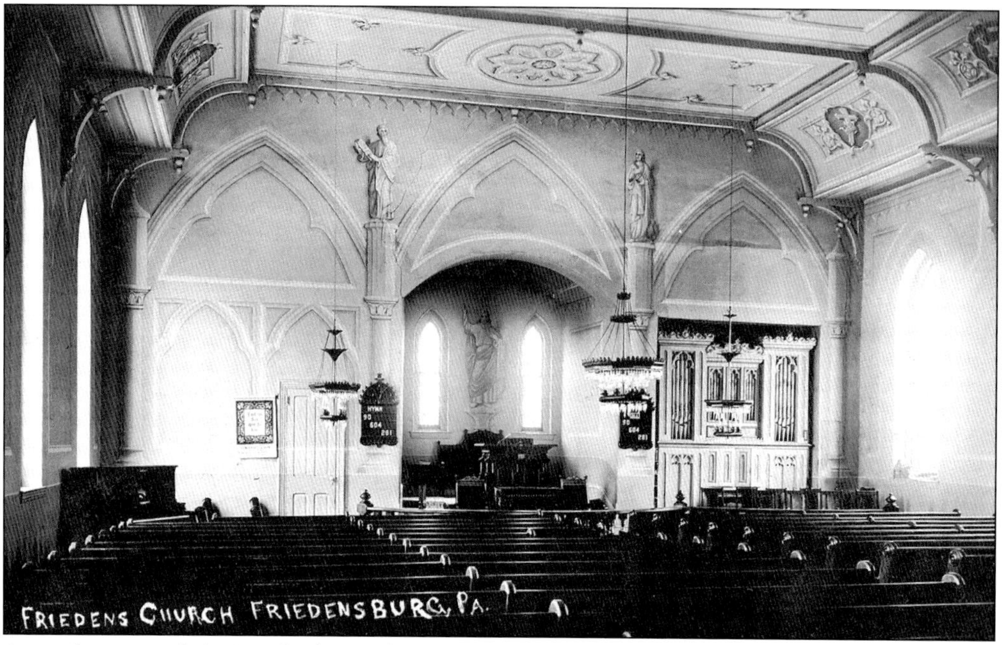

An early postcard depicts the beautiful interior of Friedens Church. Please note especially the beautiful ceiling, figures, and wonderful chandeliers. The present church dates from 1886.

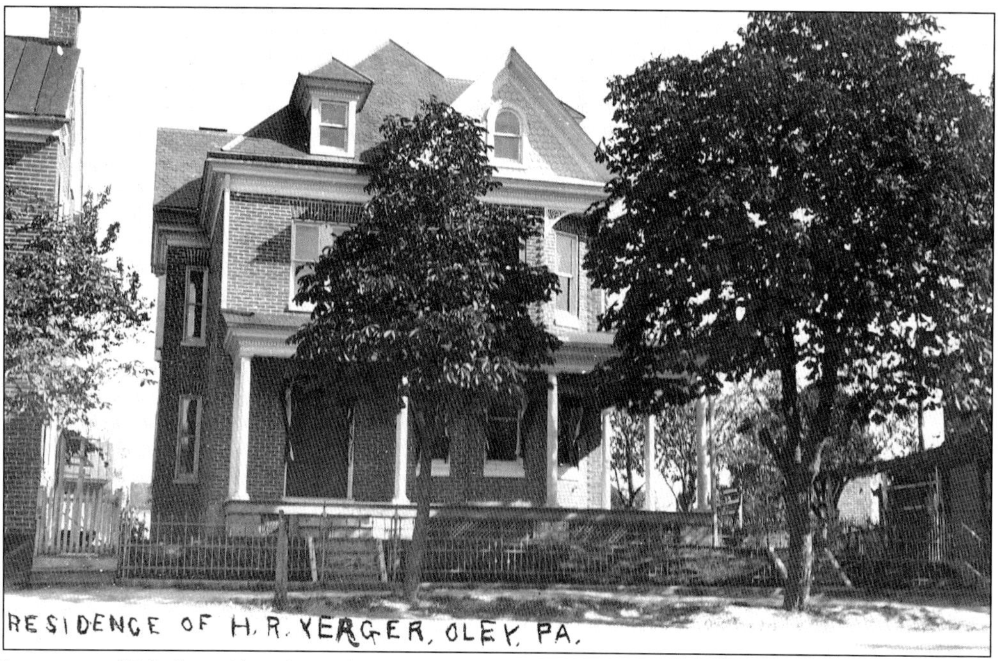

Just west of Friedens Church on the north side of Main Street is the elegant home belonging at one time to H. R. Yerger, the store owner.

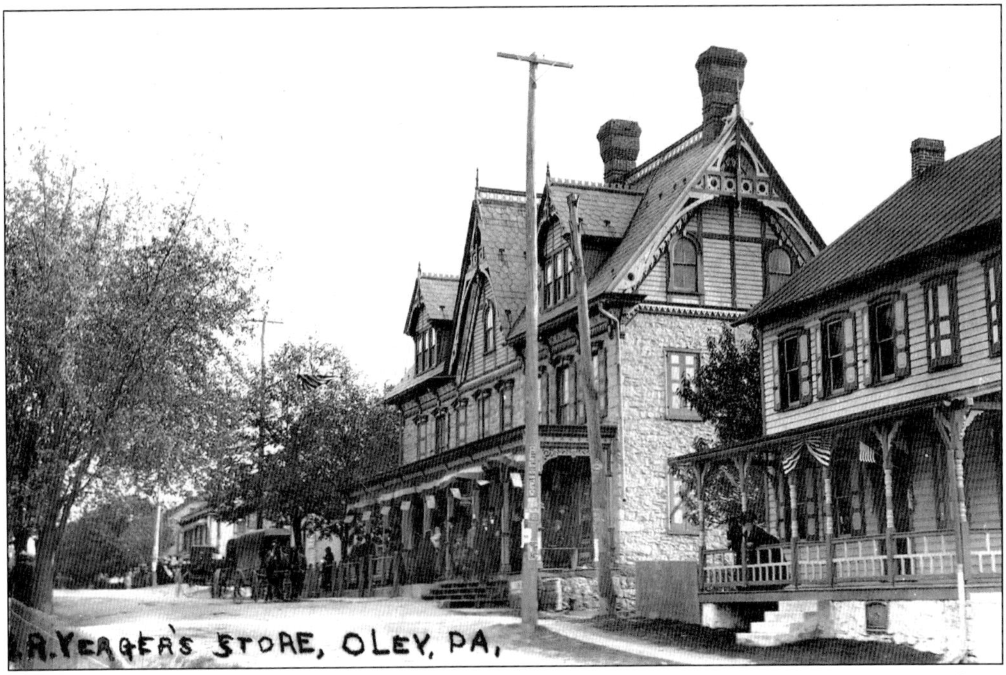

This is the former Yerger Store on the south side of Main Street, almost directly across from Yerger's residence. Please note the slate roof and the wonderful Victorian gingerbread trim on this still-standing stone building. This building is a wonderful example of the beautiful grey stone present in many early Oley Valley residences, barns, and commercial buildings.

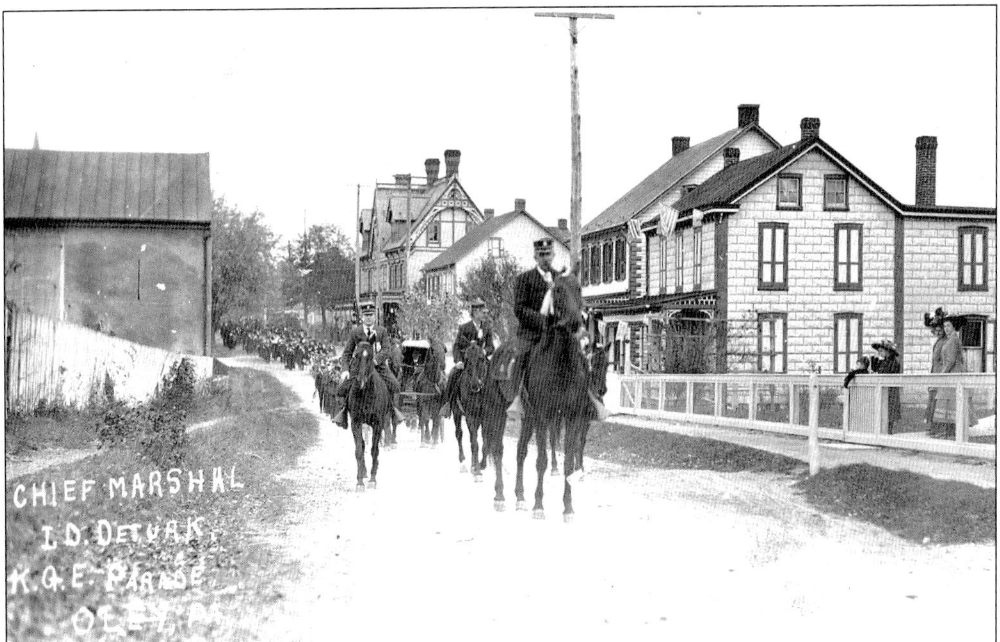

Leaving the westerly edge of town, the Knights of the Golden Eagle can be seen as they parade west on Main Street. I. D. DeTurk is the chief marshal. The Yerger Store is seen in the center background of this early card.

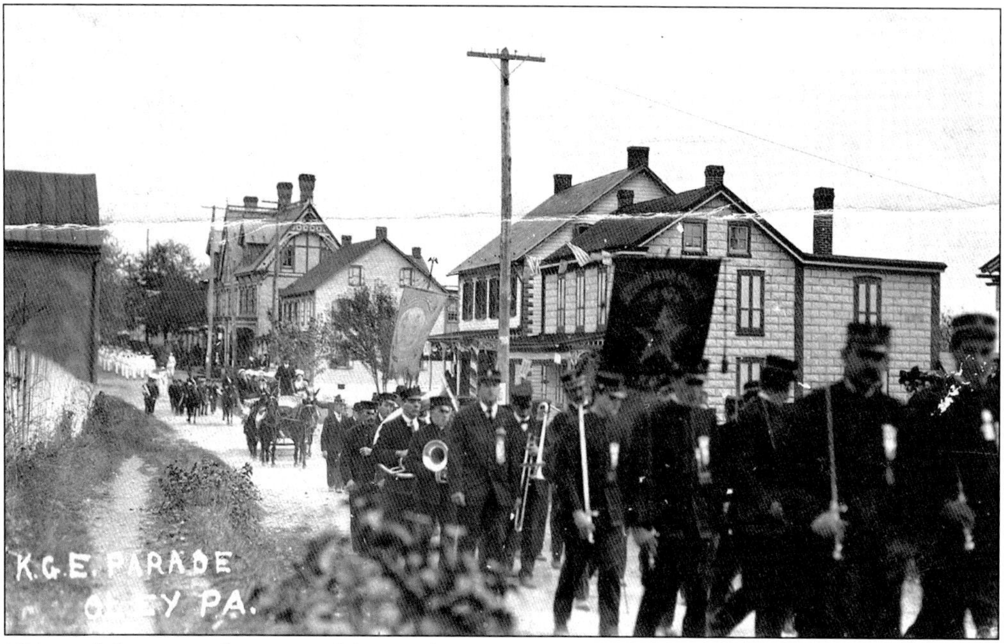

This card shows another view of the gentlemen in the parade. It has been said that there were so many lodges and fraternal orders in the late 1800s and early 1900s that a man could have every evening taken with one meeting or another.

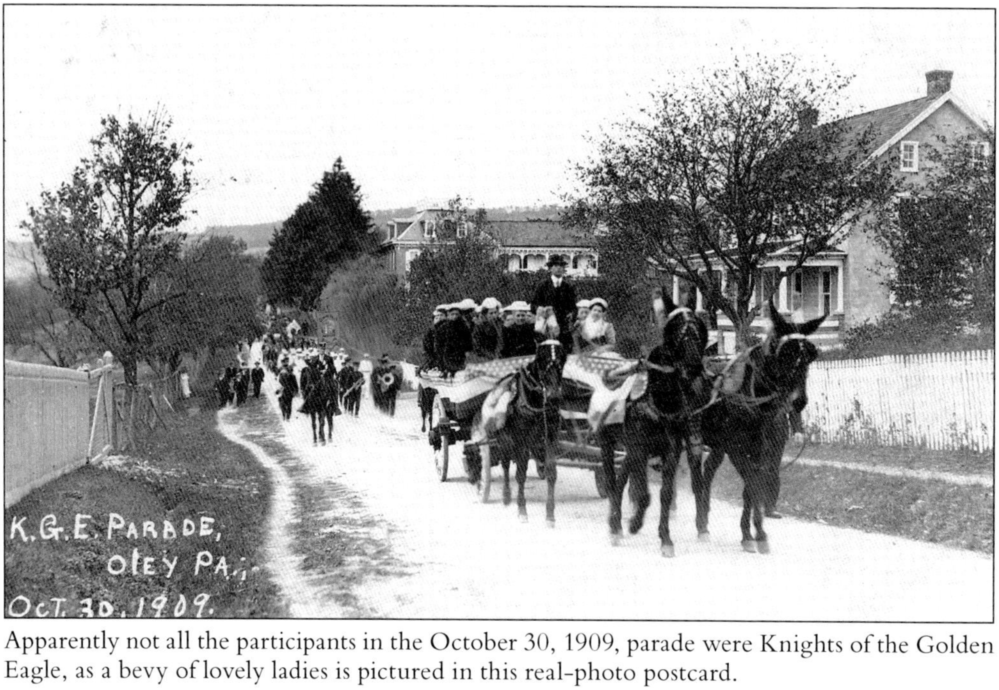

Apparently not all the participants in the October 30, 1909, parade were Knights of the Golden Eagle, as a bevy of lovely ladies is pictured in this real-photo postcard.

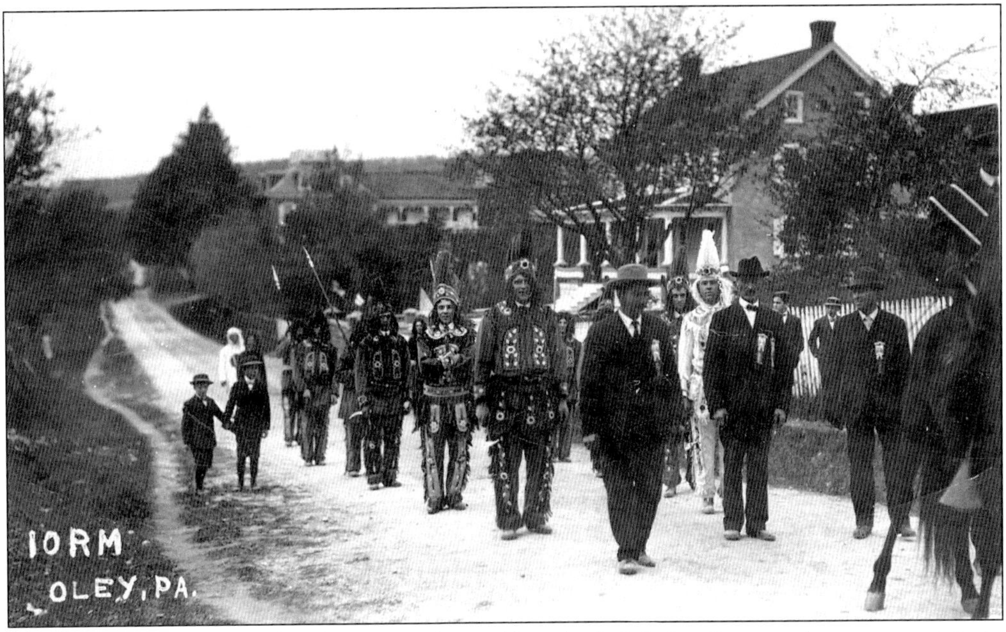

The Independent Order of Red Men are pictured here in their lodge finery as they, too, participate in an Oley parade. It is not known if they celebrated with the Knights on the previous page or if this was an independent parade.

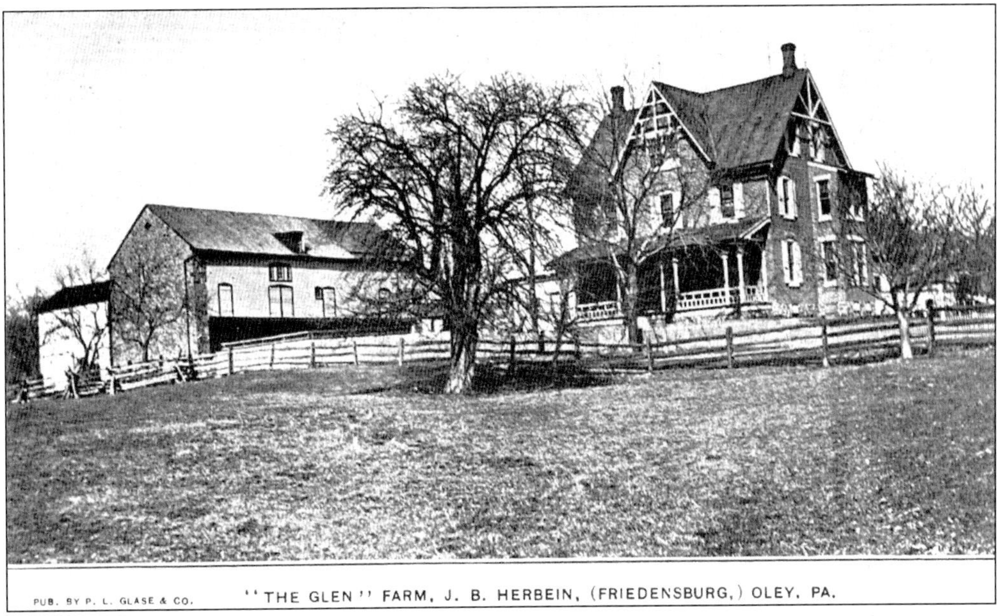

"The Glen," a farm previously owned by J. B. Herbein, graces the north side of West Main Street. It is still standing.

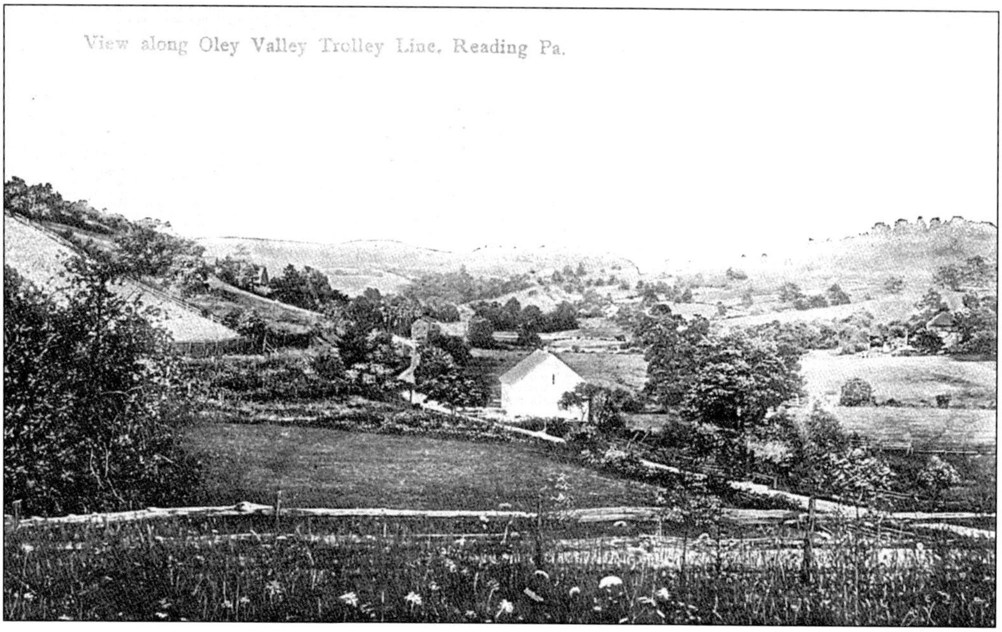

The Oley Valley Trolley Line ran through the Oley Valley from Reading, the county seat, to Boyertown. It came through many small hamlets including Limekiln where the old bed can easily be seen. It certainly would have been a much faster form of travel than the horse and buggy or even the early automobiles.

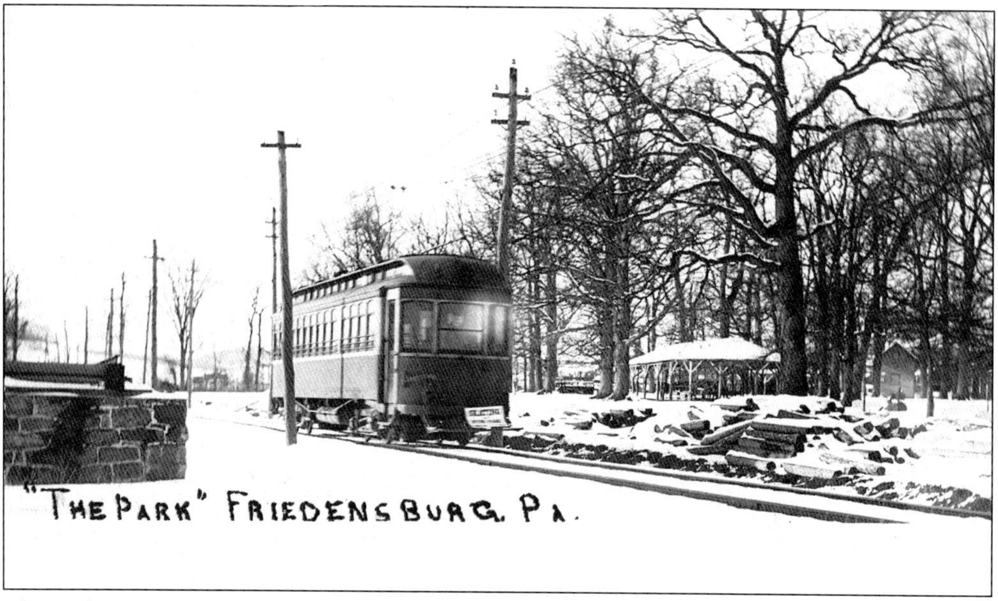

The park at Friedensburg was a delightful spot to picnic with friends, although perhaps not in the snow. It was located about halfway between Reading and Boyertown.

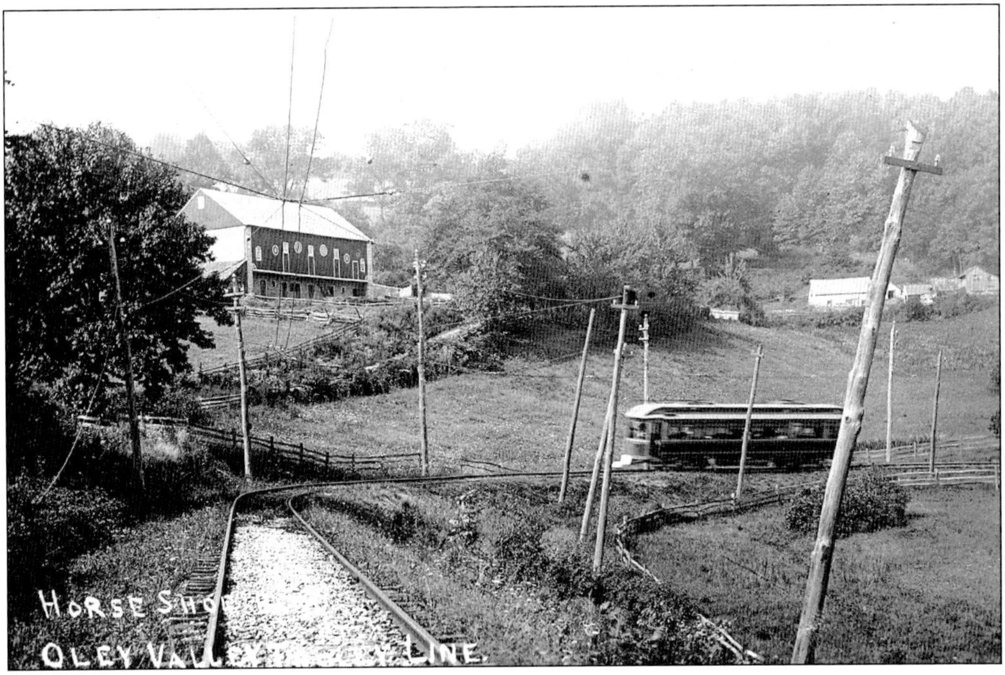

While there is a much more famous Horseshoe Curve on a railroad in Pennsylvania, this would have been very special to those riding the local rails. This trolley line traversed some of the most beautiful farmland in the county, as well as the country.

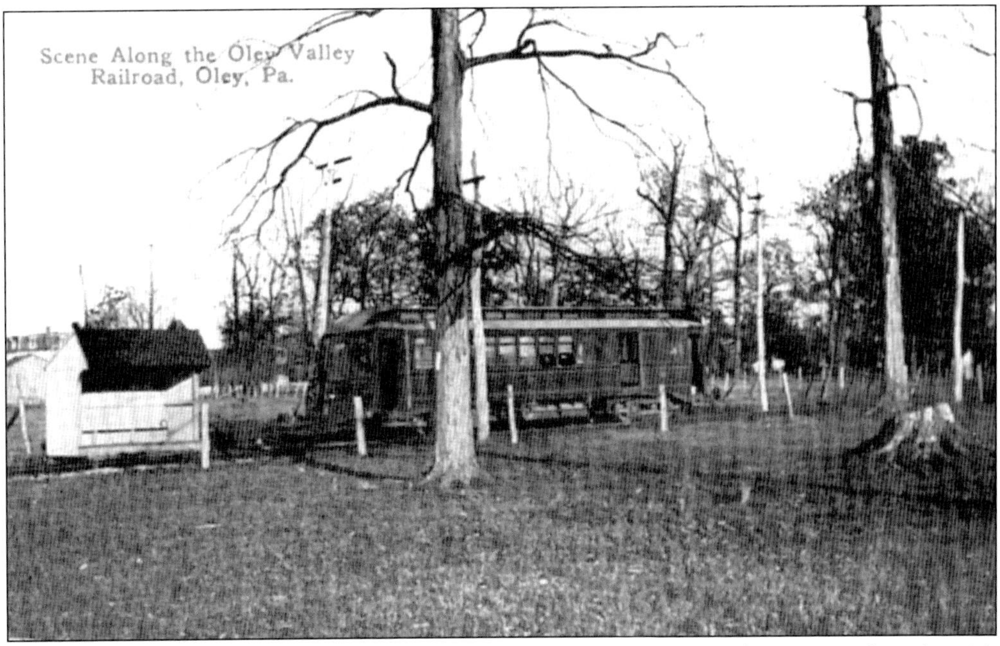

Another scene of the railway is offered. Here is a shelter for use in inclement weather. As with other trolley services in Southeastern Pennsylvania, the Oley Trolley Line probably encouraged visiting the Oley Park as a way to garner more fares.

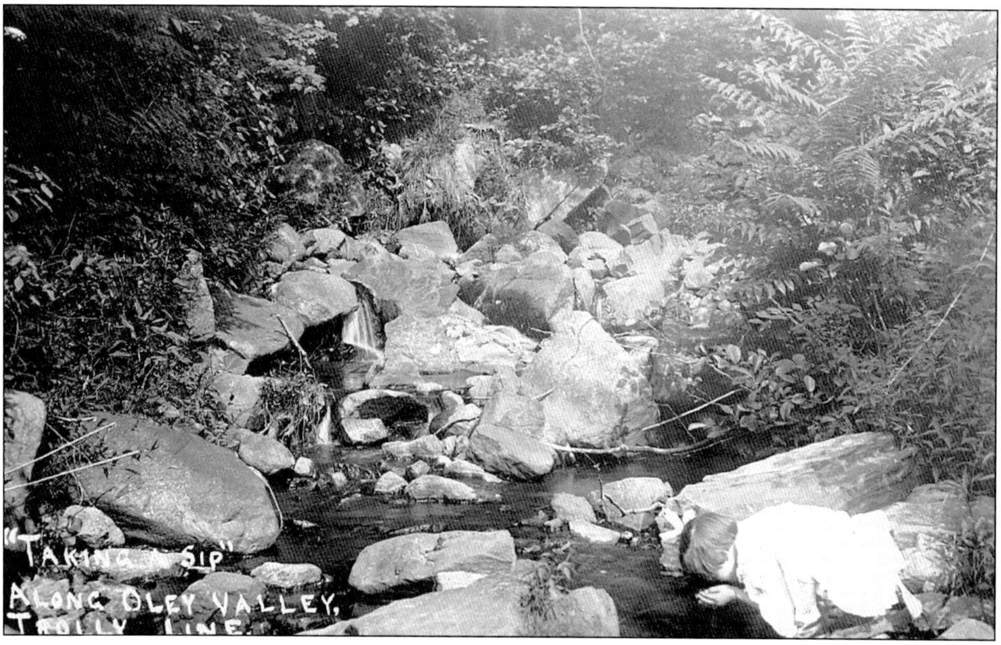

This is not a recommended way of quenching one's thirst in the 21st century. It took less than 100 years to contaminate this pure water. No responsible parents today would allow their child to drink like this.

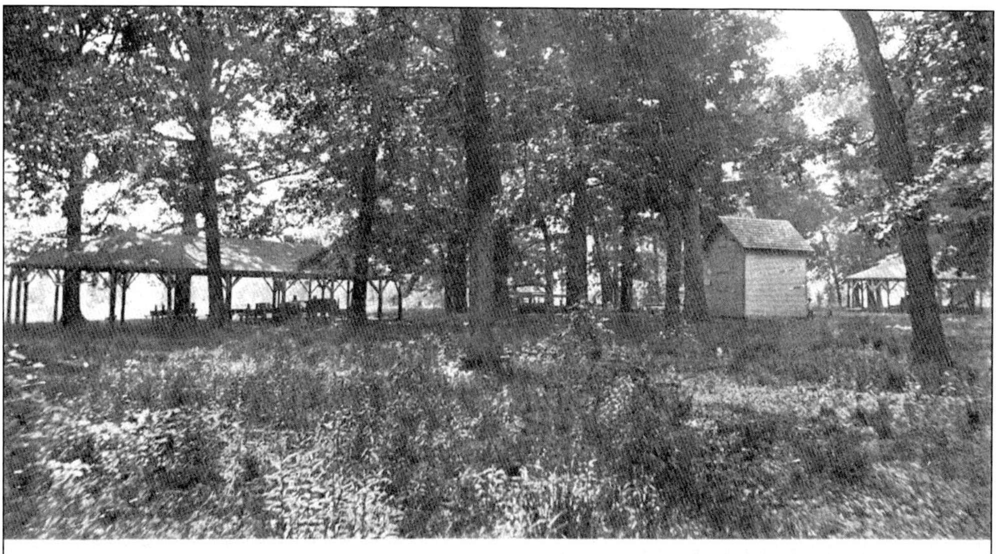
PUB. BY P. L. GLASE & CO. PICNIC GROUNDS, OLEY VALLEY PARK, OLEY, PA.

Seen here are the lovely picnic grounds folks came to enjoy. The park was south of present Route 73, and it made a lovely halfway meeting point for friends and relatives residing in Reading or Boyertown.

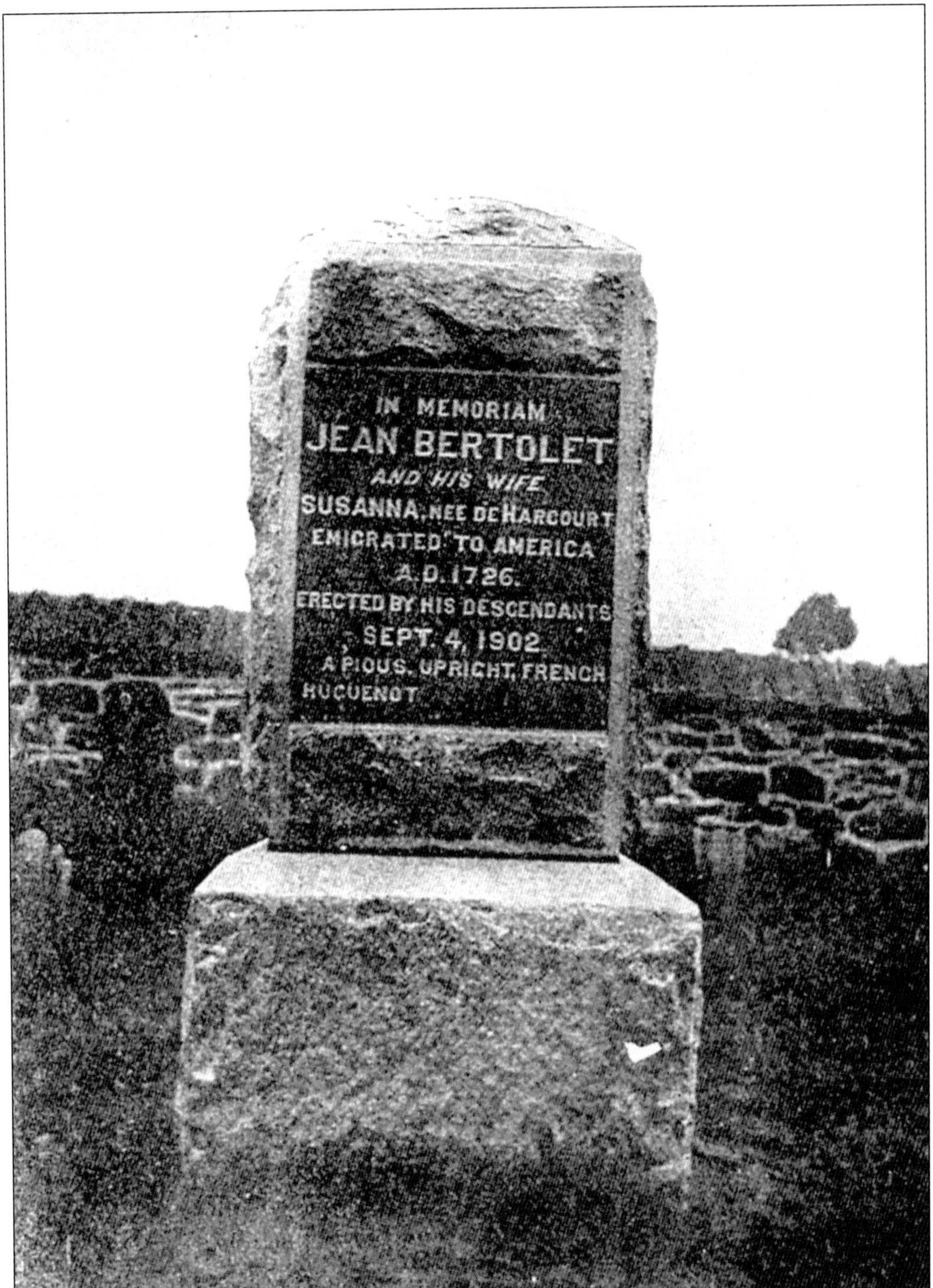

Shown here is the memorial headstone of Jean and Susanna de Harcourt Bertolet erected by his descendants in an old family burial ground on the family farm along Blacksmith Road. In 1726, they were one of the earliest Huguenot families to come to Oley Valley by way of Germantown, Pennsylvania. The Bertolets probably chose Oley because Susanna's sister and her husband, Isaac DeTurk, had come to Oley just a few years earlier.

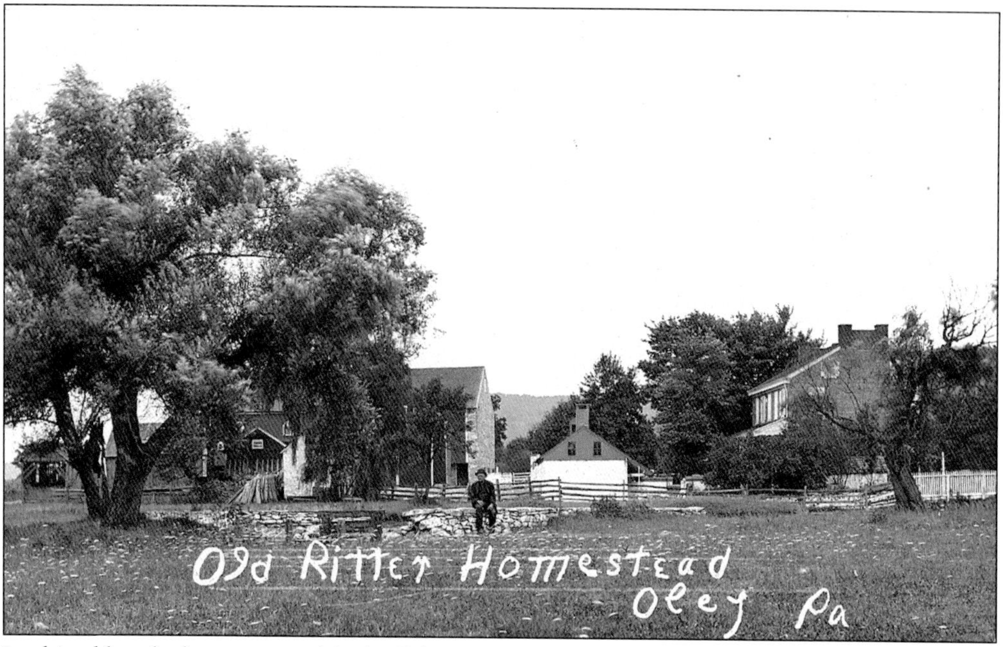

In this old real-photo postcard is the Ritter Homestead. Perhaps that is Mr. Ritter himself in the front yard. Until the cemetery was built in Oley village, it was customary to have a family plot on the family farm, as is mentioned with the Bertolets. Although not included in this book, a postcard depicting the Ritter family cemetery has been seen.

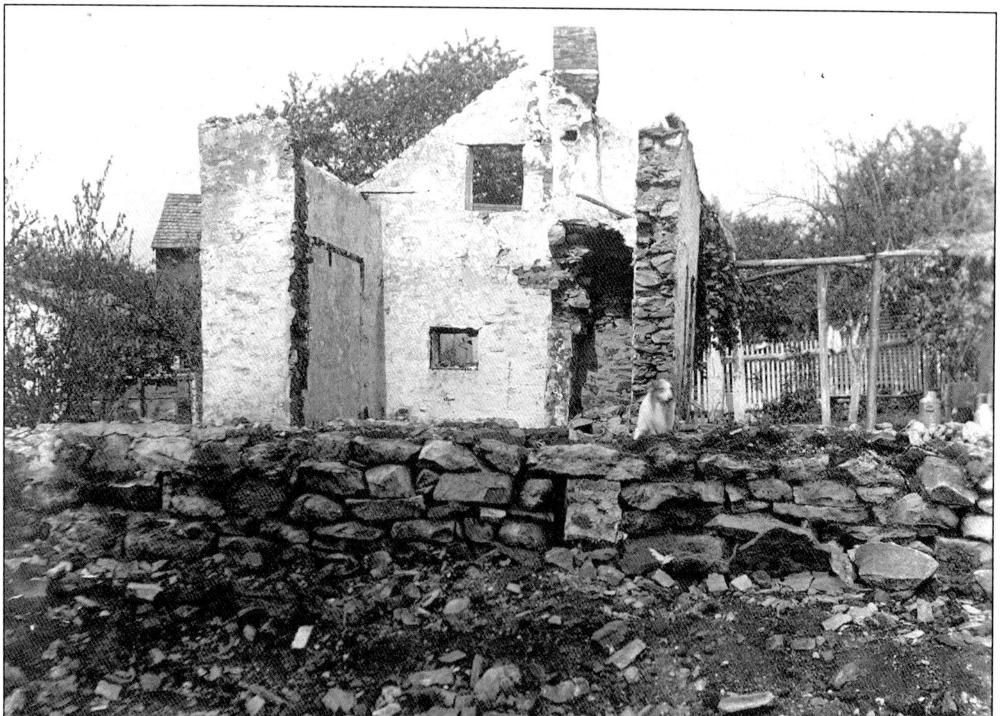

The Price homestead is shown here after a devastating tornado, or cyclone as it is described, laid waste to it. The dog seems to be searching for his human family.

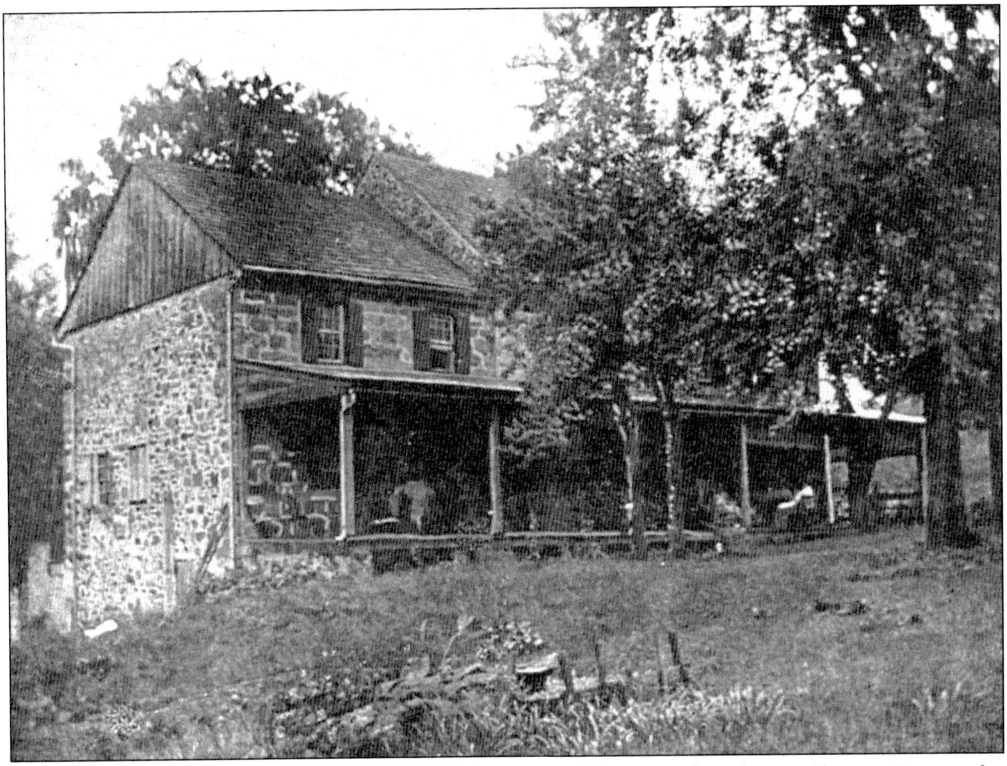

Peter Holl had quite a lovely stone farmhouse. It would appear that the smaller section on the left may be the original home with a larger addition on the right.

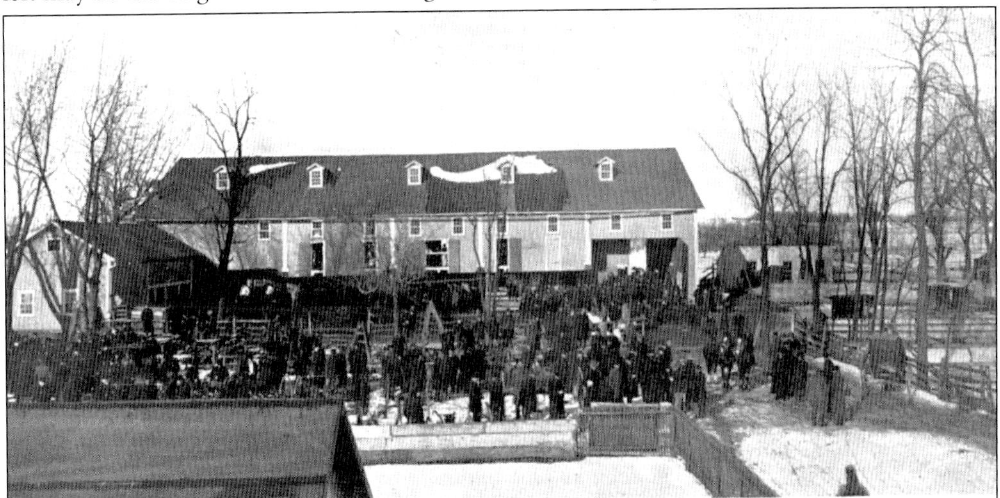

Public Sale of H. Reist Landis, February 18, 1907, on the Farm of Isaac Erb

EXPRESS PRINTING CO.

What farming community would be complete without a farm auction? All members of a community were drawn to this major social event to disperse the material goods belonging to their friends and neighbors, who were forced either by a death or a move to sell these items. Livestock, machinery, tools, furniture, and household bric-a-brac found new owners, usually in the next generation to take up farming or go to housekeeping.

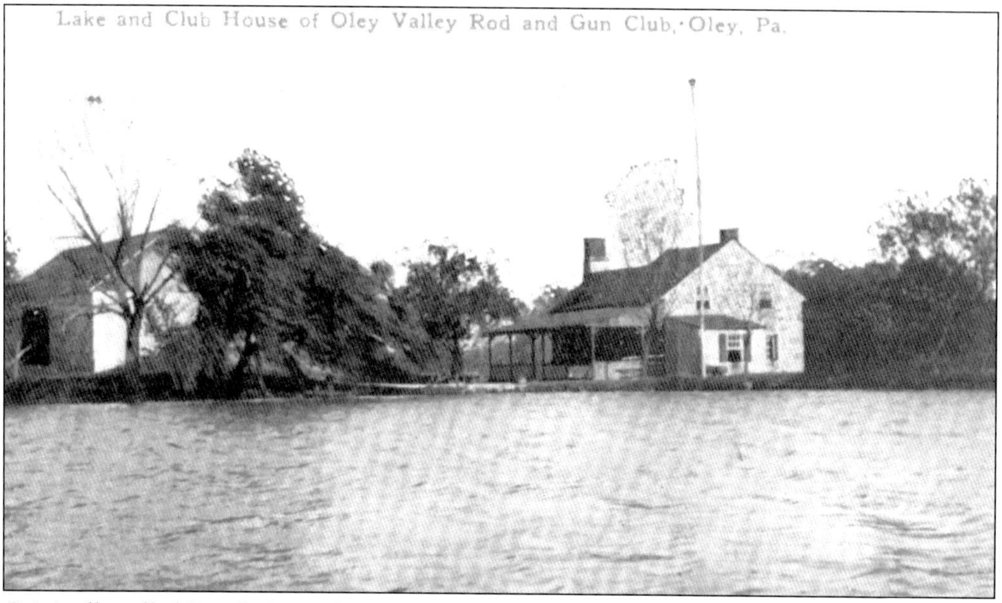

Originally called Peter's Dam, the property was sold to the Oley Rod and Gun Club, which is seen in the picture. It appears, from an earlier picture of the same site, that the farm home was converted to a clubhouse.

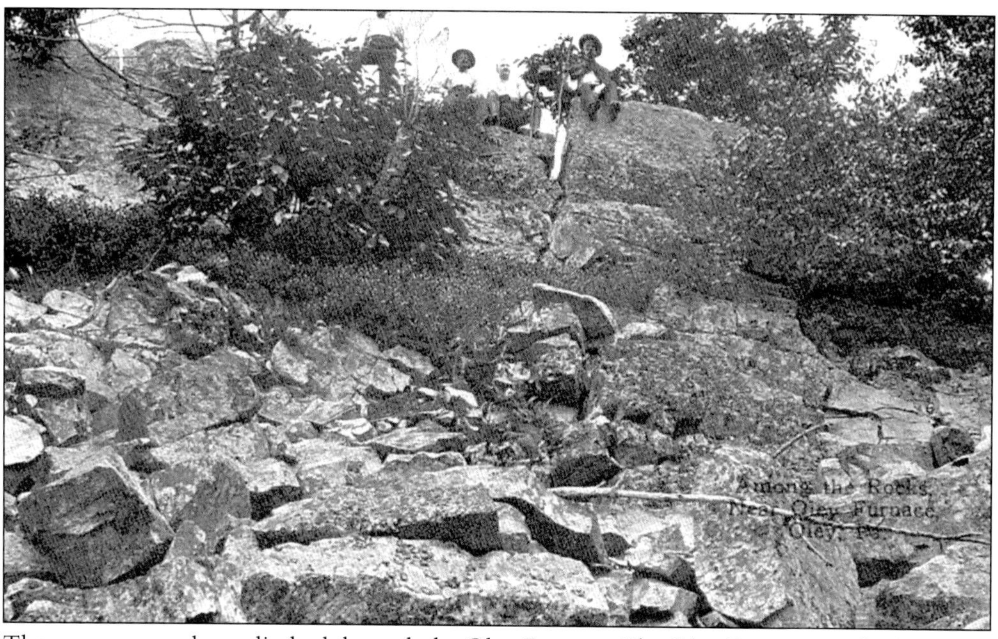

These young men have climbed the rocks by Oley Furnace. The Oley Furnace was built in 1744 to manufacture stoves. Its best-known owner was Maj. Gen. Daniel Udree, a Revolutionary War hero, who acquired it in 1778. In 1828, at the time of his death, he was the largest landowner and consequently the largest taxpayer in Berks County.

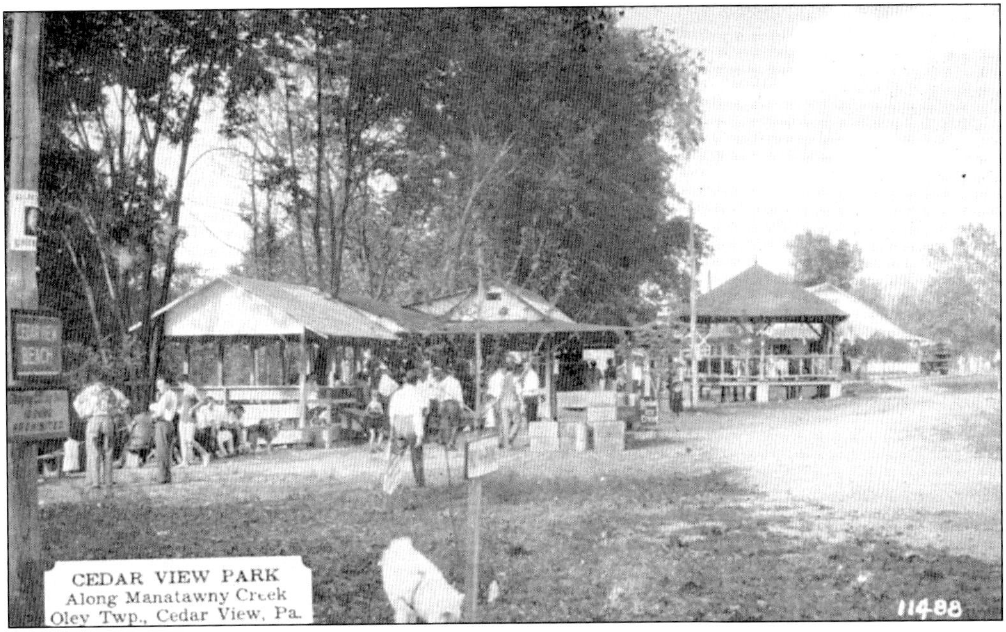

Cedarview Park along the bank of the Manatawny Creek seems to have been a popular spot for picnicking. Many family reunions were held here. Although there is an Oley reference on this postcard, it is believed to have been closer to Earlville.

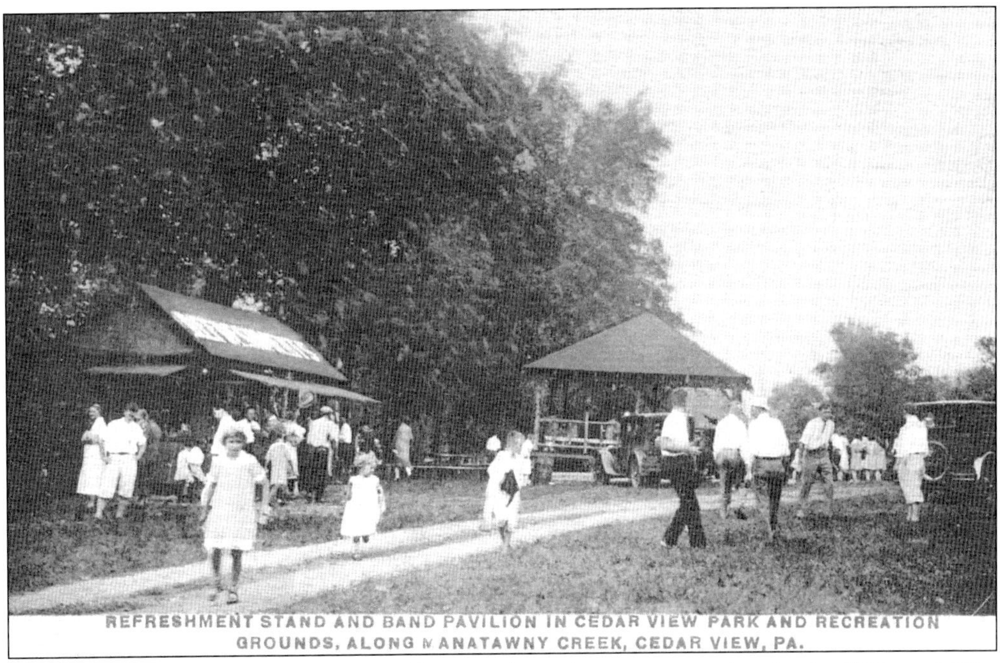

Another view of the park, this time with cars, places the scene sometime in the 1920s or 1930s. The refreshment stand seems to be doing a good business.

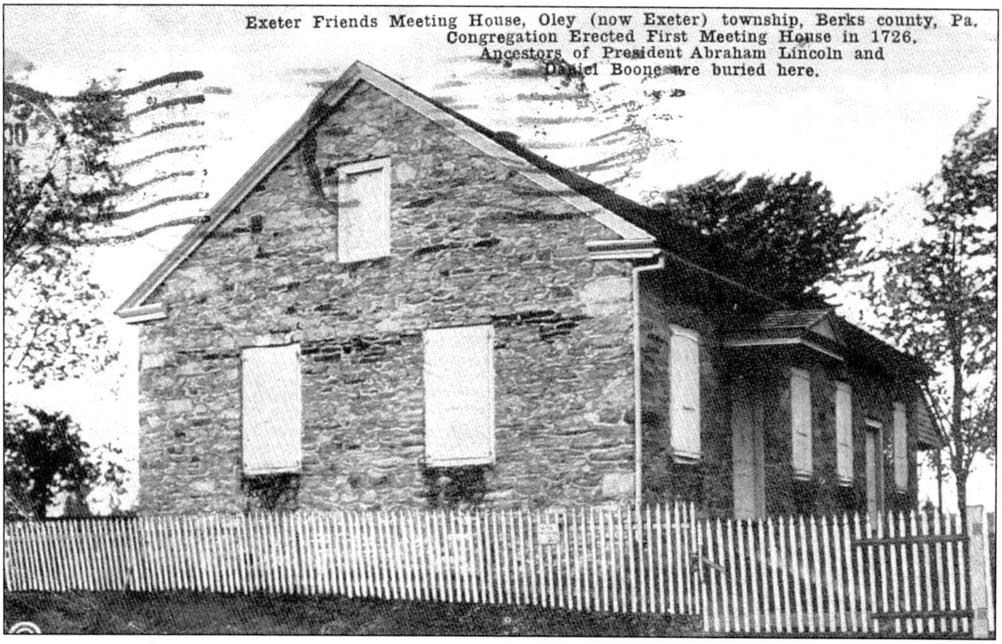

Exeter Township was once part of Oley Township until about 1750. In this area, many people of English descent settled. Many of the early residents worshipped and are buried at this Quaker meetinghouse. The Quakers held worship meetings in this area as early as 1725. In 1759, a meetinghouse was built on land given to them by the Boone family, ancestors of the famous frontiersman Daniel Boone.

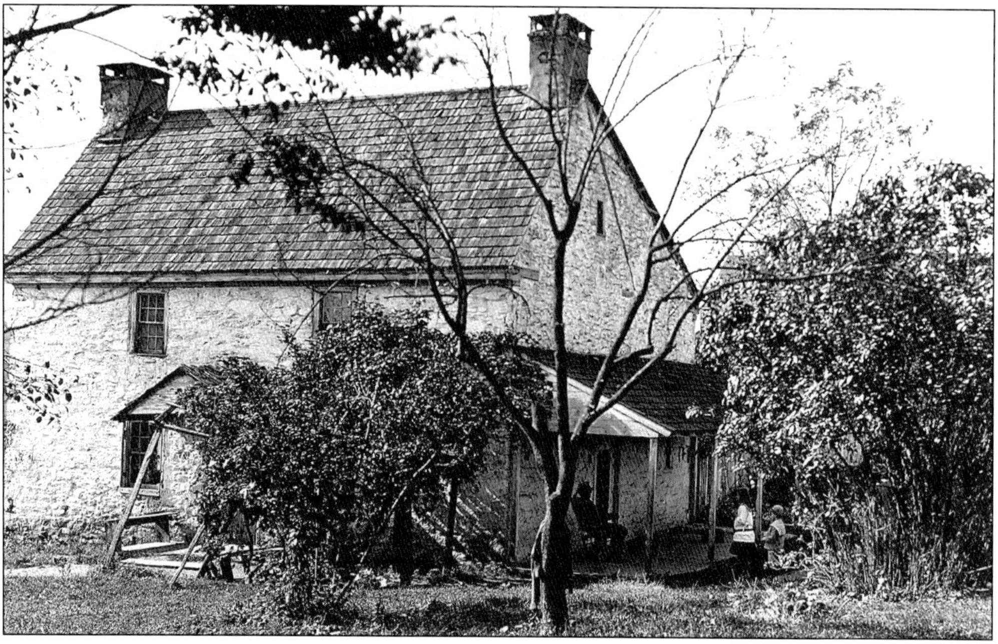

George Boone, Daniel Boone's grandfather, came to the colony in 1717 at the urging of his friend William Penn. This was reported to be George's second home in Exeter after his log cabin burned to the ground sometime before 1727. According to the legend on the card, this home was built in 1733, the year that Daniel was born.

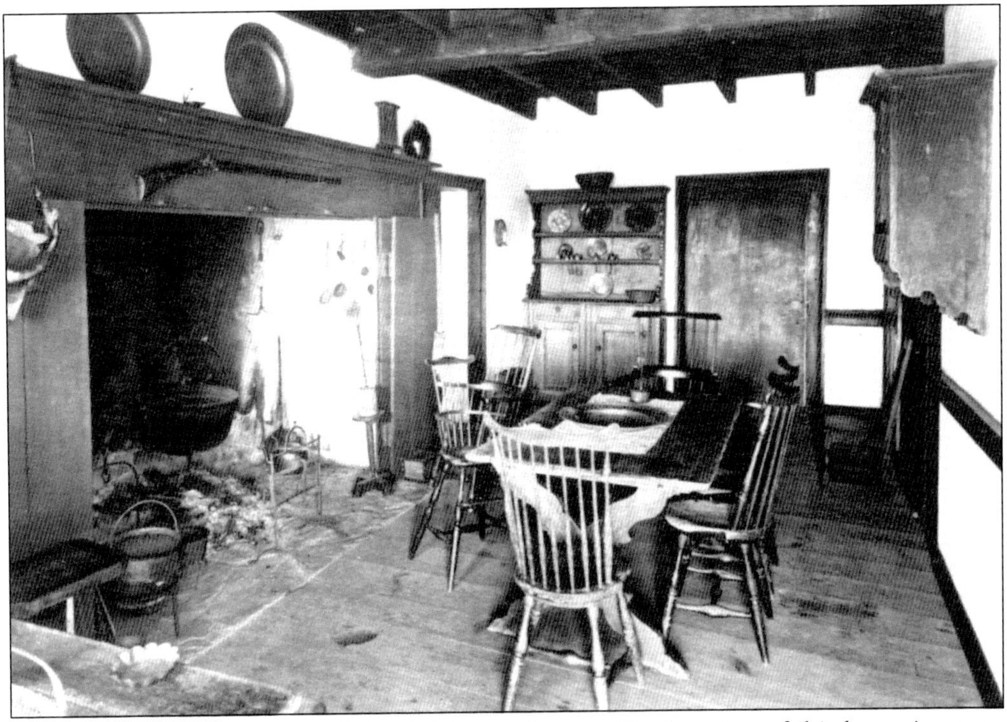

Daniel was born to Squire and Sarah Morgan Boone. The location of this home is now a Pennsylvania State Historical Site with a lovely park, which draws many people for recreation and enjoyment of the scenic beauty that it offers. Here is the cooking and dining area of the restored Boone Homestead. In pre-Colonial and Colonial times, all of the family would have gathered here except when attending to farming chores and sleeping.

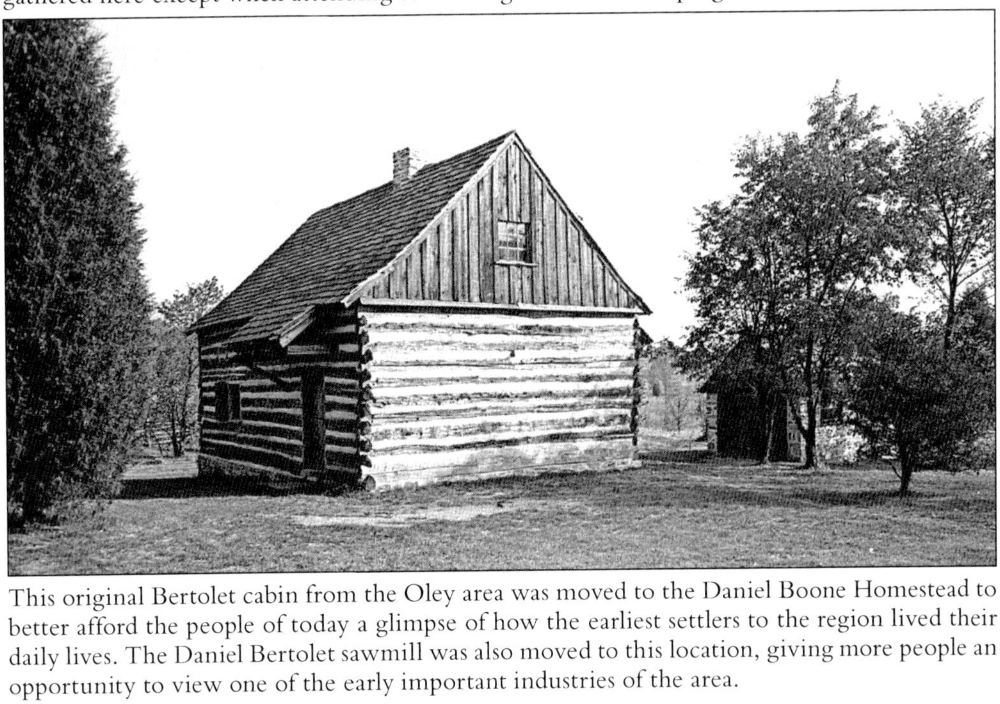

This original Bertolet cabin from the Oley area was moved to the Daniel Boone Homestead to better afford the people of today a glimpse of how the earliest settlers to the region lived their daily lives. The Daniel Bertolet sawmill was also moved to this location, giving more people an opportunity to view one of the early important industries of the area.

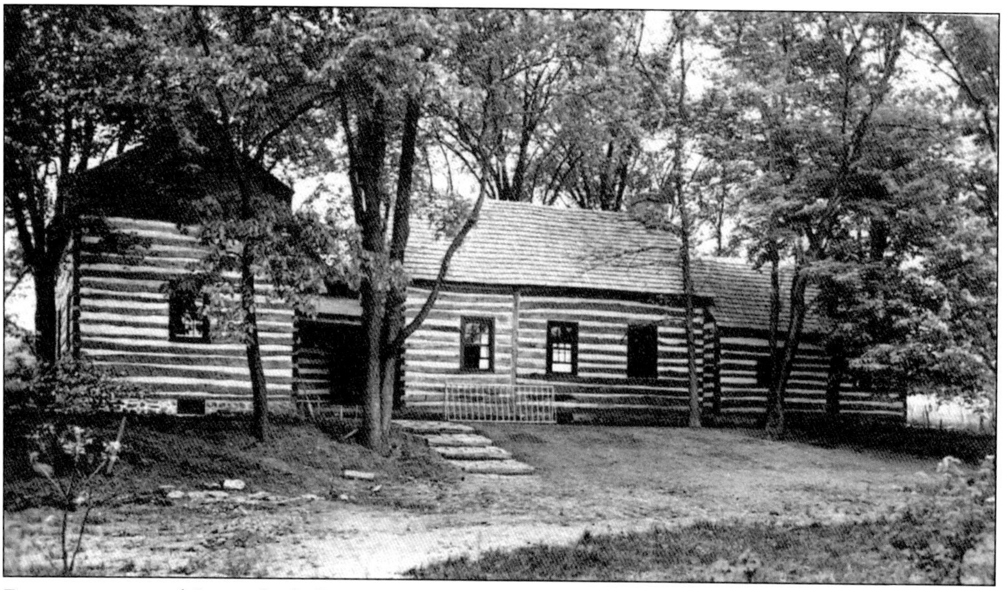

For many years this youth shelter was present at the Daniel Boone Homestead. It was used by scouting and other organizations for overnight camping trips. It is remembered fondly by those who were able to participate in its use.

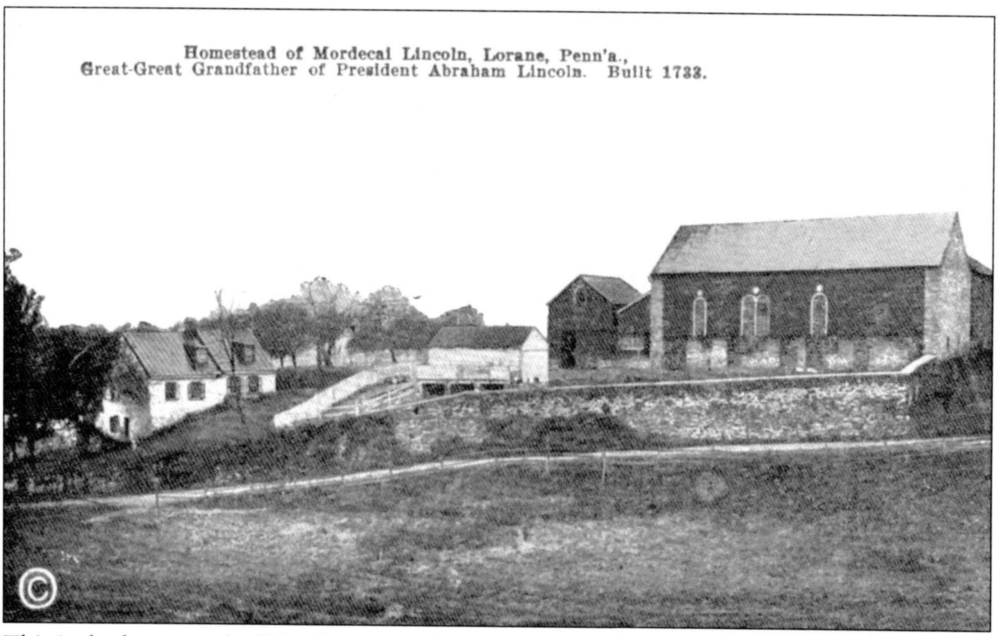

This is the homestead of Mordecai Lincoln; it was built around 1733 in Oley Township, now Exeter Township. Mordecai was a slaveholder, while his great- great-grandson Abraham Lincoln was the Great Emancipator. Mordecai Lincoln and George Boone were peers, and several of their children intermarried, although none of these unions was a direct line to Abraham.

Two

Yellow House, Earlville, and Amityville

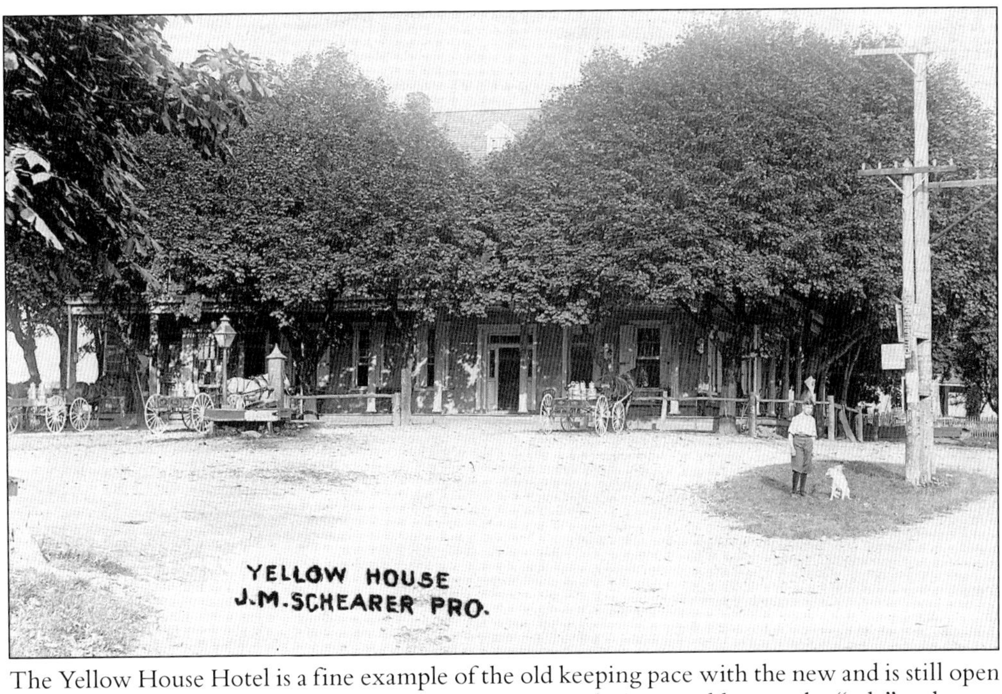

The Yellow House Hotel is a fine example of the old keeping pace with the new and is still open for business. The Yellow House Sale was across the road. One could go to the "sale" to buy or sell one's vegetables and meats for the week, meet one's friends, check out the medicine man's panacea, hear the latest in country music, or perhaps buy some used furniture for one's home.

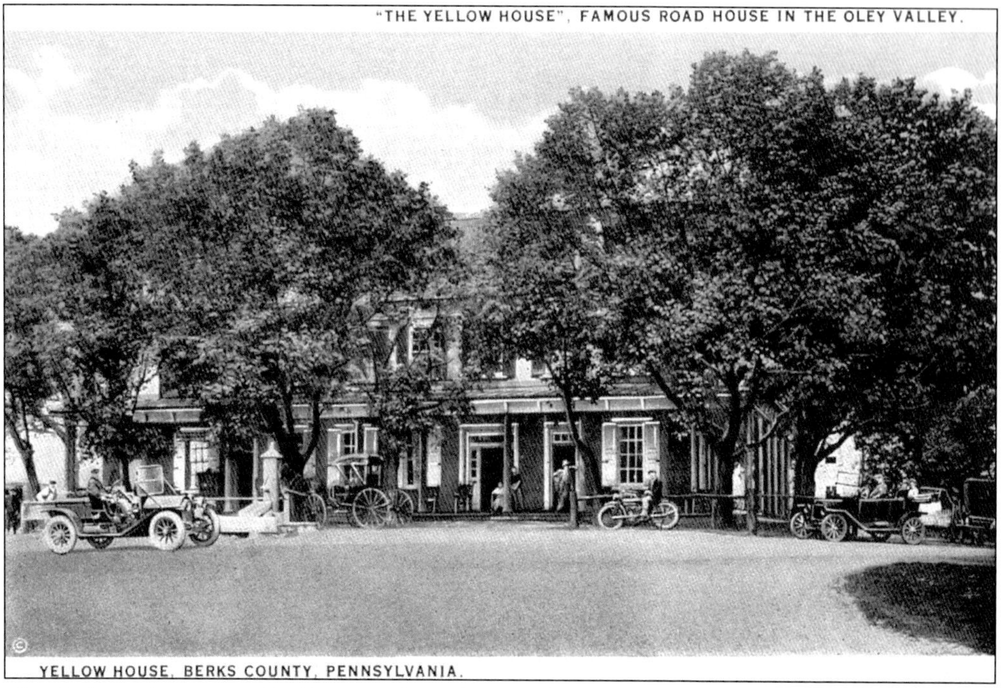

The Yellow House, so called because it really is yellow, is seen here with a new kind of traffic and is called a roadhouse. Please note the hitching posts for the horses and buggies have been replaced by automobiles and motorcycles.

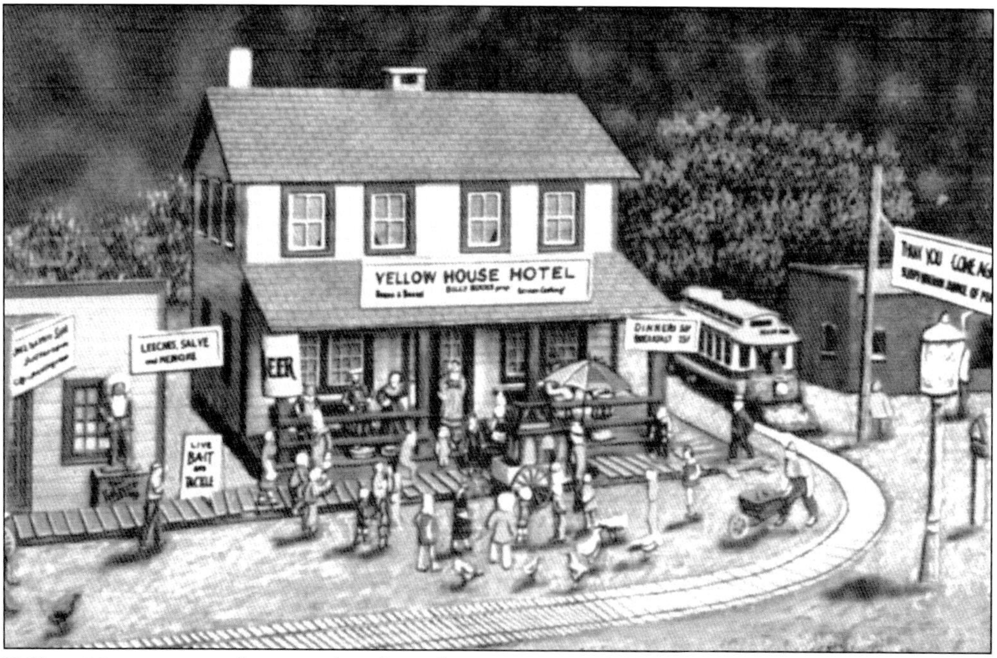

Yellow House was such a popular place that it commanded a model in Roadside America in Hamburg, Pennsylvania. A bit more stylized, perhaps, than the real thing, the people appear to be using the front of the hotel as a market. Perhaps that is where the "sale" really started and then moved across Route 562.

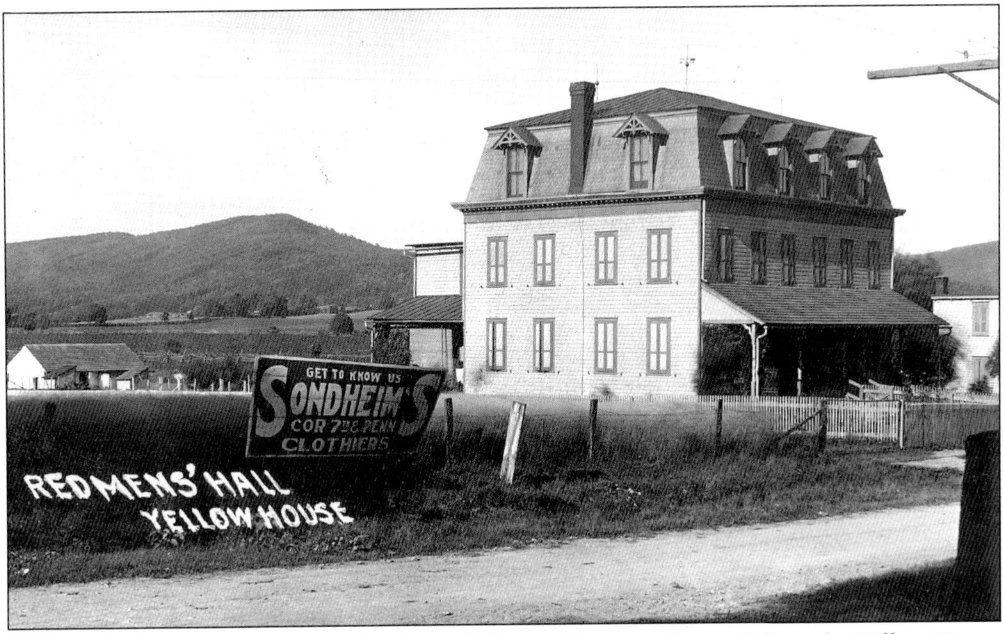

Pictured here is the Redman's Lodge located diagonally across the road from the Yellow House Hotel. The building remains, but the lodge no longer functions in this locale. This edifice is a double home with three front doors. The center front door leads to the former lodge on the upper floor.

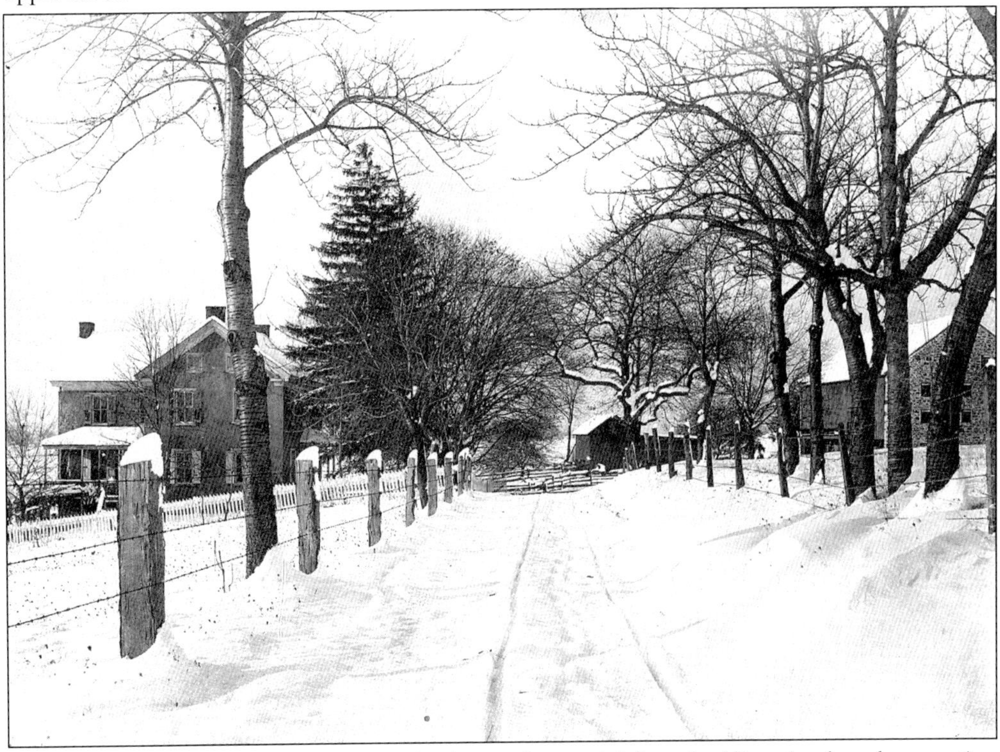

This is such a peaceful winter scene with a horse-drawn sleigh trail adding depth and perception to an artistic landscape.

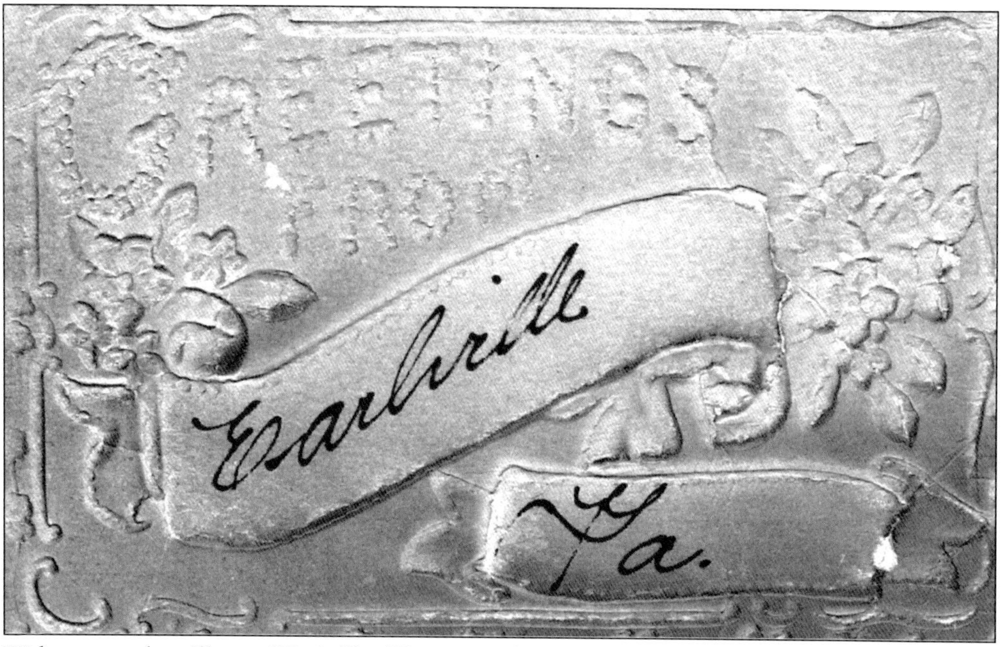

Welcome to the village of Earlville. "Greetings from" postcards from such small communities are always a delight to find. It appears to be a stock card on which you wrote the name of the locale you were visiting before you sent it off to friends or family.

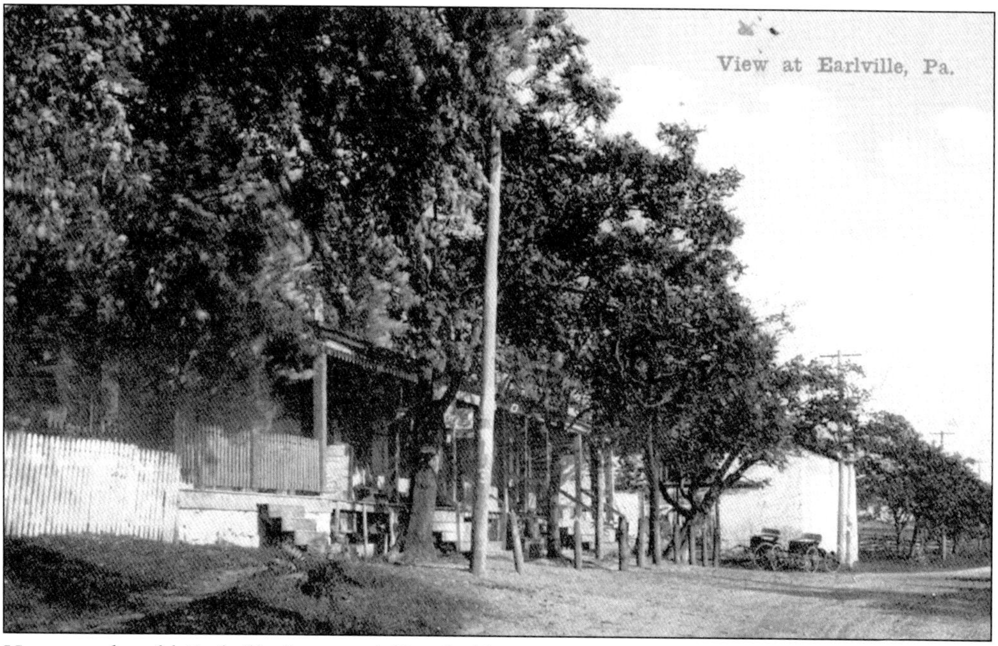

Here are the old Earlville Store and Hotel. Along Route 562, it still stands with a restaurant on one side and the post office on the other side. It is good to see community life retained at this old gathering place and nice to have a post office preserving the name of the community. Too often when the post office leaves a locale, it is not too many years before people forget just where that place actually was.

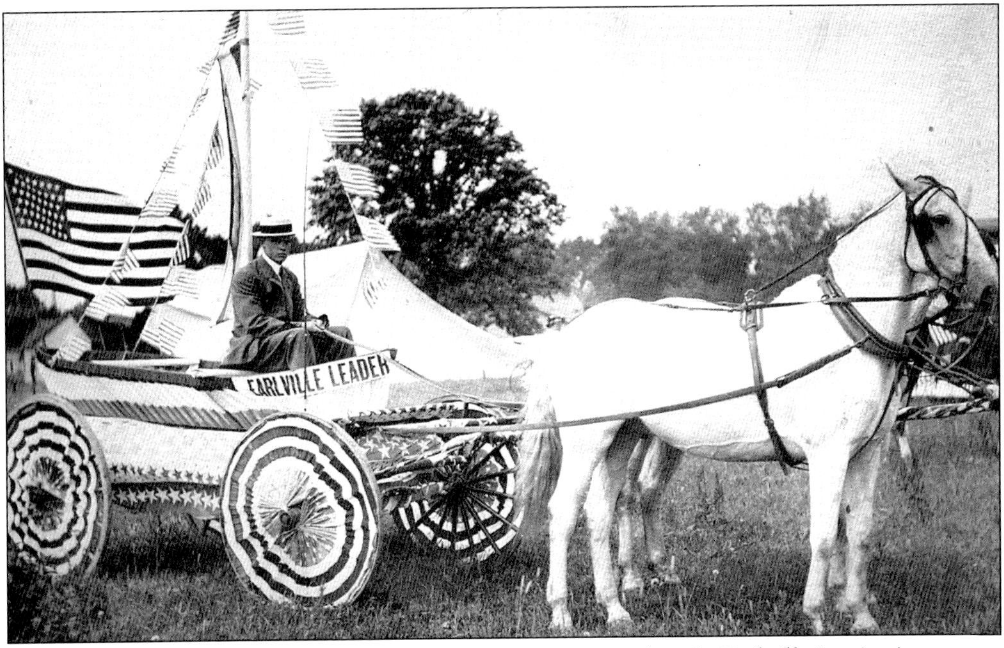

On the journey through southeastern Berks County, one arrives in Earlville just in time to see the quite impressive Earlville Leader float ready for a parade.

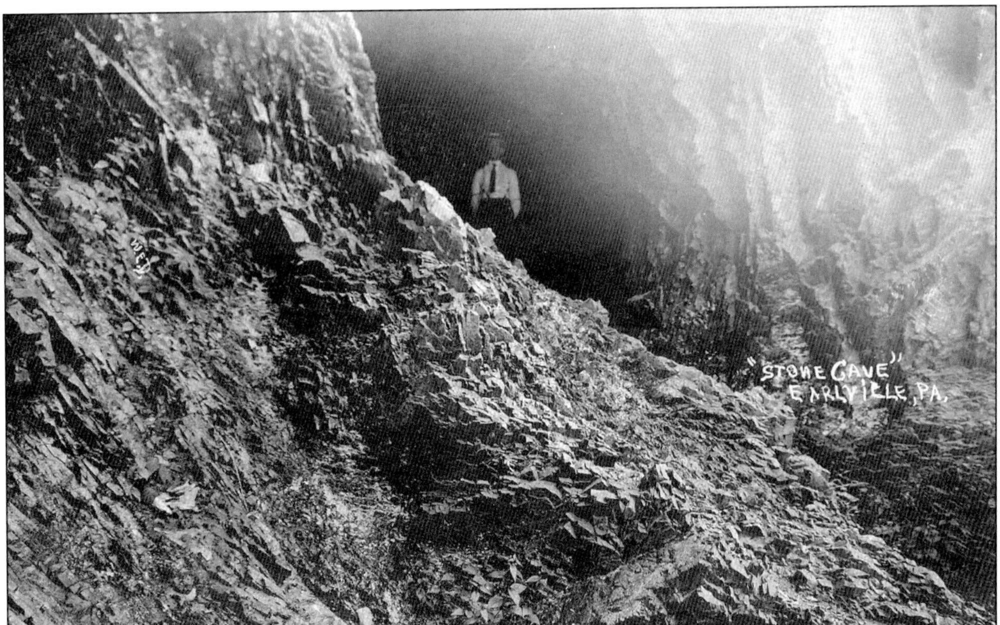

The "Fancy Hills" lie behind Earlville. It is thought that perhaps these caves are in that area. In the early 1900s, blueberries abounded on these hills and it was an annual event to take the horse and buggy as far as possible and then go into the hills to gather the berries for pies and preserves.

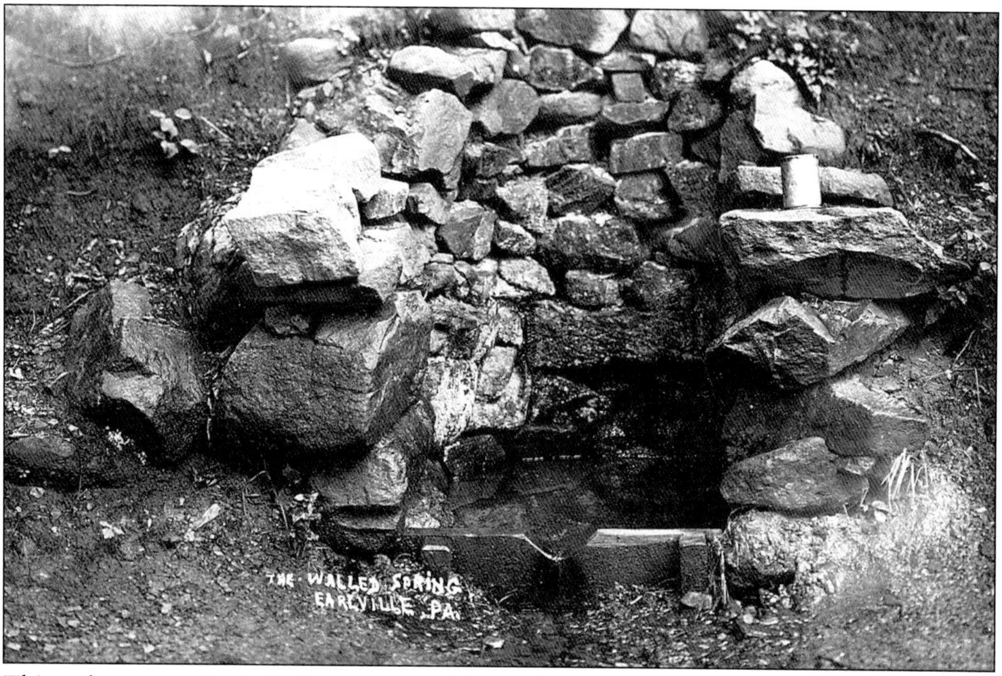

This early spring at Earlville looks as though it would have been a great place to get a cool drink on a hot day. Please note the battered can used as a communal cup.

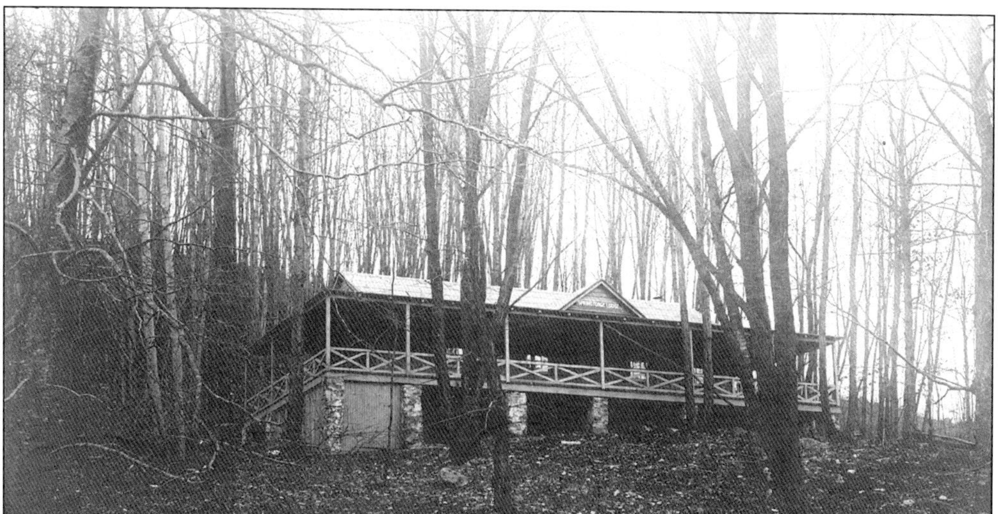

Earlville was once a great getaway spot for residents of more populated areas. Here is the Spring Forge Lodge, one of many vacation hideaways. Many of the summer cabins along the Manatawny Creek have been converted into year-round homes.

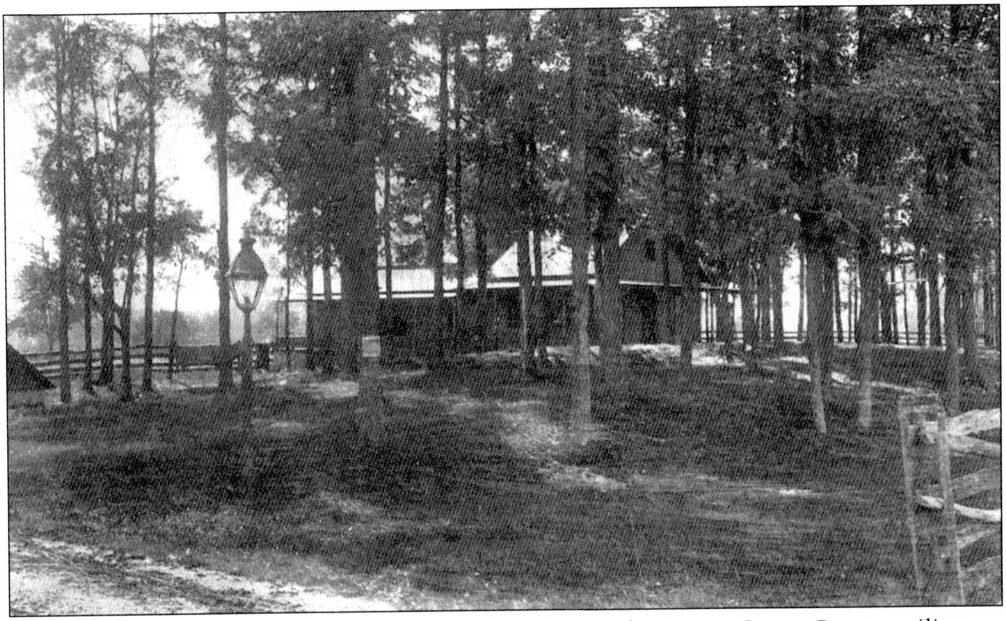

Earlville also had its share of summer camps. Seen here is the Locust Grove Camp pavilion.

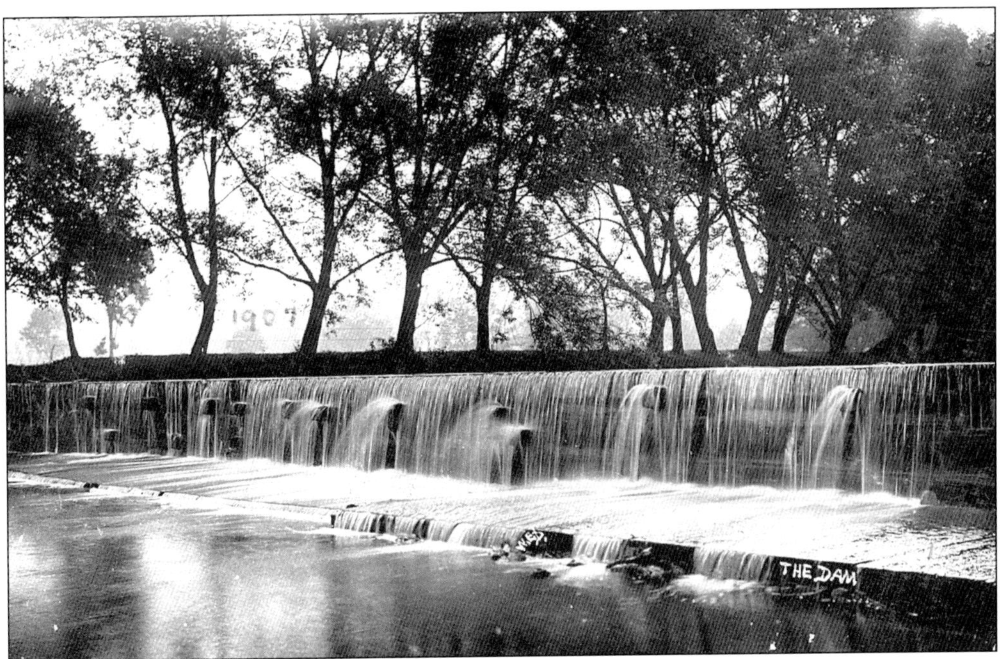

This card pictures the Earlville Dam in 1907. This must have been a timber and earthen dam judging from the protruding logs.

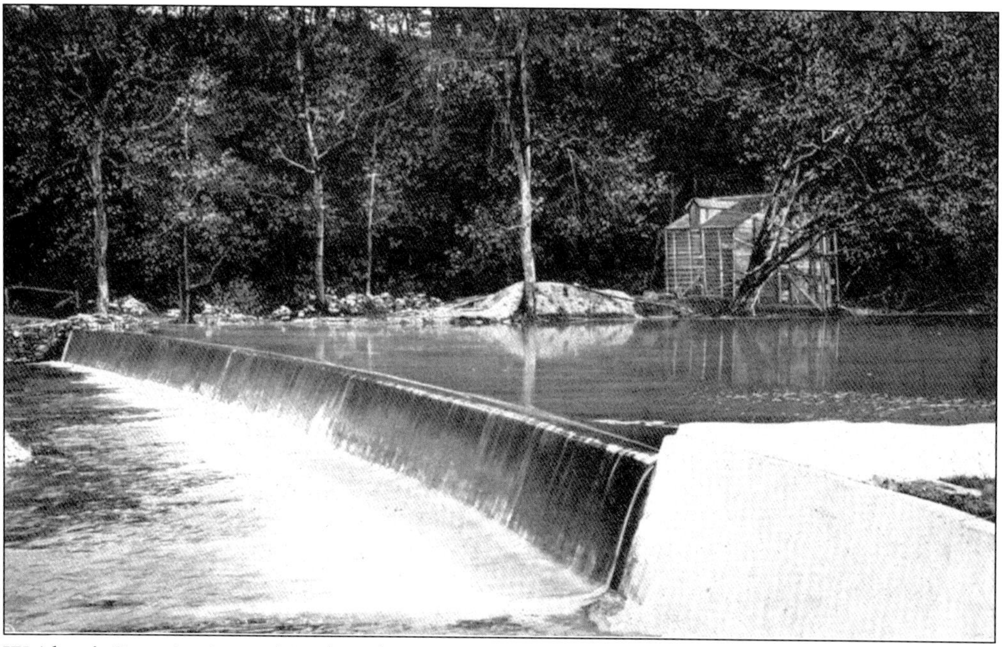

Weidner's Dam is pictured in this photograph card. The logs have been replaced with a more substantial material. Entitled "An Afternoon Outing in Earlville," this very early, slightly hazy card below captures the essence of relaxation that a little fishing along the Manatawny Creek offers.

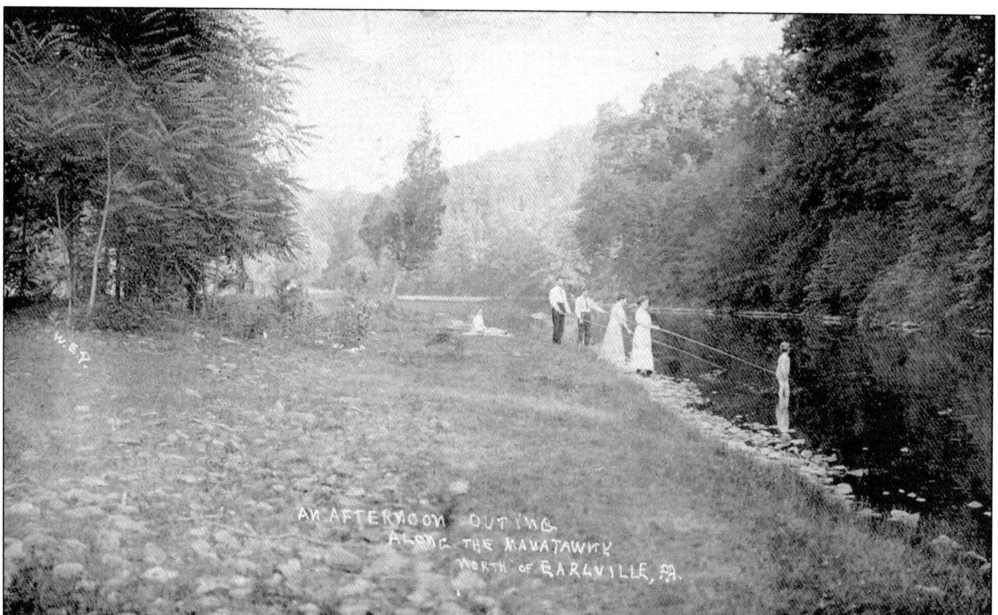

These brave ladies and fine gentlemen have no waders, fancy fishing vests, or even tackle boxes, yet they appear to be having a good time trying their luck with the trout. A smaller child is seen back on the blanket.

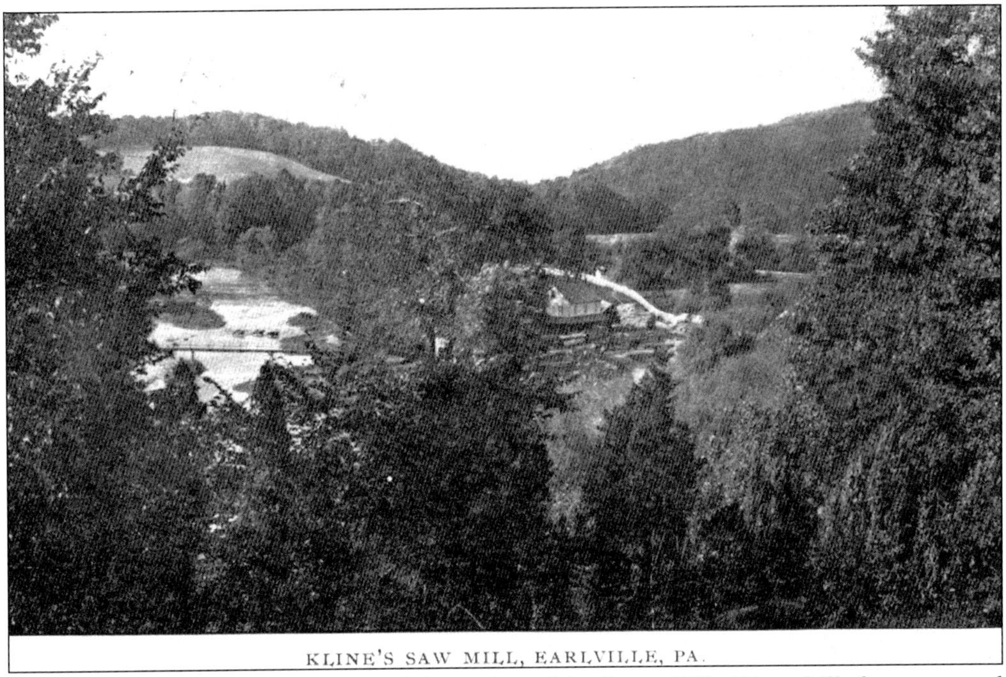

Klein's Saw Mill is pictured here amid the setting of the Fancy Hills. These hills form a natural wall along the eastern Oley Valley.

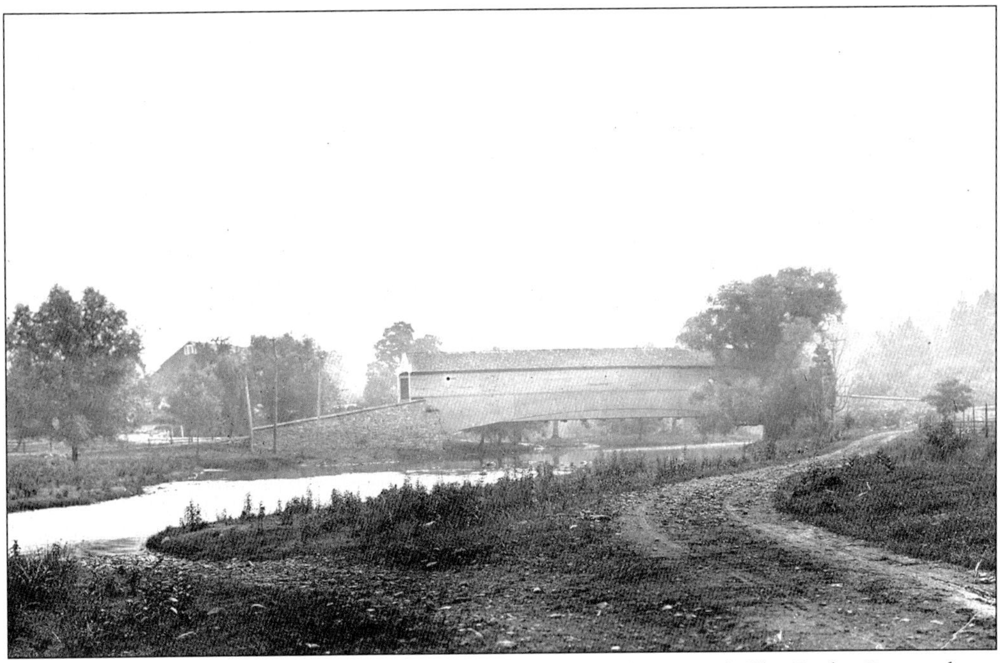

This is a very early real-photo postcard of the covered bridge at Earlville. Berks County has a number of remaining, rebuilt covered bridges, and this is one of them.

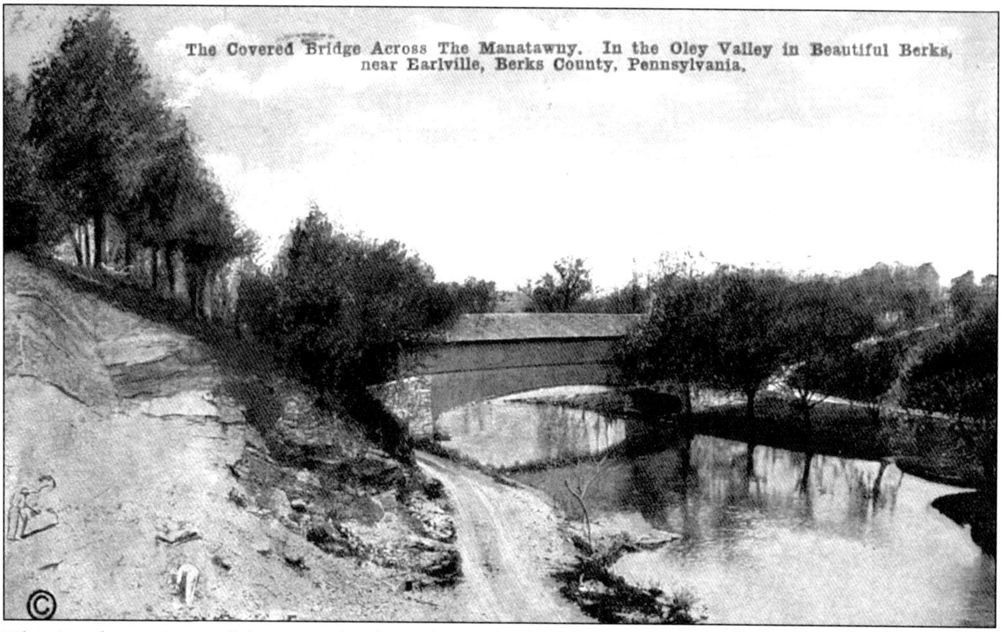

This is a later view of the same bridge after some alterations. Using this bridge on the way to Amityville and following the custom of passage through a covered bridge, holding one's breath, making a wish, or kissing one's favorite person would be in order.

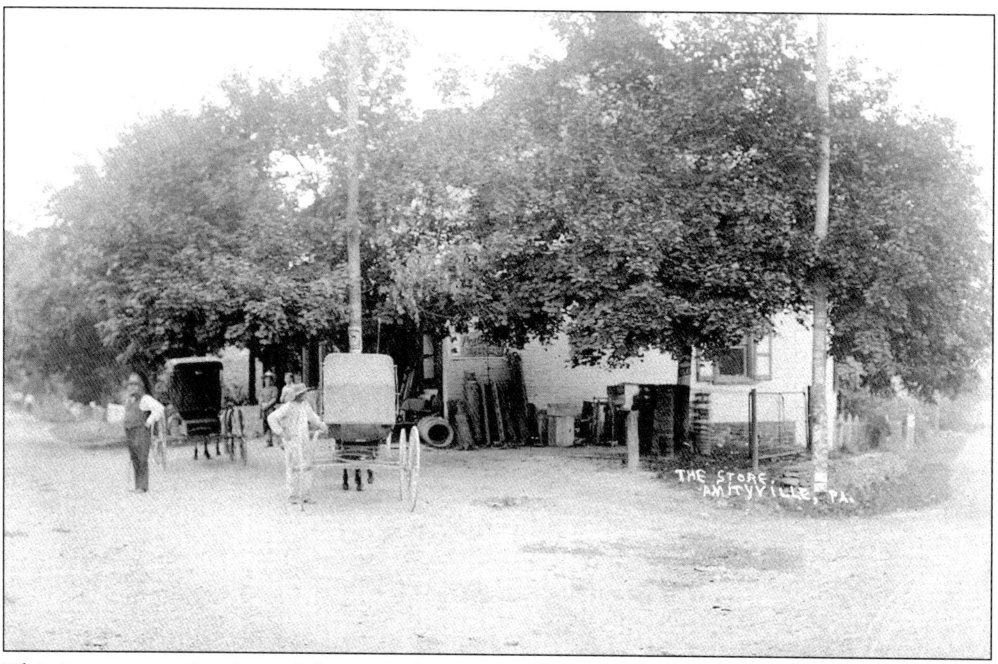

This is a very early view of the store in Amityville, a popular meeting place to discuss the weather, crops, politics, family, and other social topics.

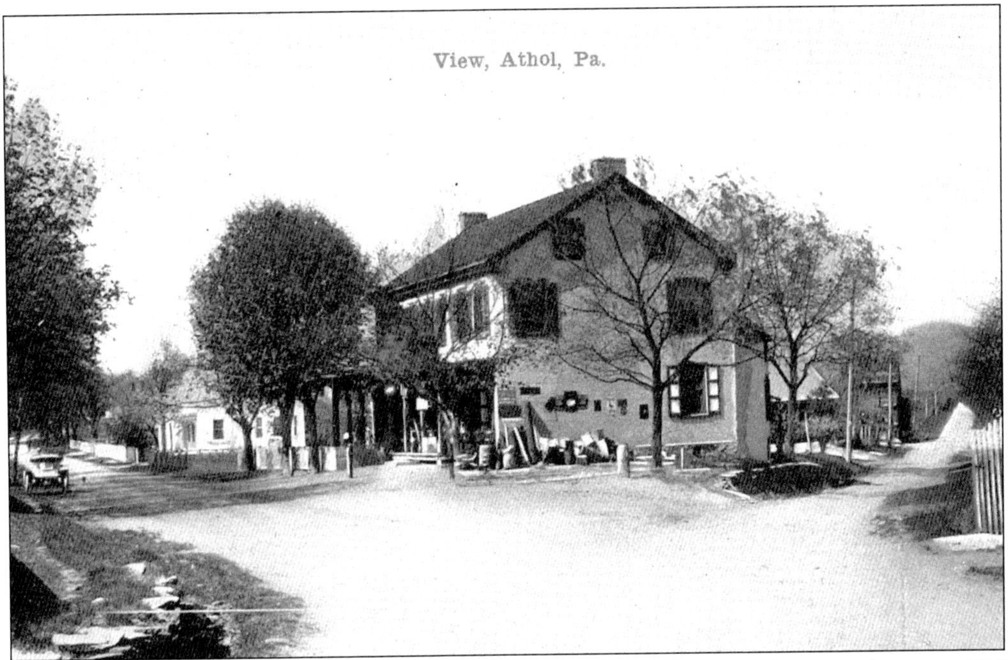

For many years Amityville was known as Athol. Here is a later view of the general store at Old Swedes Road and Blacksmith Road, the road one took from Earlville to Amityville. A very early automobile is seen to the left of the picture.

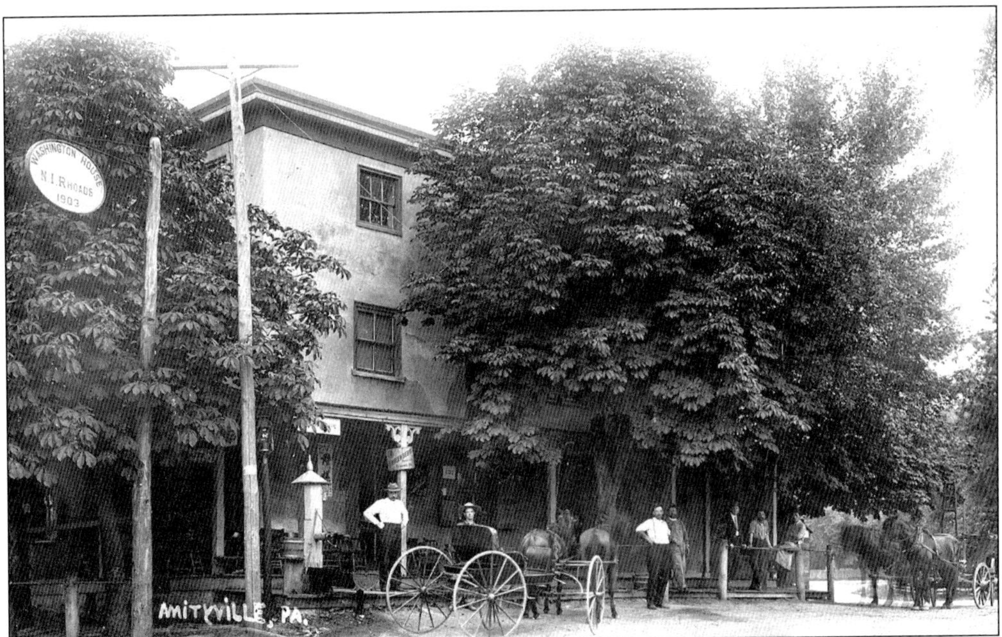

Seen here is another favored gathering place in Amityville (Athol), the Washington House Hotel, kept in 1903 by Newton Rhoads. Supper in those early days consisted of griddle cakes, a plate of chops, bread and butter, various fruit jellies and preserves, and pie. A plate of tripe was passed up according to an early journalist.

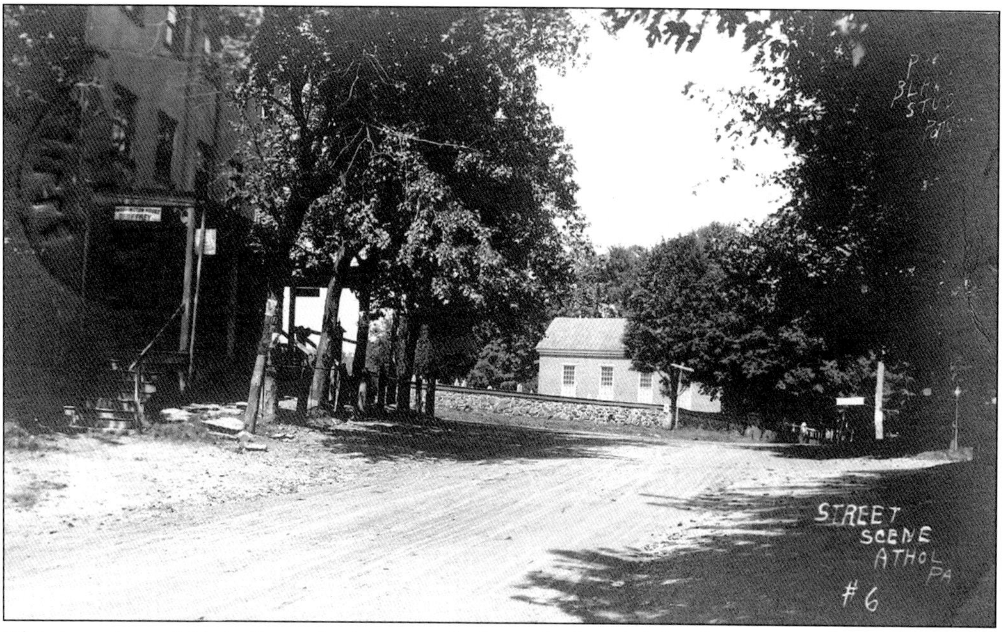

This is a view of Main Street looking north from the hotel. The diarist cited on the card that the charges were $1.75 plus a 5¢ fee for two people and 5¢ for a drink for the horse. It was also noted that a child in the next room whooped (coughed) all night. Inoculations against whooping cough have changed all that.

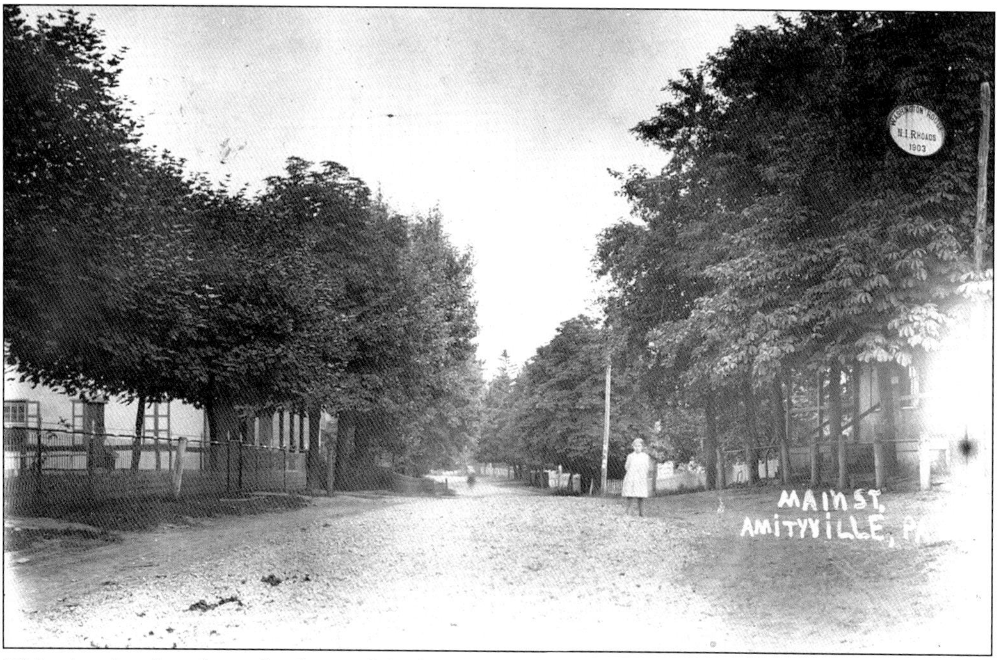

This view is taken from the front of the hotel and looking to the south toward the church spire, which can be seen in the far distance. These early folks must have looked ahead when they planned the road, for it seems much wider than in some villages. This fact kept many homes from destruction when modern highways were built.

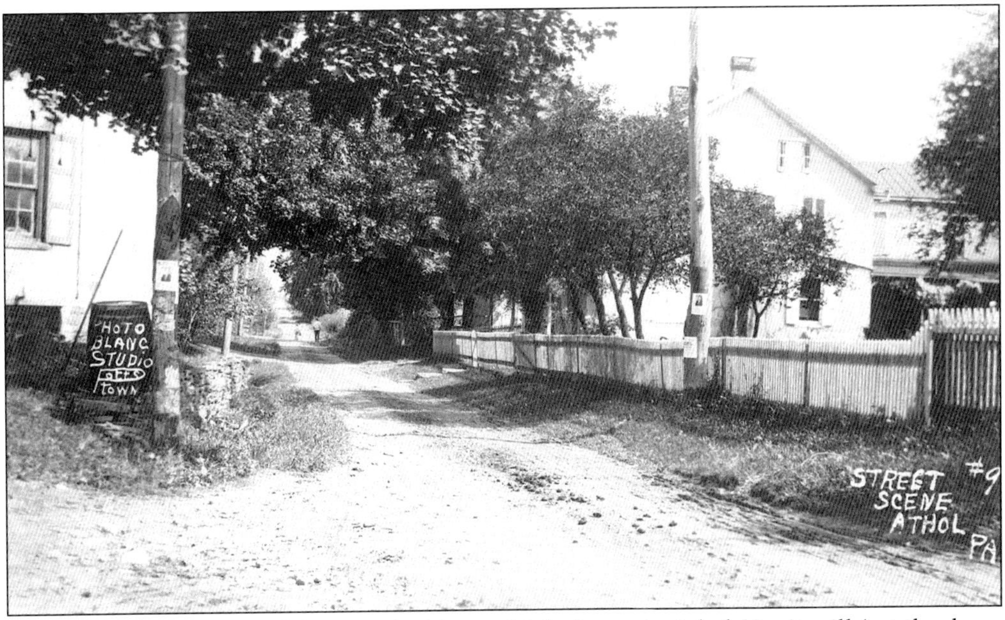

Once the Oley to Philadelphia Road, this was Main Street in Athol (Amityville) at the dawn of the 20th century. Old Swedes Road or Route 662 leads from Douglassville to Oley. The old-timers would be amazed at the nice stretch of macadam roadway existing over this dirt one, but their horses probably appreciated this one more than they would have the new one.

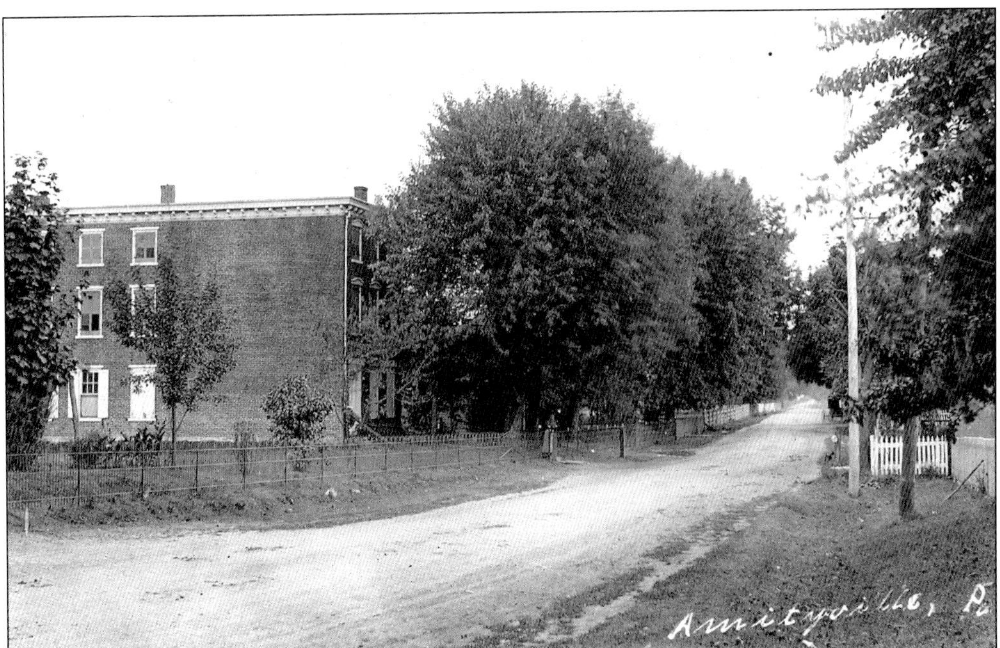

Another peaceful scene showing Amityville's Main Street is offered here. In 1903, the village was described as having but a dozen homes.

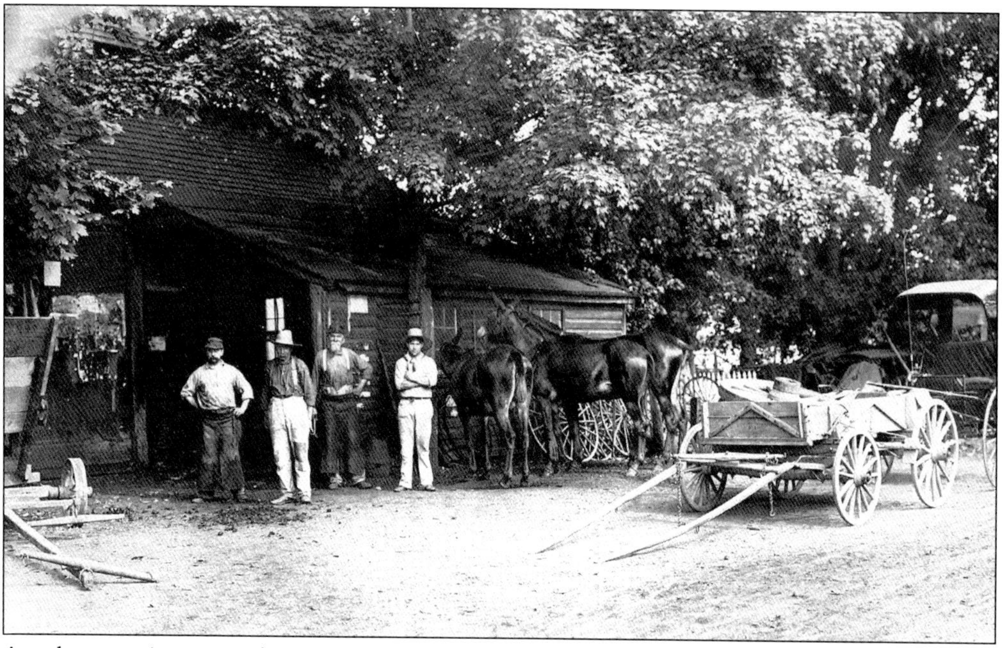

Another very important business in the community was the blacksmith shop. In this early card postmarked 1906 are Isaac Rhoads, Nathan Swavely, Uriah Wise, who is the proprietor, and an unknown gentleman, possibly a customer. This is the scene pictured on the back cover of this book.

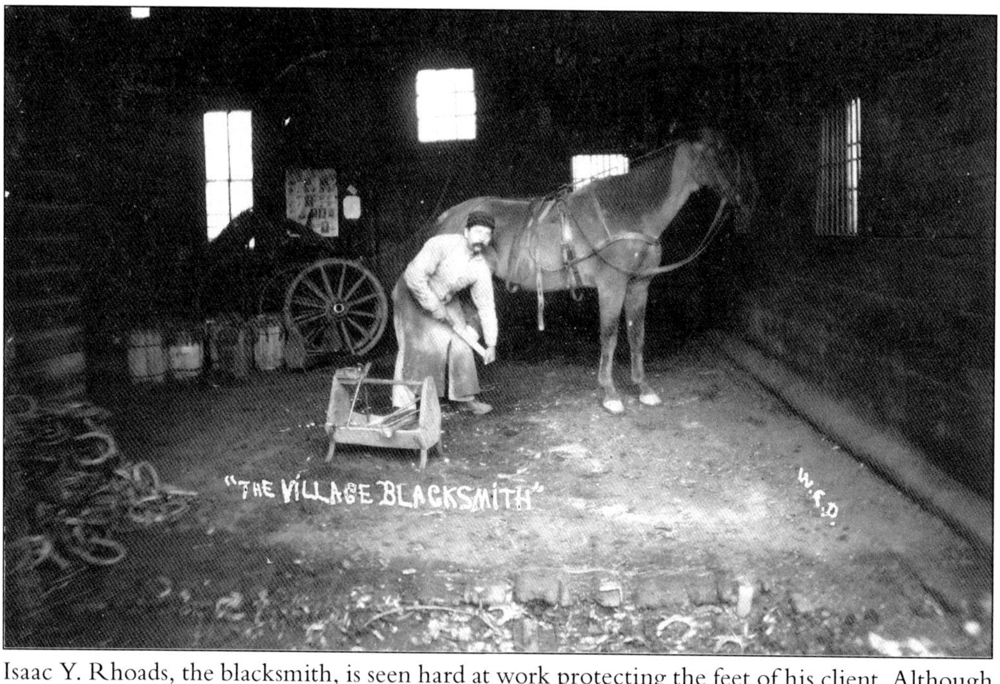

Isaac Y. Rhoads, the blacksmith, is seen hard at work protecting the feet of his client. Although clothed, it is possible to see the muscles that his occupation has built in his upper body. No doubt he did not have many takers for arm wrestling. Please note the long leather apron protecting his lower body.

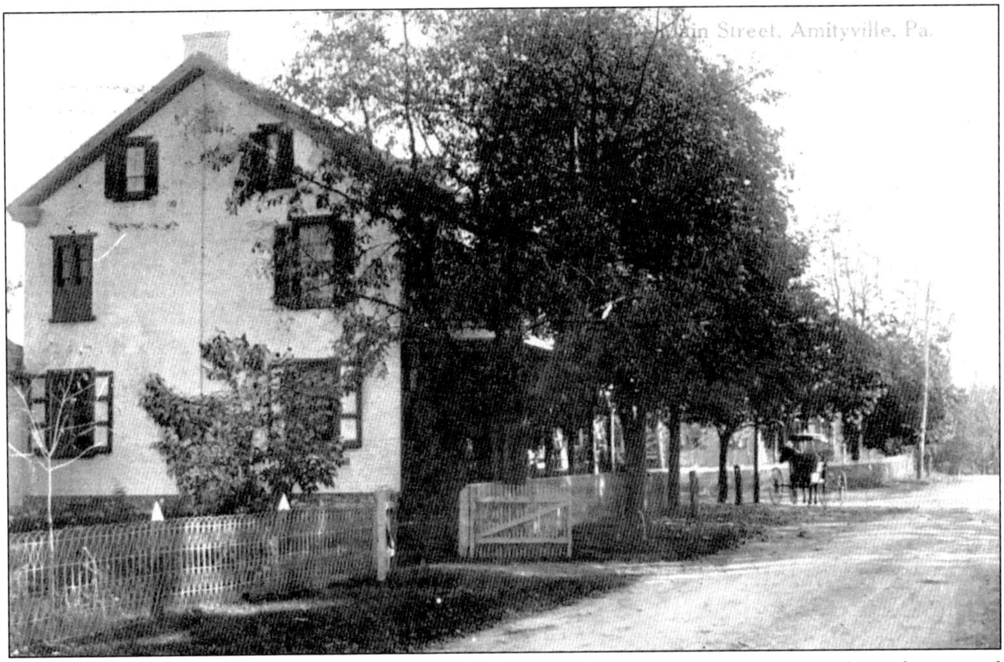

A later scene of Main Street is seen here. The street appears a bit wider perhaps, but a horse and buggy are still the main means of transportation in this rural community.

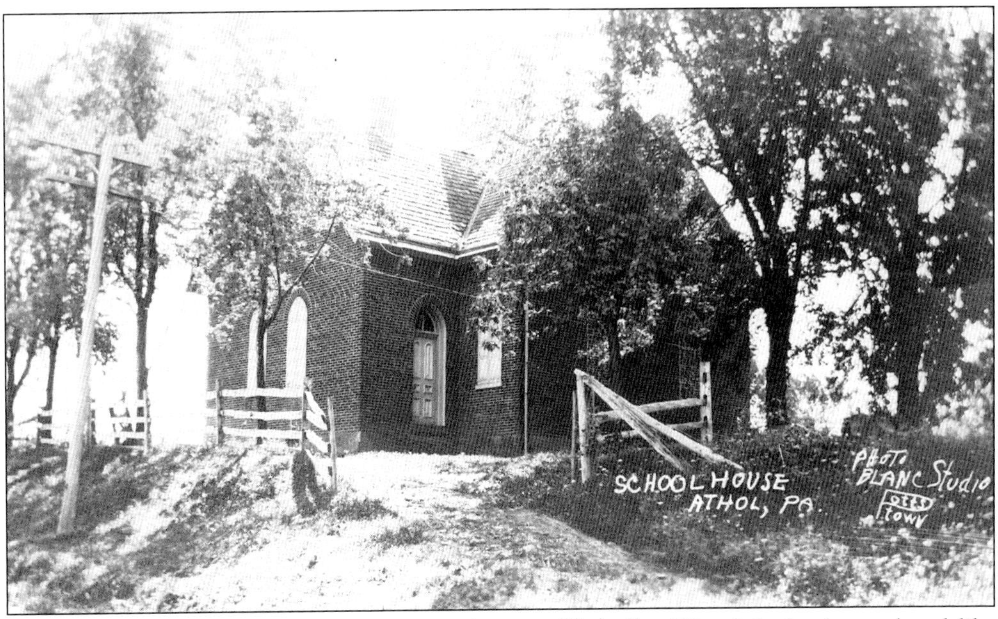

The Athol School House seen here appears to be a sturdily built edifice. It looks almost chapel-like in structure.

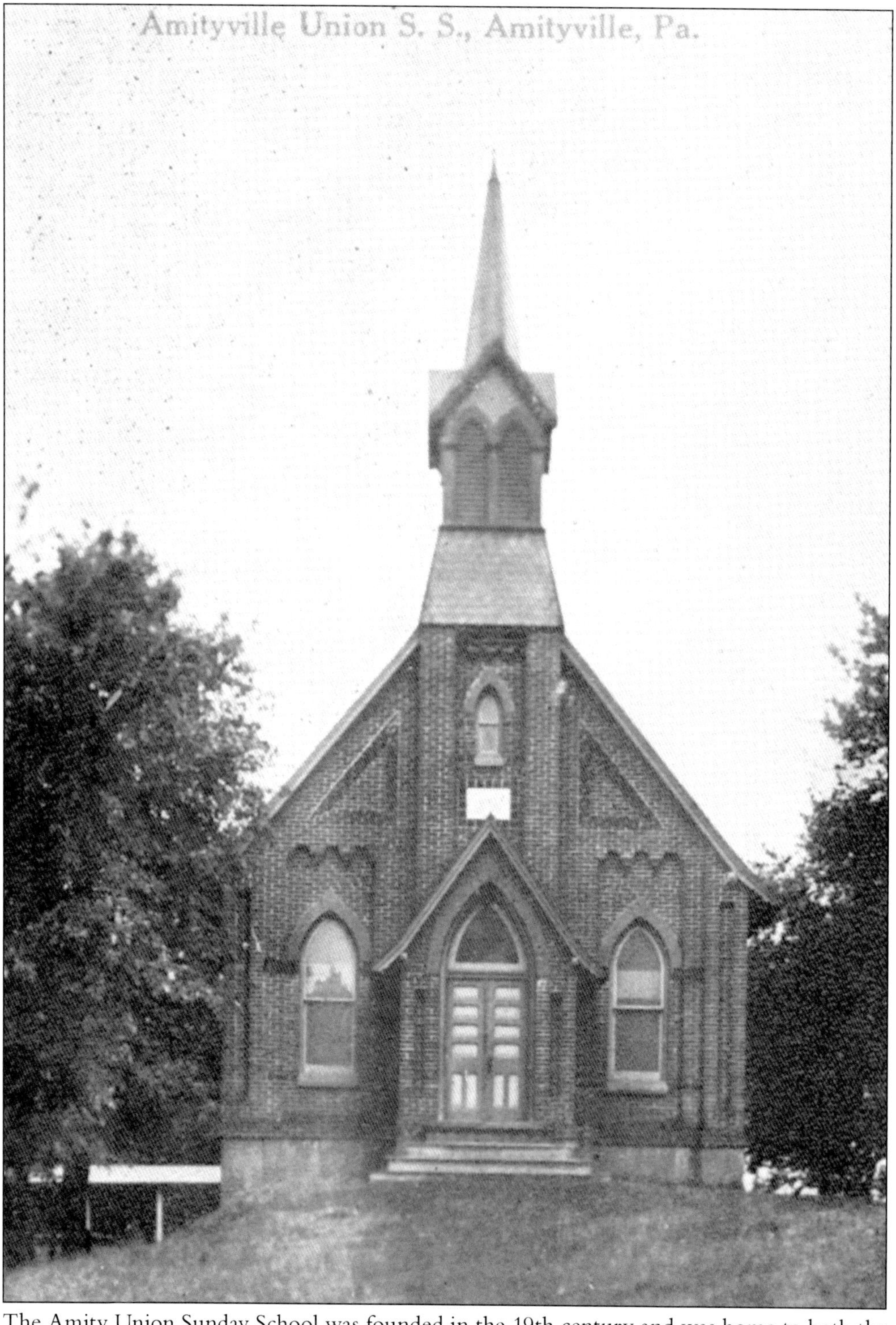

The Amity Union Sunday School was founded in the 19th century and was home to both the Lutheran and Reformed congregations in Amityville. The groups met on alternate Sundays for worship. The lovely quaint building is still standing.

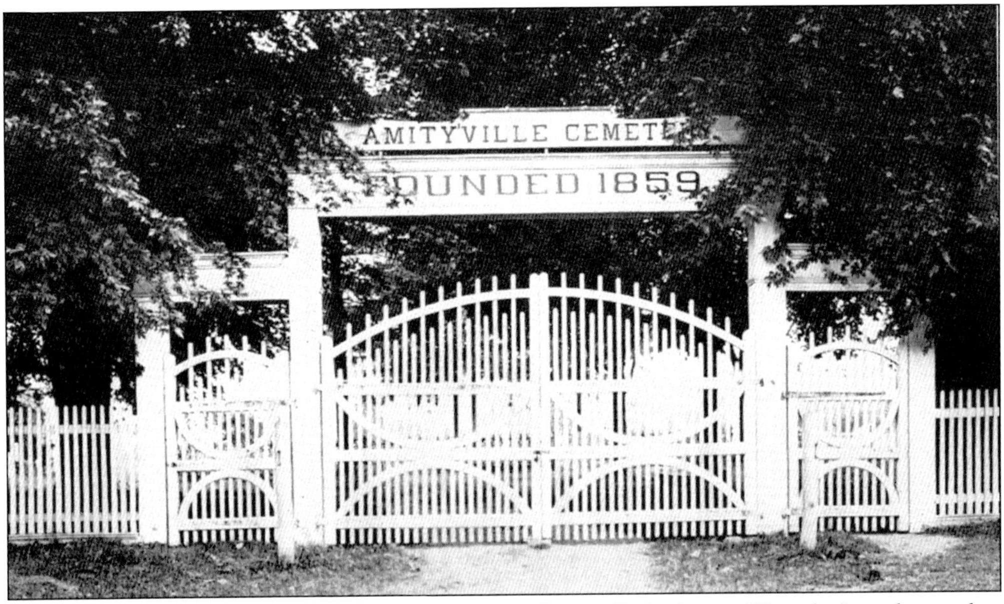

The Amityville Cemetery, dating from 1859, is at St. Paul's Lutheran Church. It no longer has the picket fence seen here. The oldest part of the cemetery is right along Route 662.

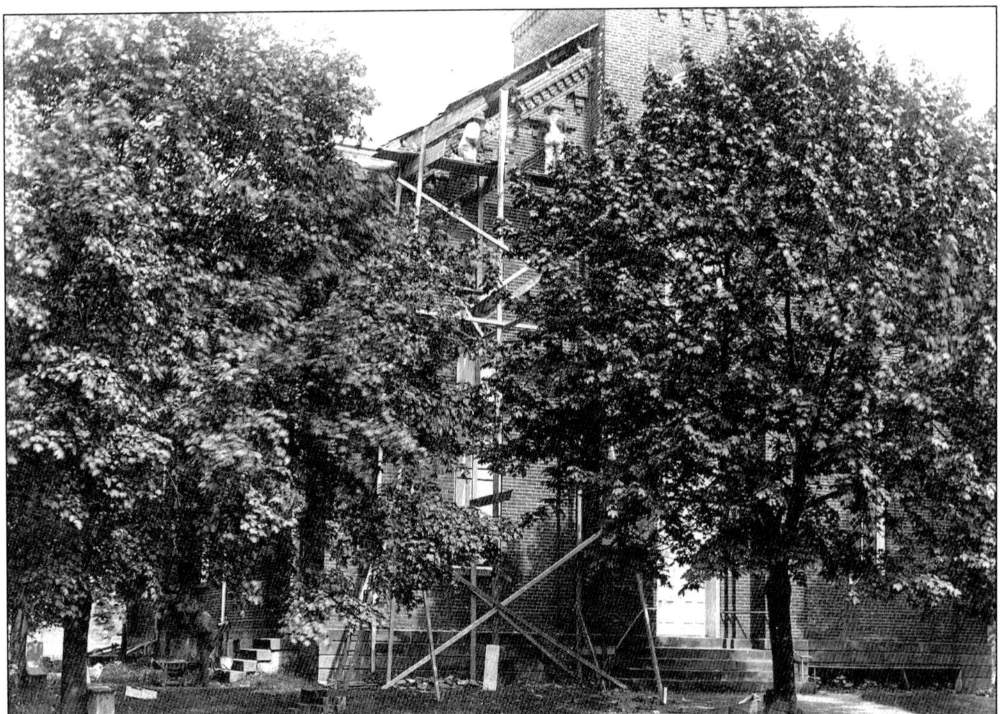

Pictured on this card are workmen on scaffolding doing some finishing work along the roofline of a new edifice to replace the Union Sunday School.

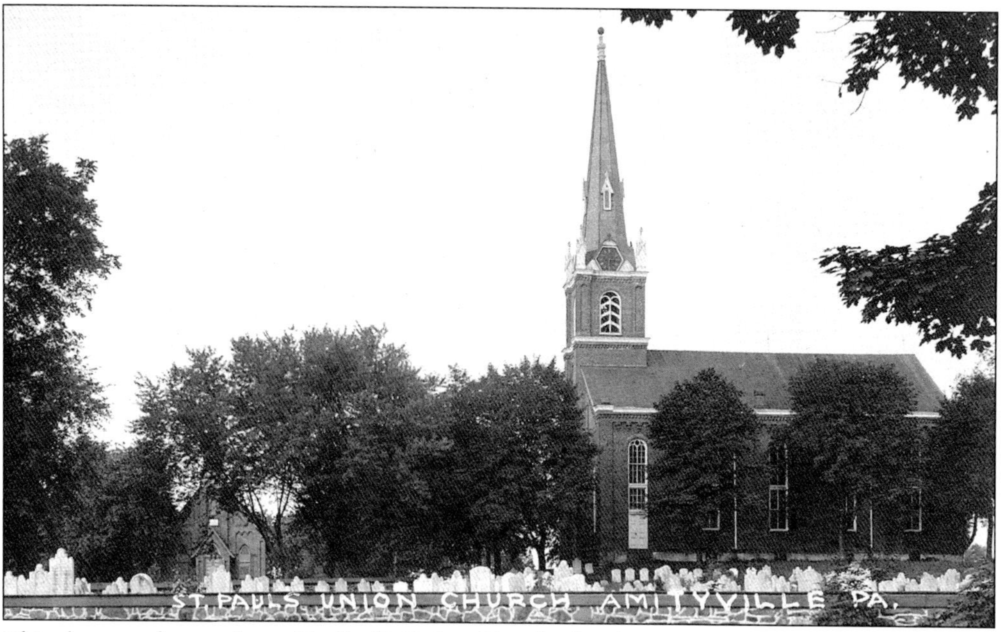

This photograph was taken of St. Paul's Union Church after the construction of the new sanctuary, but prior to June 11, 1922. The Old Union Sunday School is seen to the left in this picture.

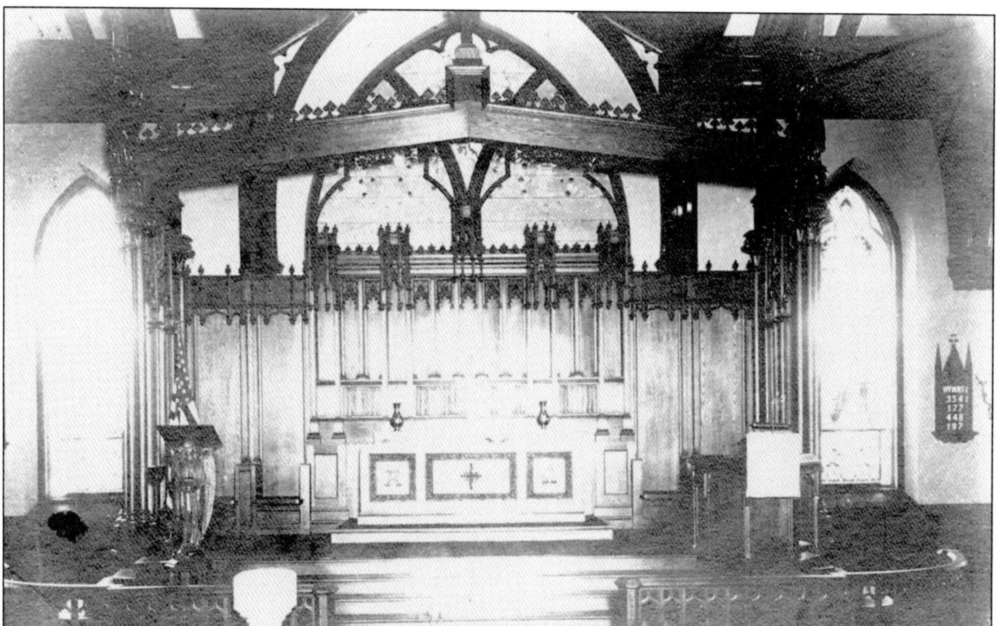

This card of the beautiful interior of St. Paul's Church was postmarked in 1909. Please note the very lovely ornate woodwork.

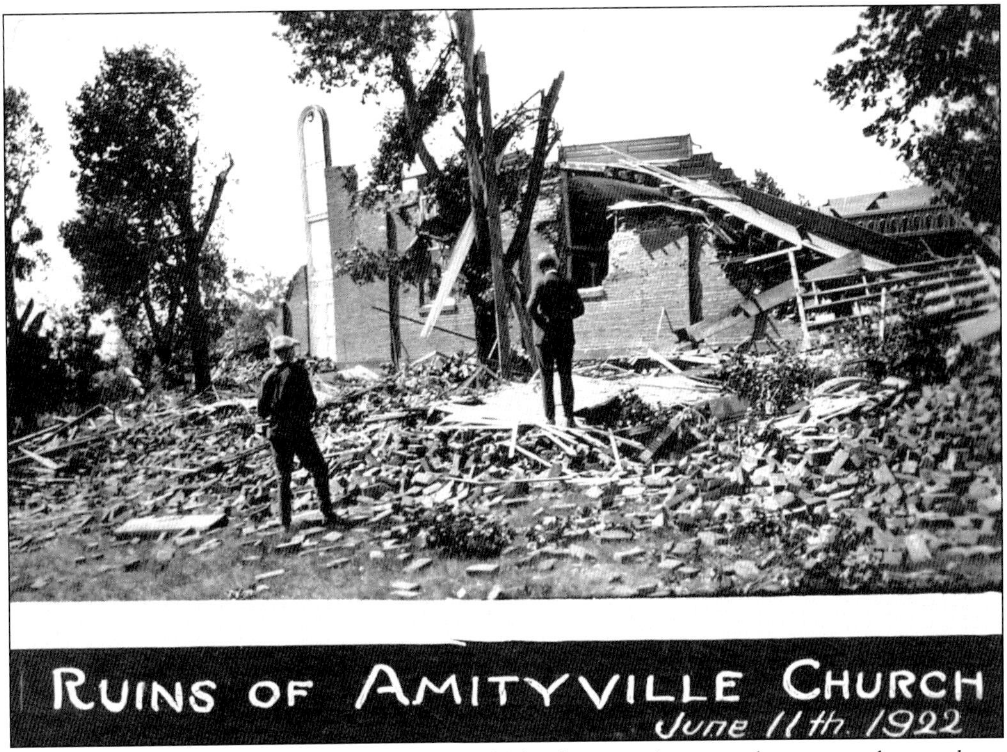

One can only imagine the anguish and despair felt by these gentlemen as they survey the wreckage of their church by a tornado on June 11, 1922.

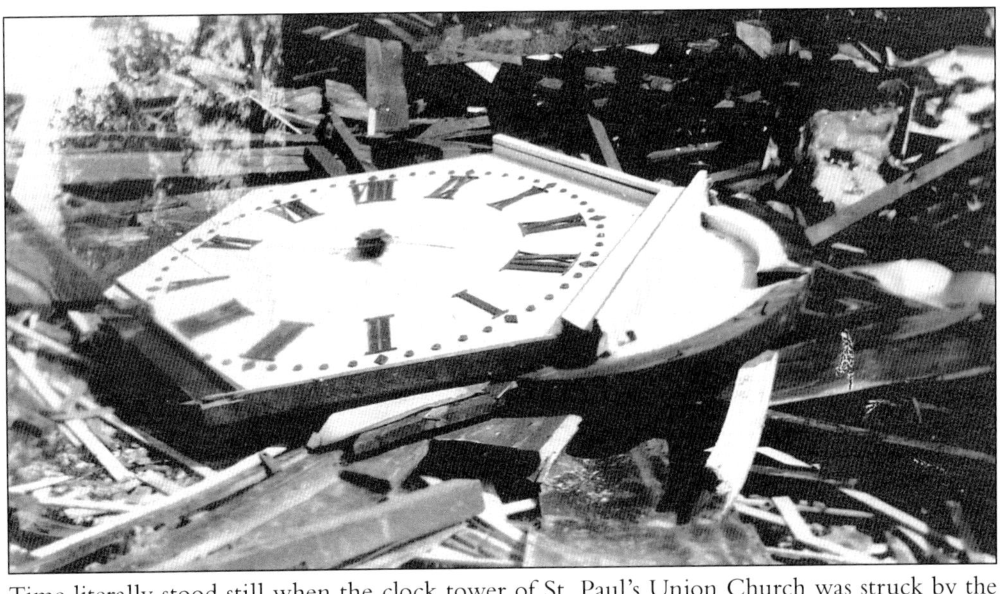

Time literally stood still when the clock tower of St. Paul's Union Church was struck by the twister in 1922.

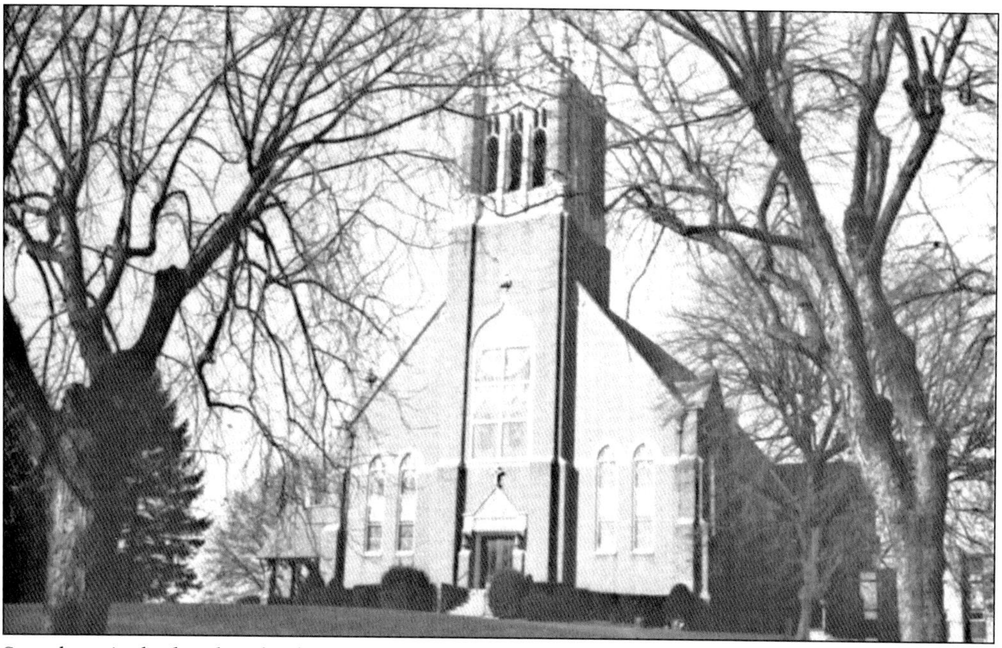

Seen here is the lovely rebuilt St. Paul's Church, which stands today in modern Amityville.

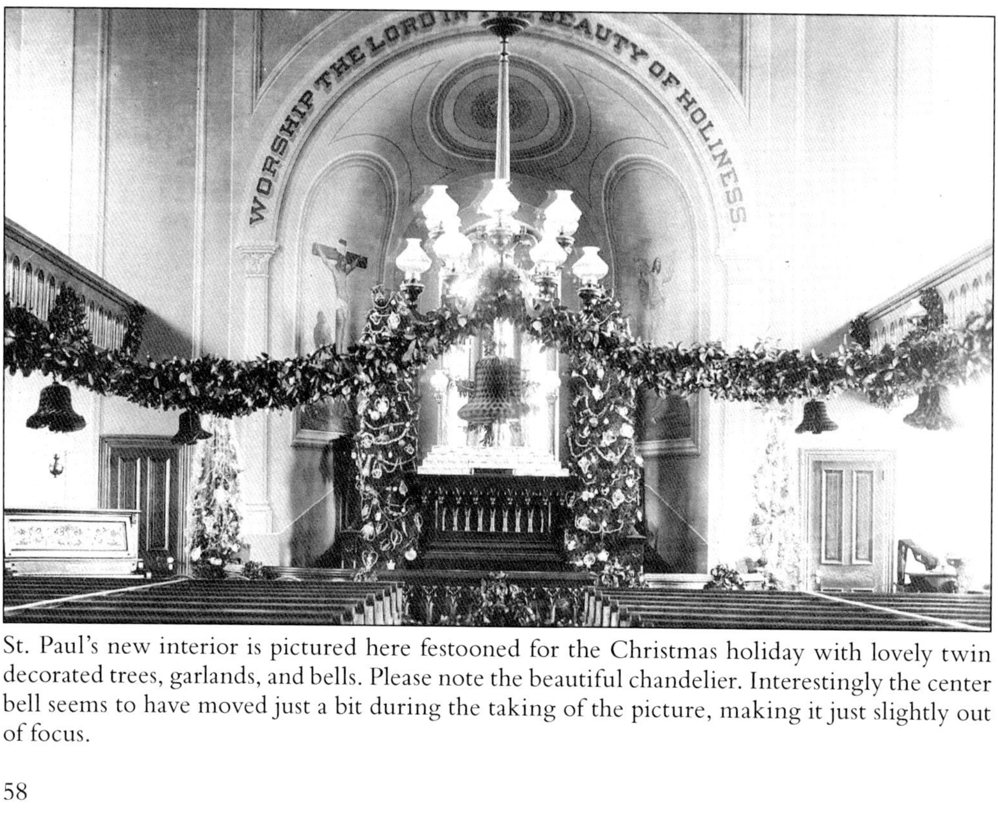

St. Paul's new interior is pictured here festooned for the Christmas holiday with lovely twin decorated trees, garlands, and bells. Please note the beautiful chandelier. Interestingly the center bell seems to have moved just a bit during the taking of the picture, making it just slightly out of focus.

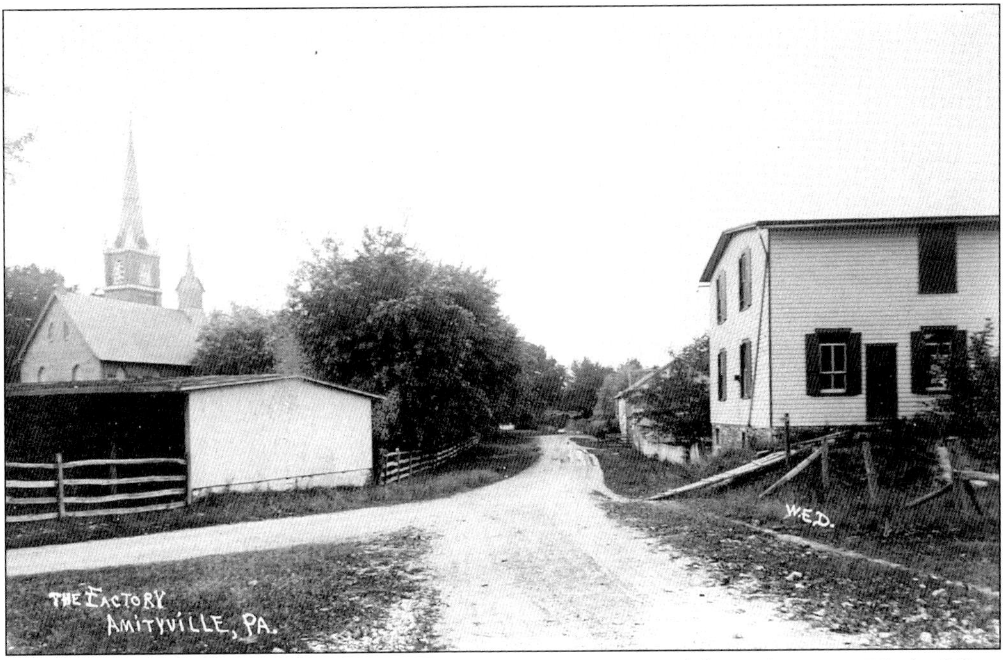

Amityville had another industry. The view is looking east toward the main street. The building on the right was known as the factory. A carriage barn is seen to the left, presumably to service the attendees of St. Paul's Church.

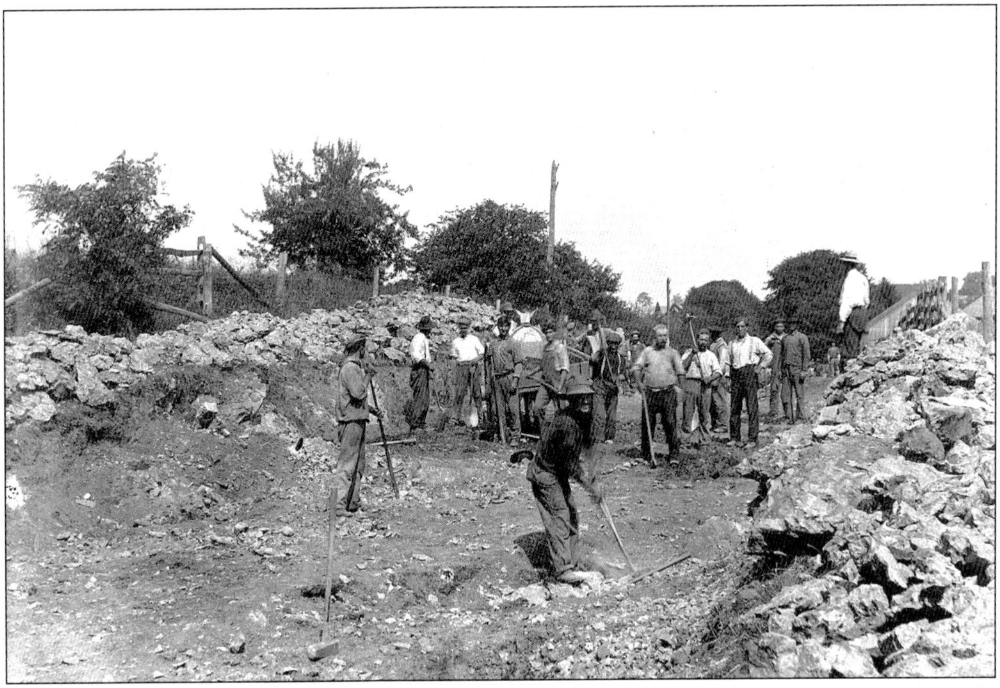

It certainly appears to be a backbreaking endeavor to construct this road in Amity. The only form of mechanization, if one could call it that, seems to be the horse-drawn cart.

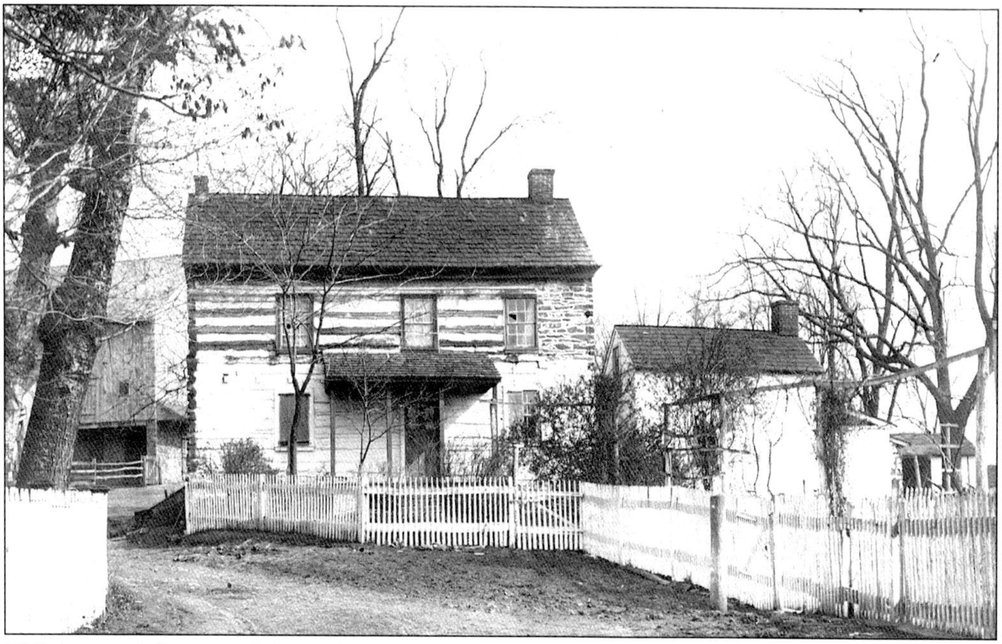

This is certainly one of the earliest homes in the Amityville area. The farmhouse, although of log construction, has a stone end. This would be to accommodate a cooking fireplace. A freestanding bread oven is pictured to the right of the home. It was the original Samuel Whitacre home built around 1739.

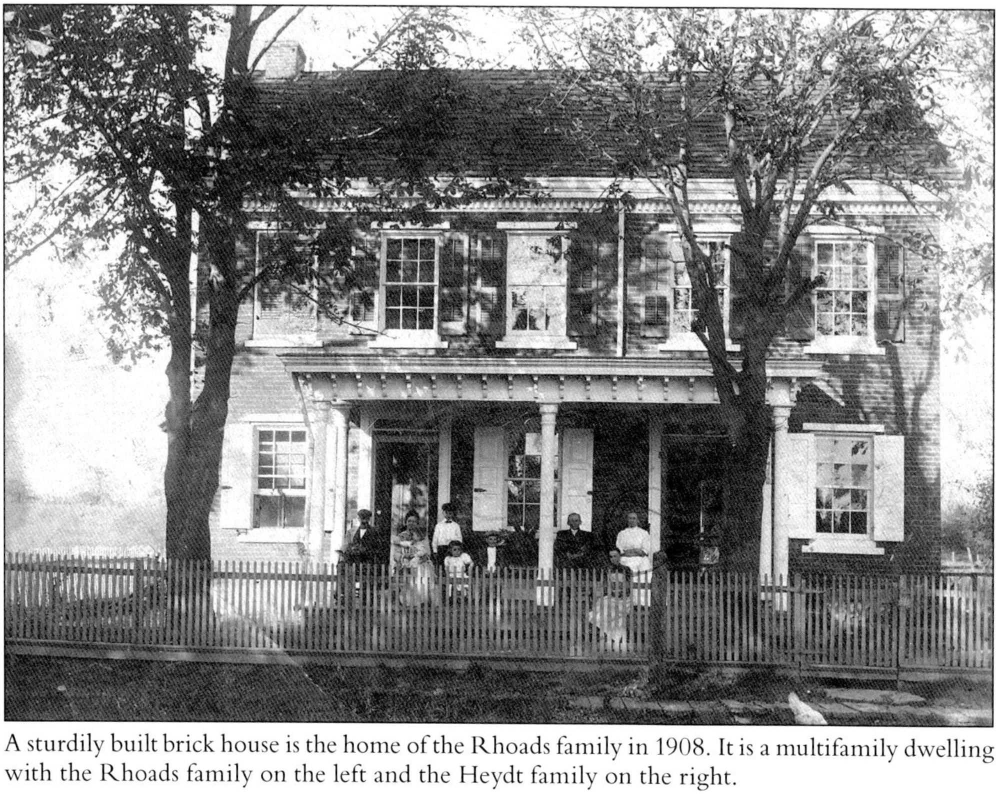

A sturdily built brick house is the home of the Rhoads family in 1908. It is a multifamily dwelling with the Rhoads family on the left and the Heydt family on the right.

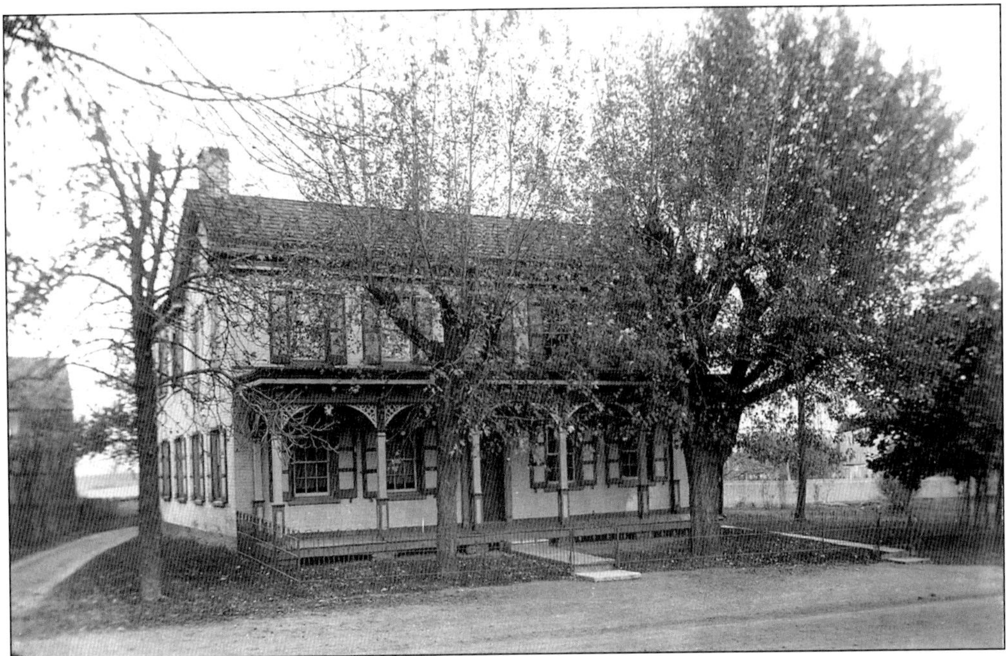

Shown here is another lovely, stately home in Amityville. Please note the Victorian accents with the fancy trim around the porch and the manner in which the shutters are painted. It is difficult to tell if the construction is frame or stucco over stone.

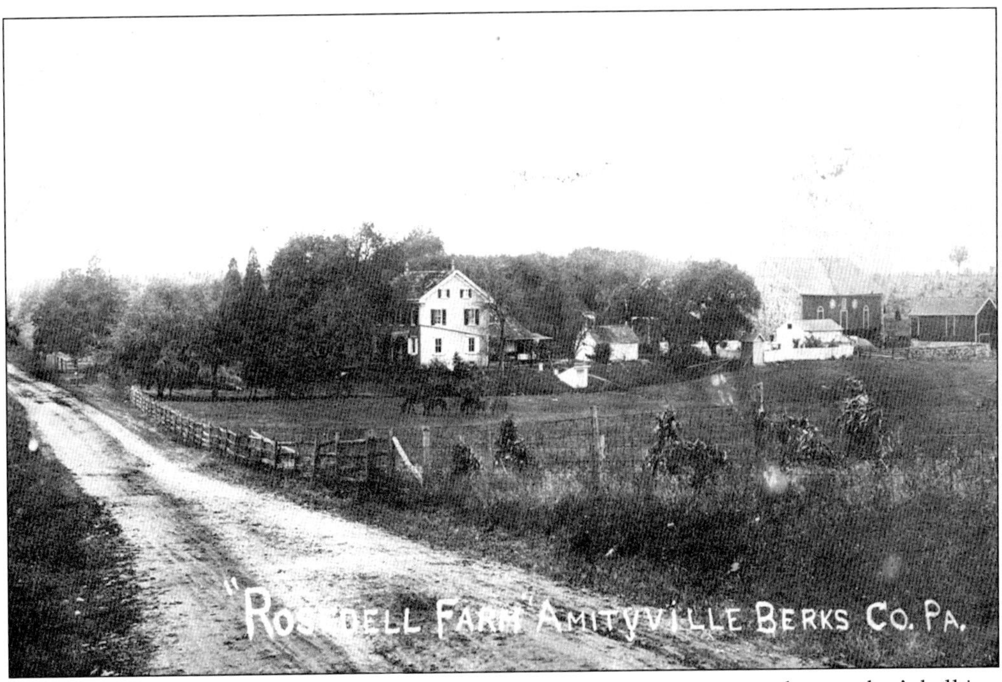

This is an early view of Rosedell Farm. A farm with a similar name met the wrecker's ball just a few years ago to make way for modern needs. That farm sat between the east and west lanes of Route 422. It is believed that this road is the Reading to Philadelphia Pike known as the High Road on a 1775 map.

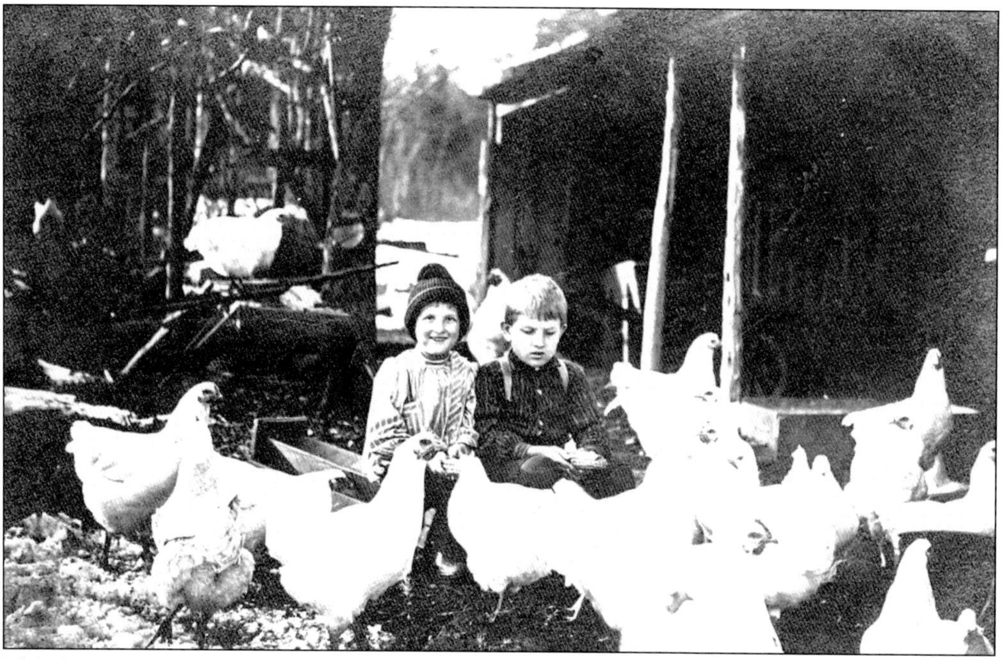

This is a great scene of rural life. The farmer Yergey of Amityville used his children on his advertising card to sell his poultry products. The youngsters probably had some chores like feeding the chickens and gathering the eggs to help the dad.

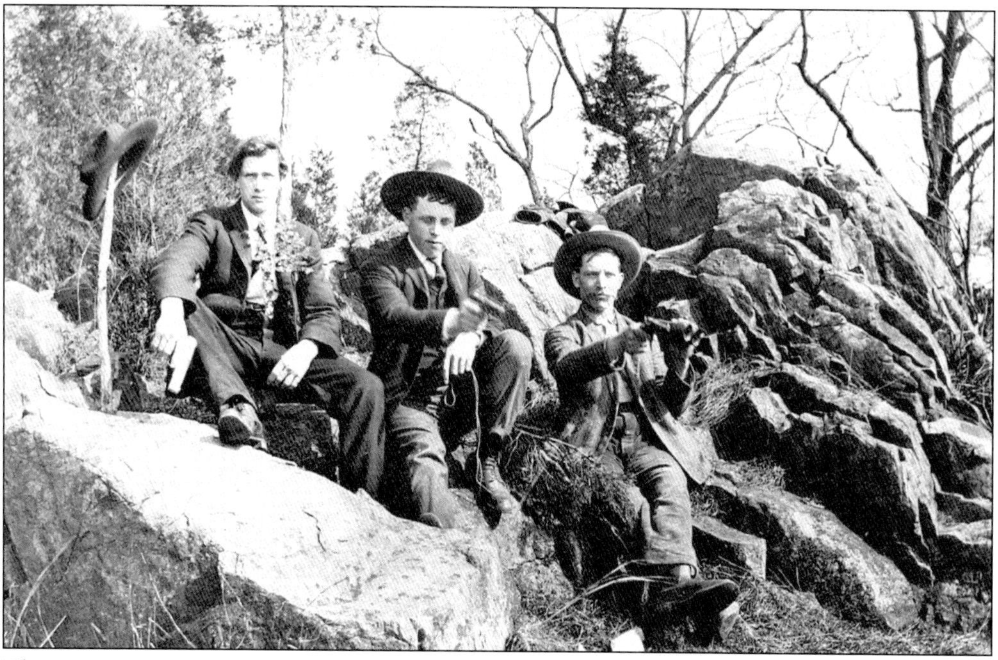

The young men pictured in this early photograph have just climbed Monocacy Hill, the highest point in Amity Township. With weapons in hand, it is assumed they were target shooting and not after the photographer. The author remembers climbing the hill one Easter afternoon with her family, just to be able to say they had done it. It is remembered as being quite a climb with no trails to guide the climbers.

Three

Douglassville, Pine Forge, Little Oley, Englesville, Greshville, and Morysville

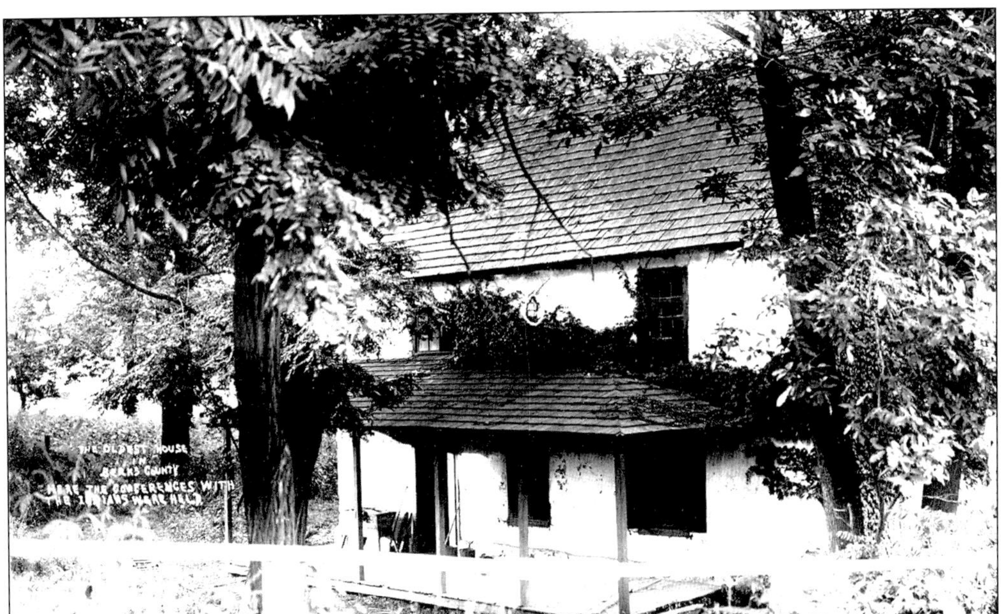

The first settlement in Berks County was by a group of Swedes in 1701–1705 at what they called Morlatton along the north bank of the Schuylkill River. The Mounce Jones House, the oldest home in Berks County, was built in 1716 and is seen here in a 1909 postcard.

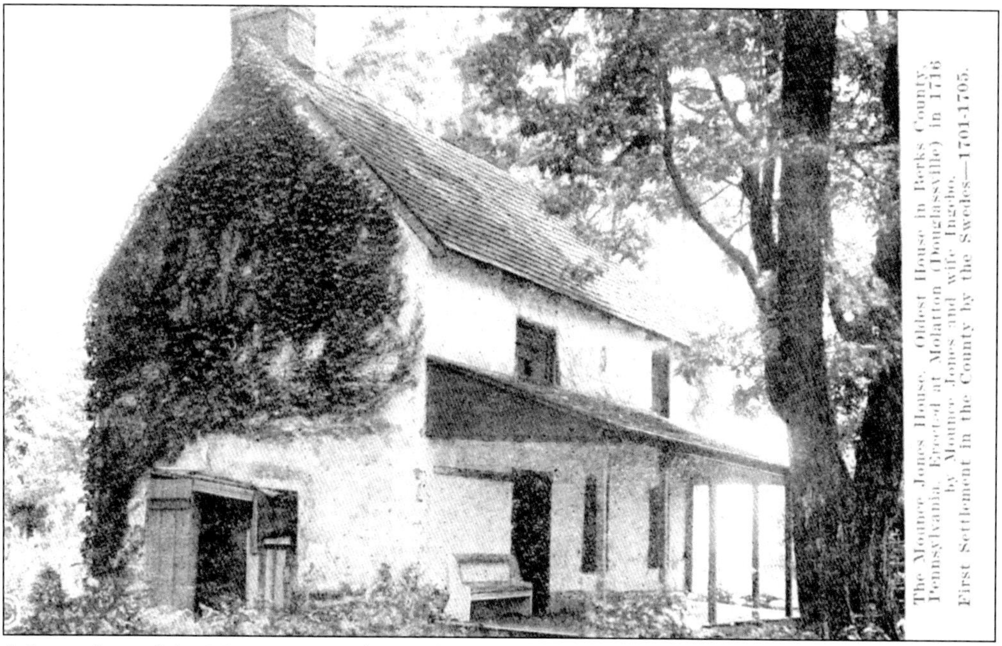

A later view of the Mounce Jones home finds it in better repair. It is still standing across from the bridge keeper's home along the road that led to the covered bridge spanning the Schuylkill River. It is now under the care of the Berks County Historical Preservation Trust, which has done excellent work in maintaining several very old structures in this area. This home looks even better today.

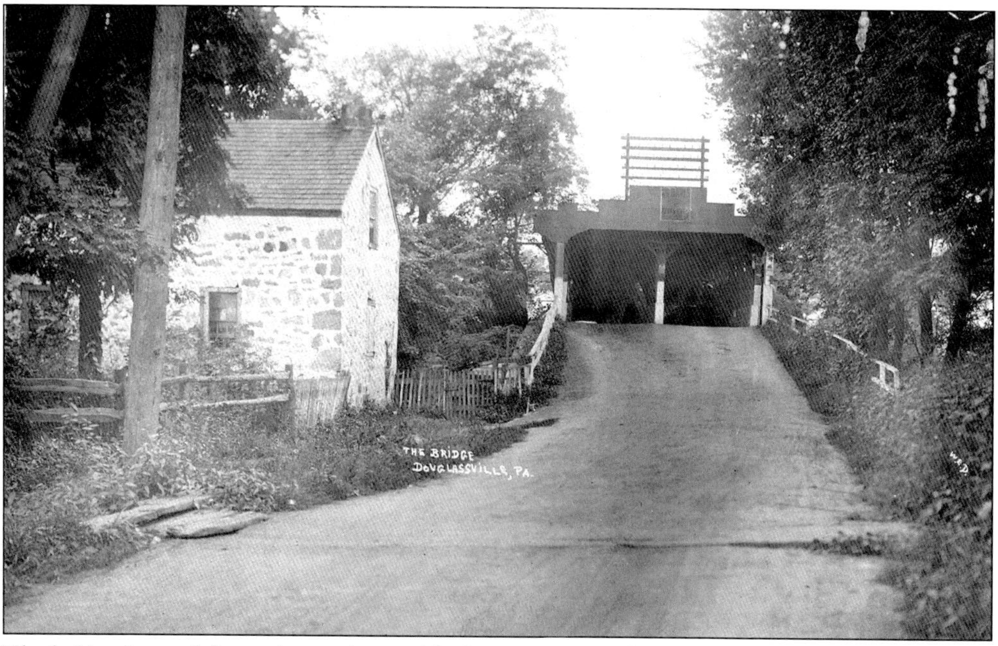

The bridge keeper's home is seen here with the entrance to the covered bridge. Both the bridge keeper's home and the Mounce Jones home stand as mute evidence of the history they have witnessed in nearly 400 years. There are celebrations here each fall for historically minded folks to learn more about and to celebrate their heritage in the Amity and Douglass Townships area.

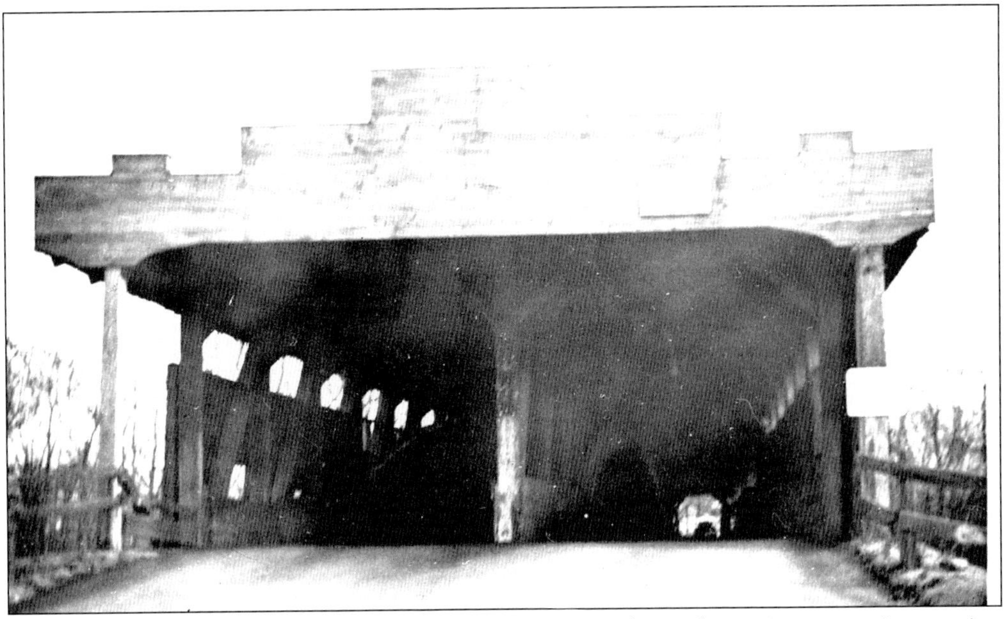

The Douglassville covered bridge was a huge structure with two lanes. It was a major crossing of the Schuylkill River between Pottstown and Birdsboro and was used until the 1950s.

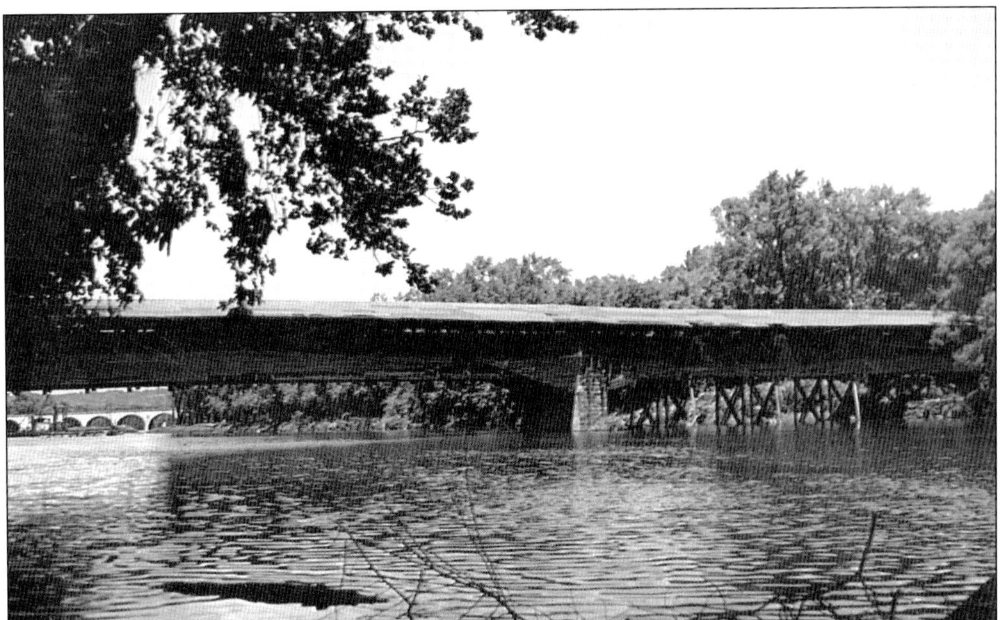

A better view of the bridge's length is afforded in this view. In the distance is a railroad bridge, which still stands today. The covered bridge met its demise in 1972 at the hands of Hurricane Agnes.

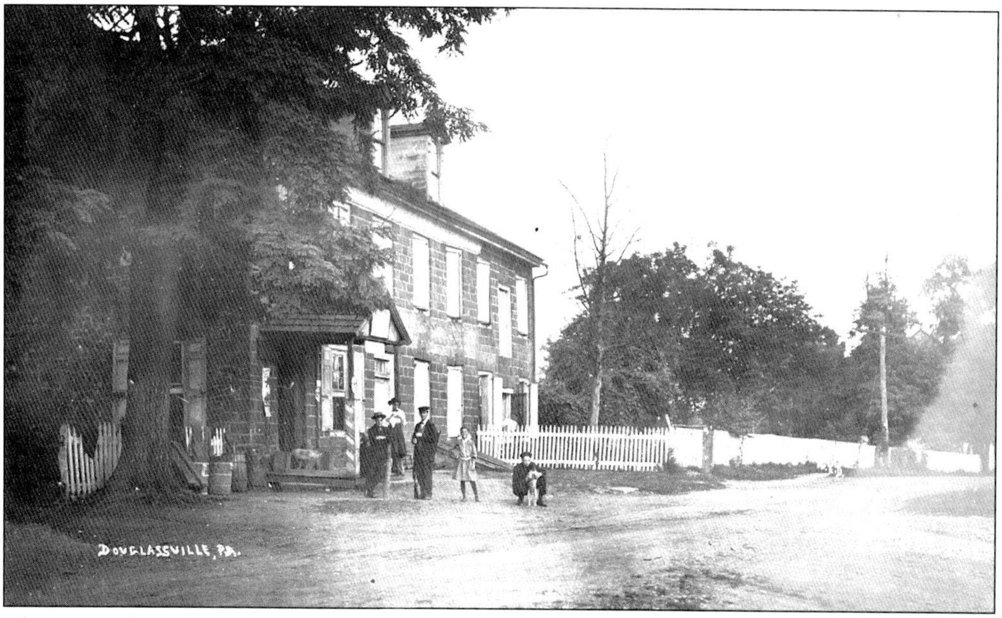

The original George Douglass Mansion was erected in 1763. The dark eaves portion of the home was added in 1834. Douglass was a storekeeper. It is unclear whether Douglass Township was named for him or another member of his family. The home would have been situated along the original Reading to Philadelphia Pike. The mansion, too, is in the hands of the Berks County Historical Preservation Trust.

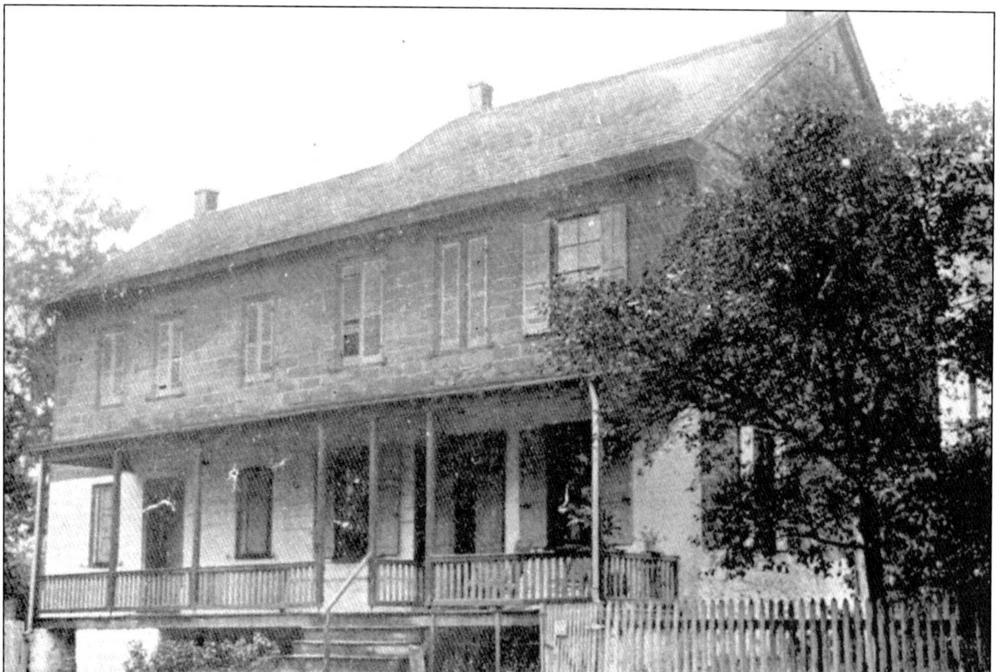

The White Horse Tavern, also under the protection of the Berks County Historical Preservation Trust, was in operation in 1740 and thrived for many of the early Colonial years. It is unknown if this is the original 1740 edifice, but it is felt that this building is no newer than 1762.

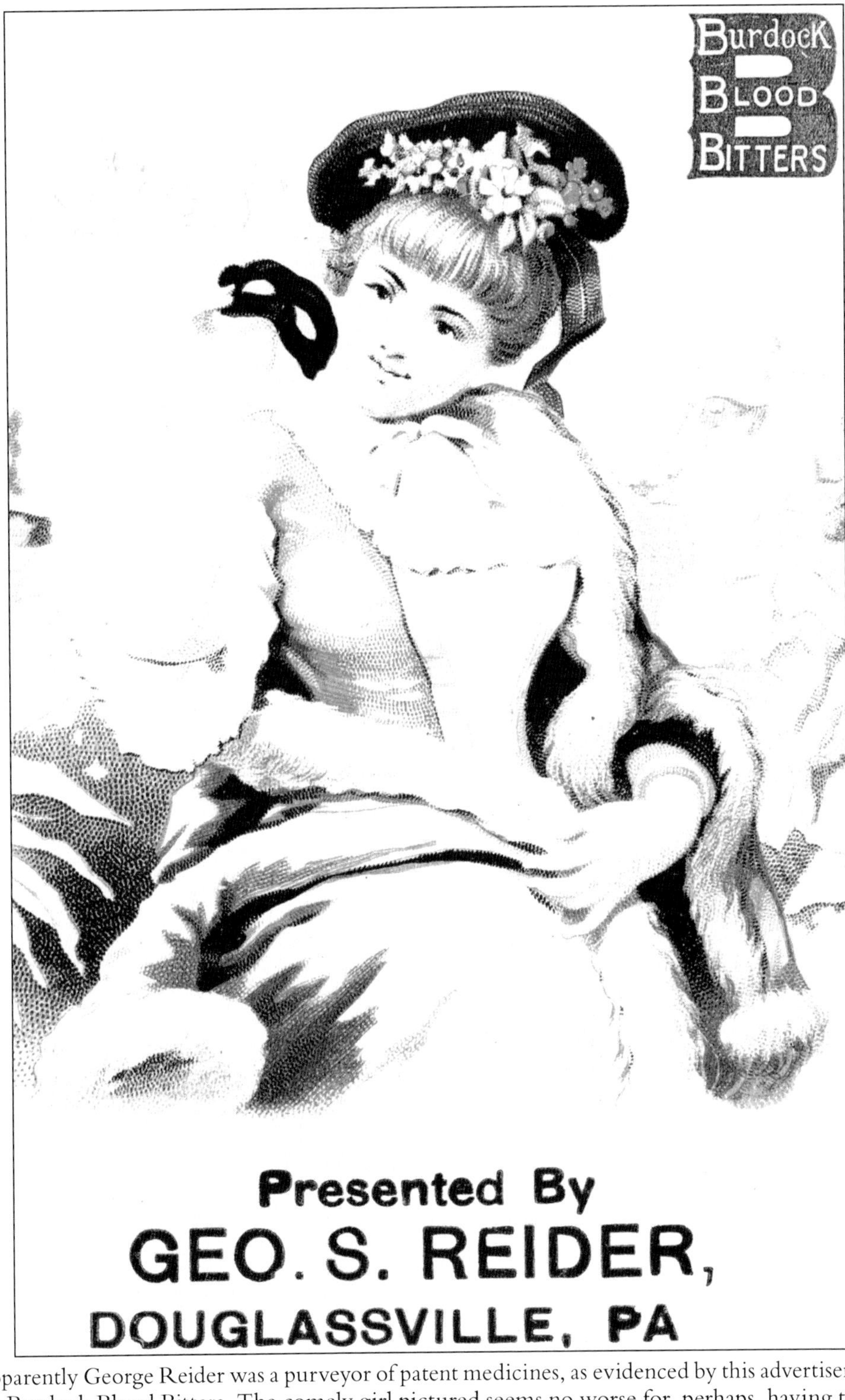

Apparently George Reider was a purveyor of patent medicines, as evidenced by this advertisement for Burdock Blood Bitters. The comely girl pictured seems no worse for, perhaps, having taken some of the bitters, but it does not sound too enticing to this writer.

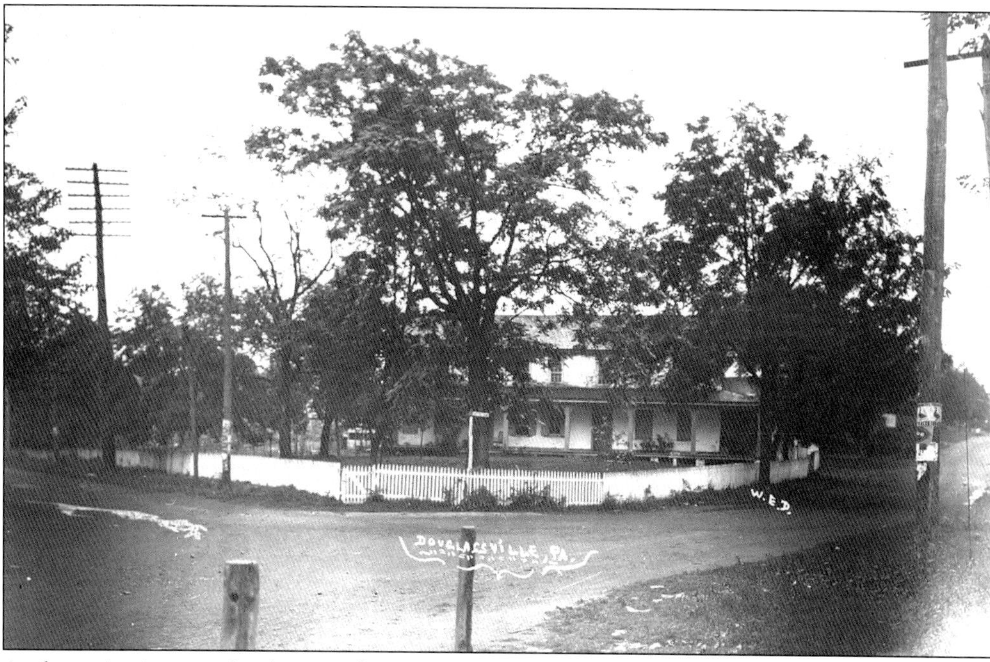

At the major intersection in Douglassville stands this building, now apartments, which housed the Farmers and Drovers Hotel. Drovers were men who drove cattle to markets to facilitate their sale for the farmers. They were similar to cowboys of the West, and there was good money in this occupation for the "boss man."

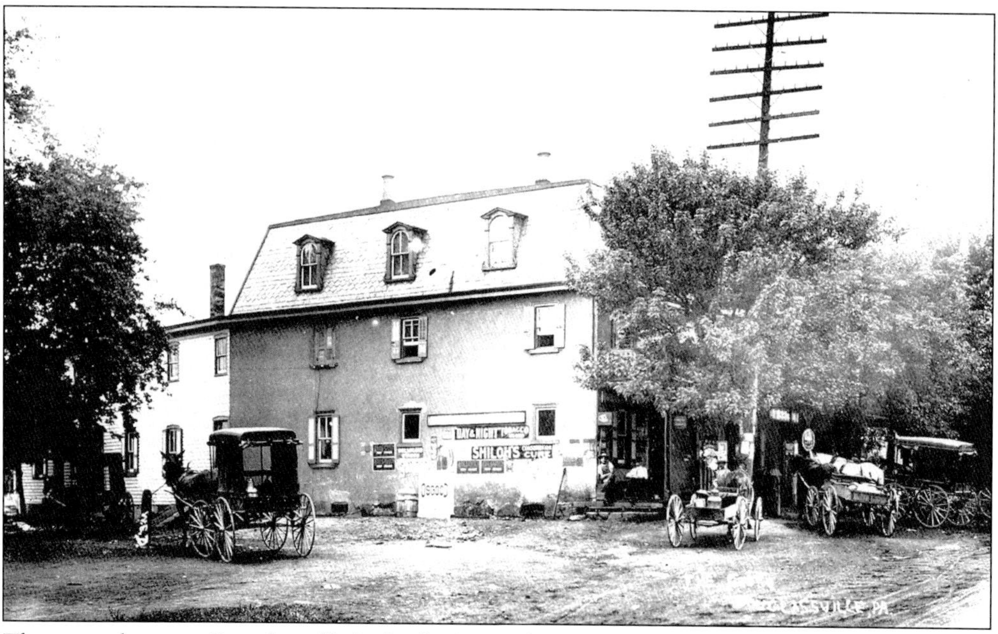

The general store at Douglassville in Amity Township is still standing and houses a 21st-century business. What a joy to see it and other old buildings preserved and utilized. It was obviously a busy gathering place as it is today. Too many historic buildings have gone the way of the wrecker, and future generations will suffer from a lack of knowledge of their locale's rich heritage.

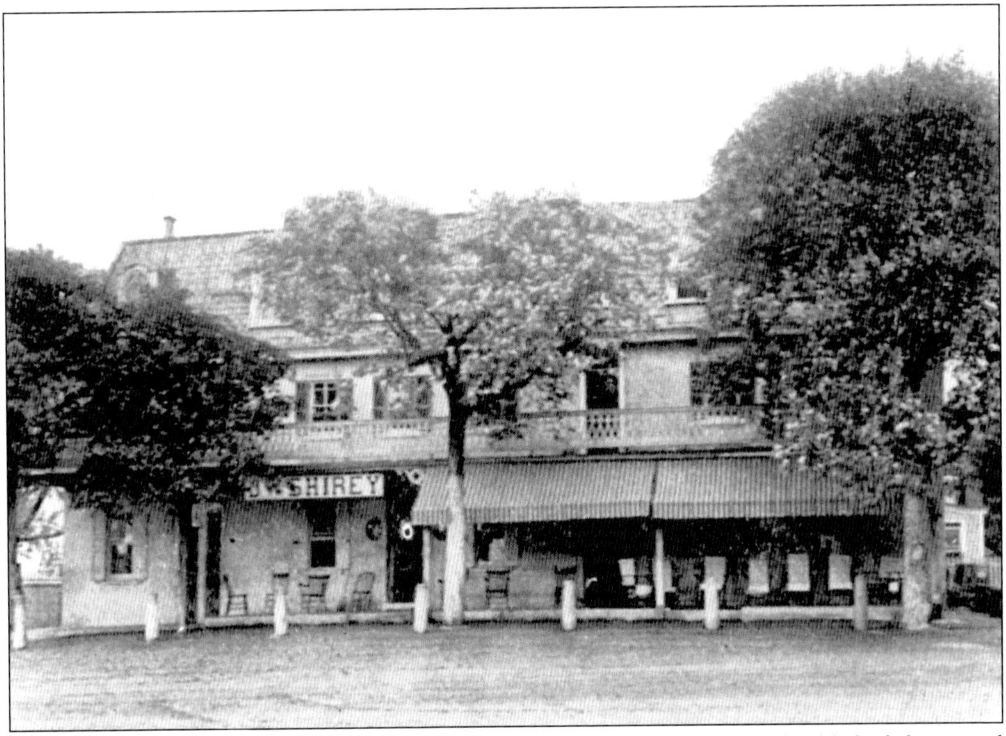

Here is the hotel under the proprietorship of D. W. Shirey. Please note the lovely old plank-bottomed chairs on the left side of the porch and the more elegant cushioned ones on the right. Hitching posts are still present, indicating a horse-drawn clientele.

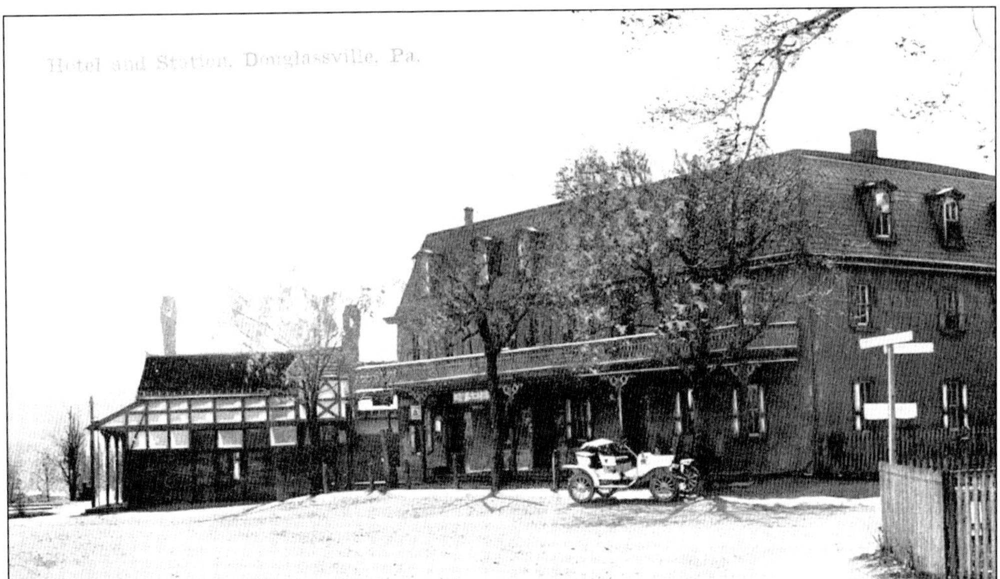

A later view of the hotel shows that the horse-drawn clientele has been replaced with newer forms of transportation. A great roadster has stopped, and the railroad station has been built to the rear of the hotel.

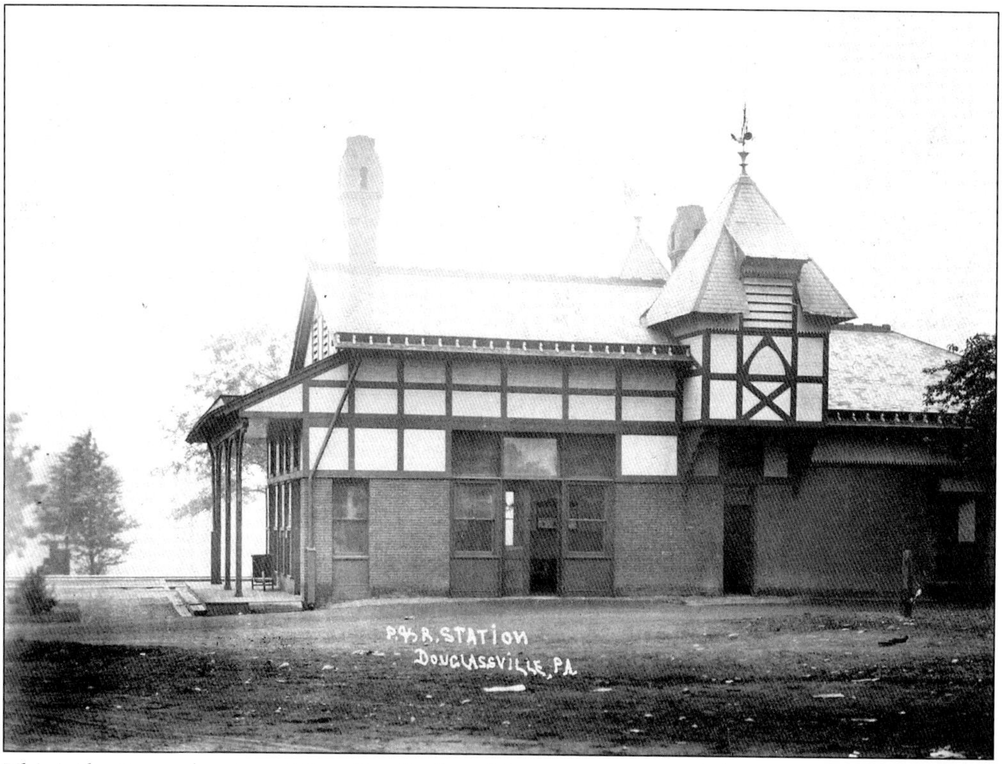

This is the Pennsylvania and Reading Railroad Station constructed about 1920. It certainly has interesting chimneys. They probably serviced big, old coal stoves used to heat the building.

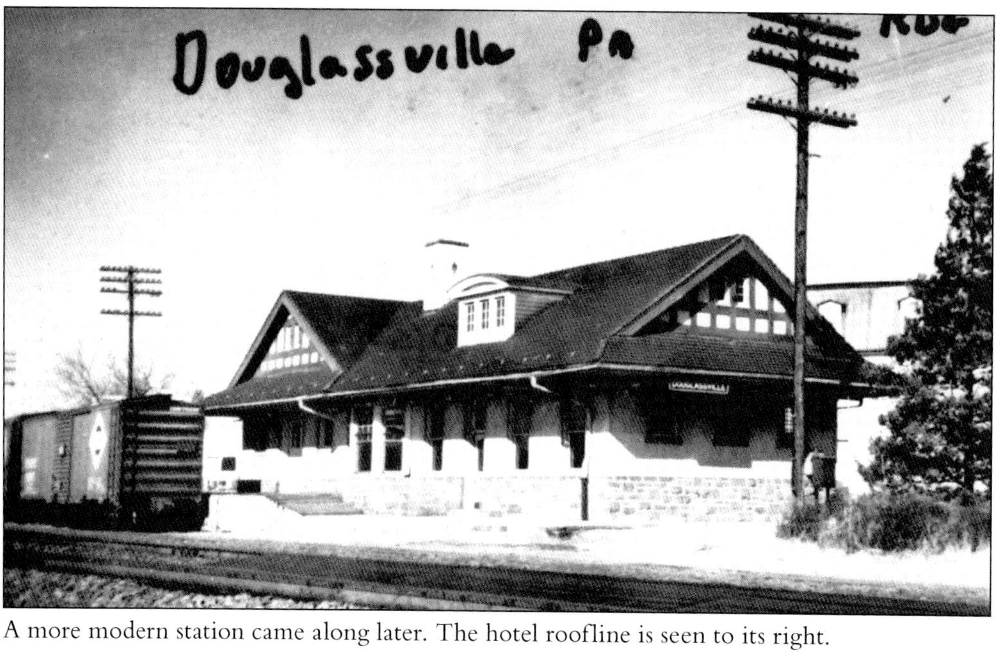

A more modern station came along later. The hotel roofline is seen to its right.

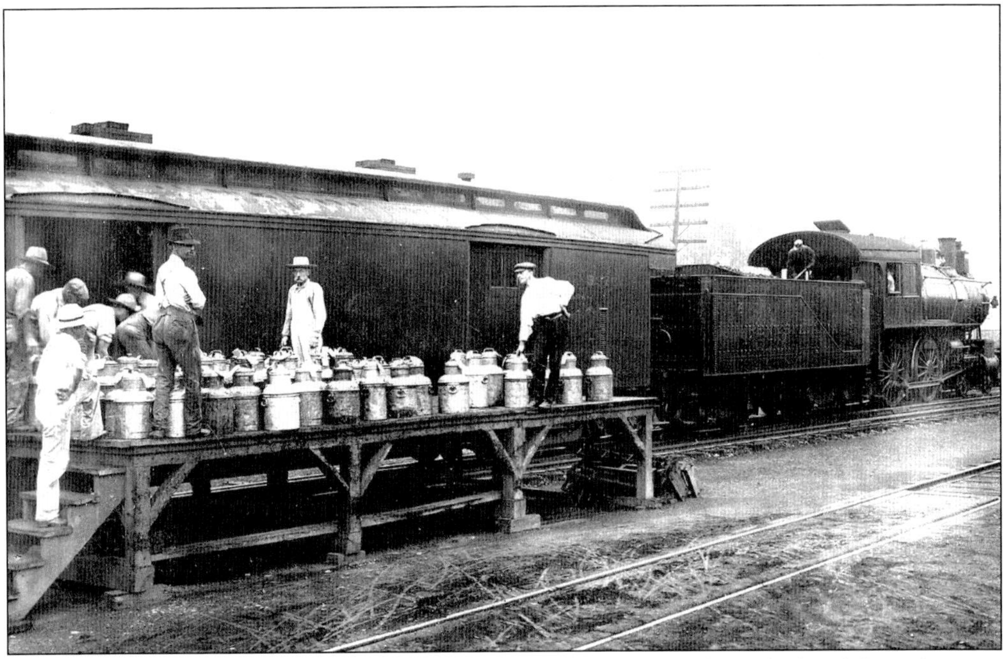

The freight train became a very efficient method of getting milk from the local dairy farms to the various cities and towns that were served by railroad.

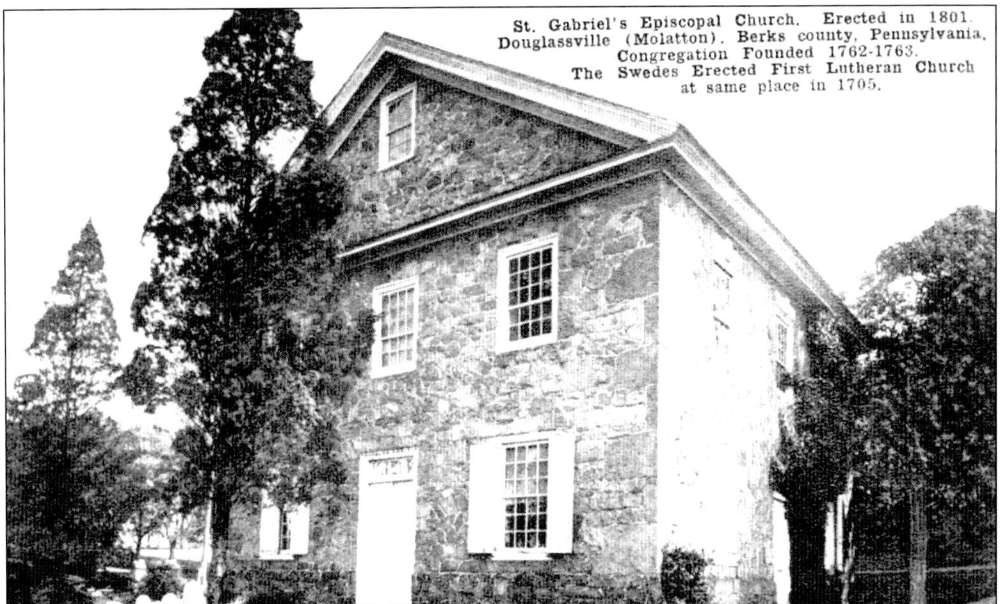

This was the old St. Gabriel's Episcopal Church built in 1801 for the original congregation founded in the 1780s. The first Lutheran church in the area was built on this same spot by the Swedes in 1705.

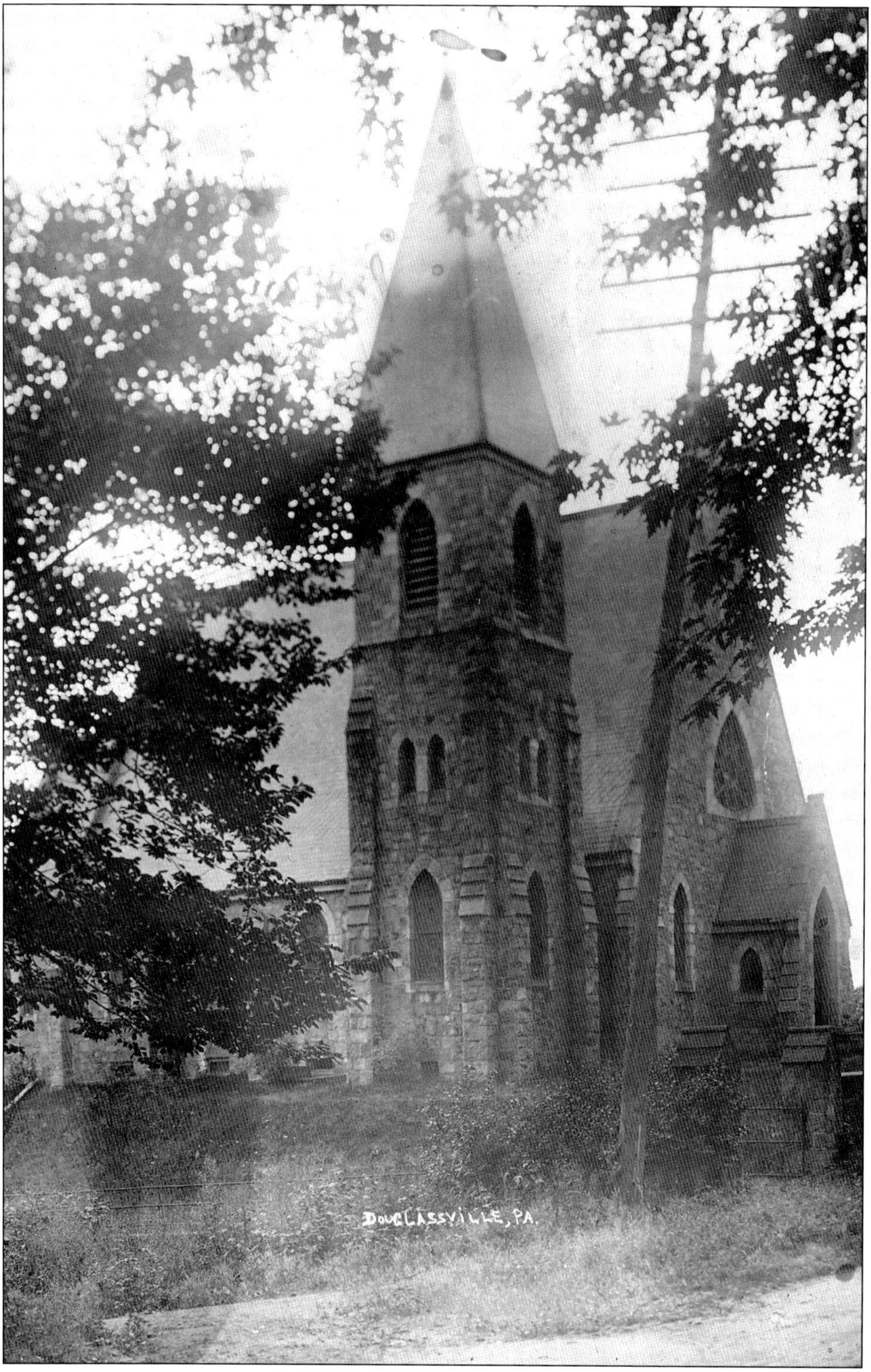

This is a very early real-photo postcard of St. Gabriel's Church built over a period of four years from 1880 to 1884.

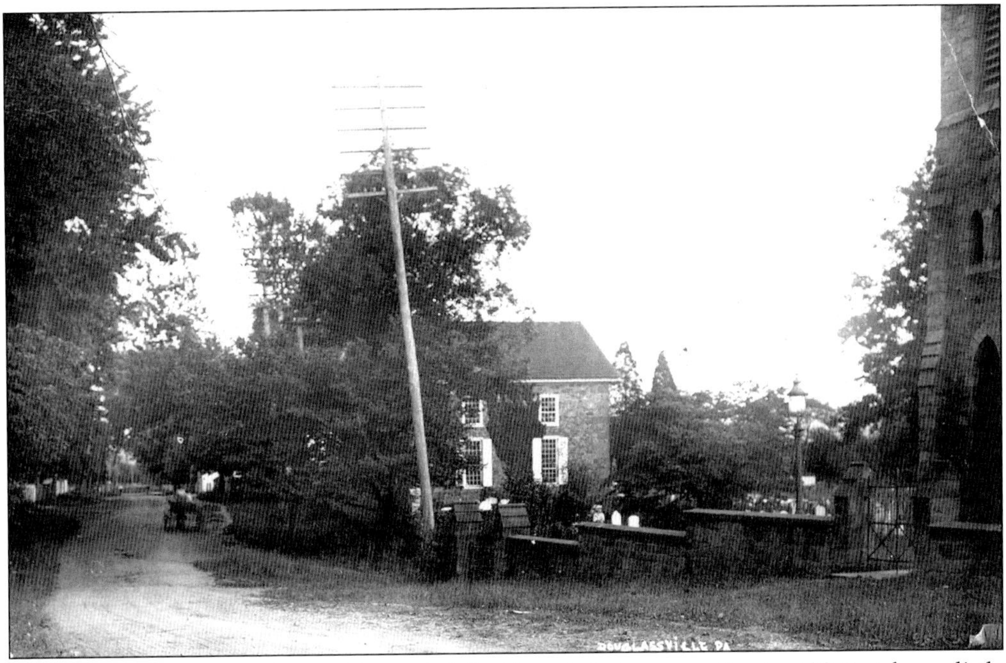

The view was taken in front of St. Gabriel's Church facing east. Route 422 East bears little resemblance to this country dirt road, The man and his cart would be swept away with the 18-wheelers coming through Douglassville today.

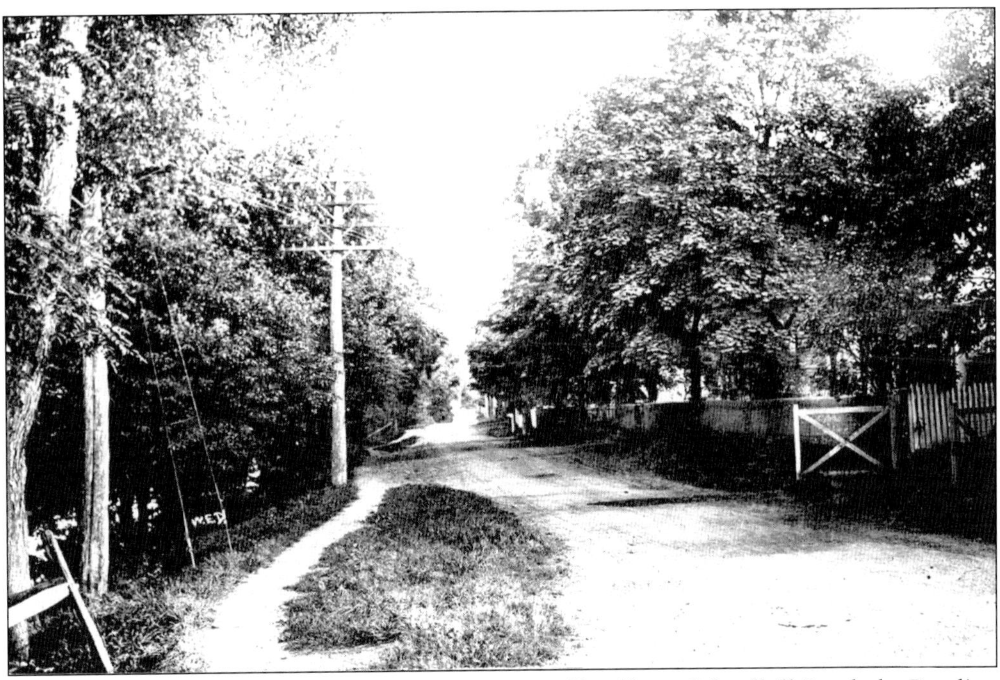

Another view of the Schuylkill Road looking east is offered here. Schuylkill Road, the Reading Philadelphia Pike, and Route 422 are all the same road from different periods of time. One's age can be measured by how she or he refers to the road.

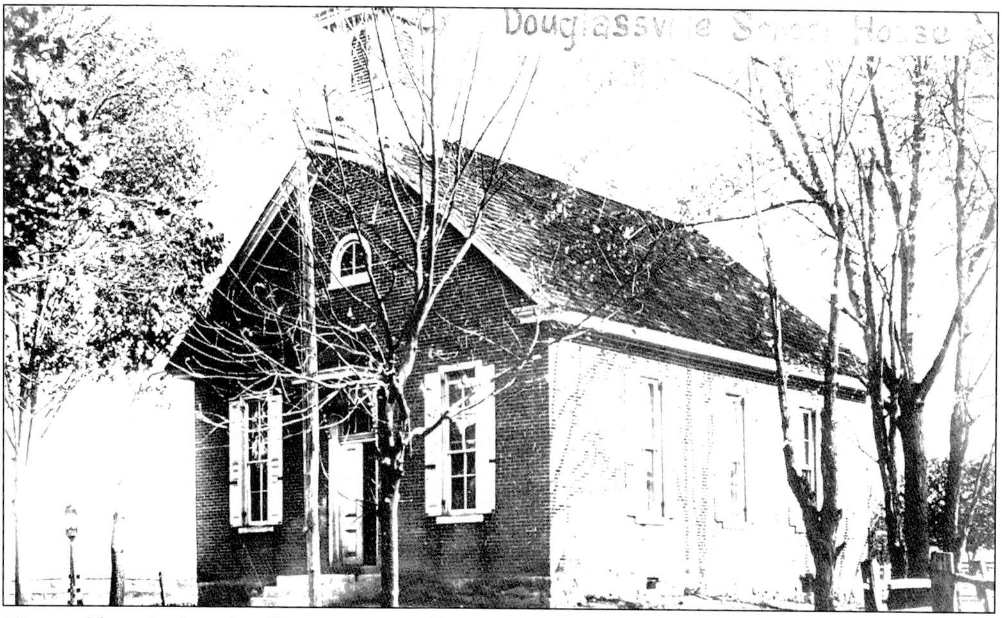

Pictured here is the schoolhouse at Douglassville.

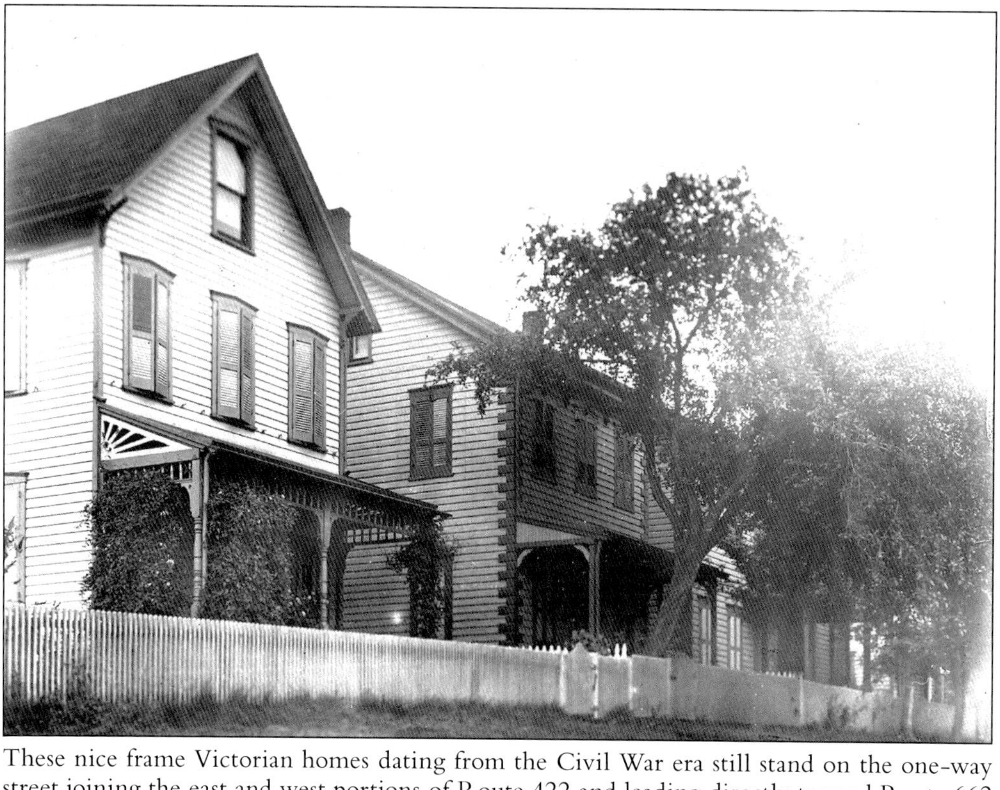

These nice frame Victorian homes dating from the Civil War era still stand on the one-way street joining the east and west portions of Route 422 and leading directly toward Route 662 and Amityville.

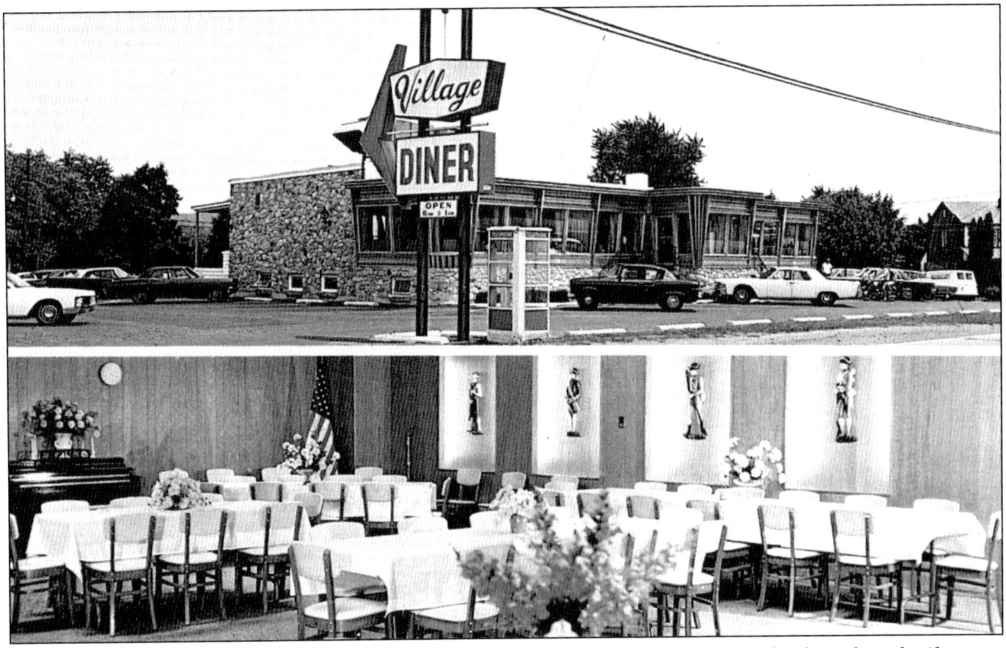

At the current intersection of Routes 662 and 422 stands this diner, which, when built, was known as the Village Diner. Under different management, it still stands and offers a nice affordable menu.

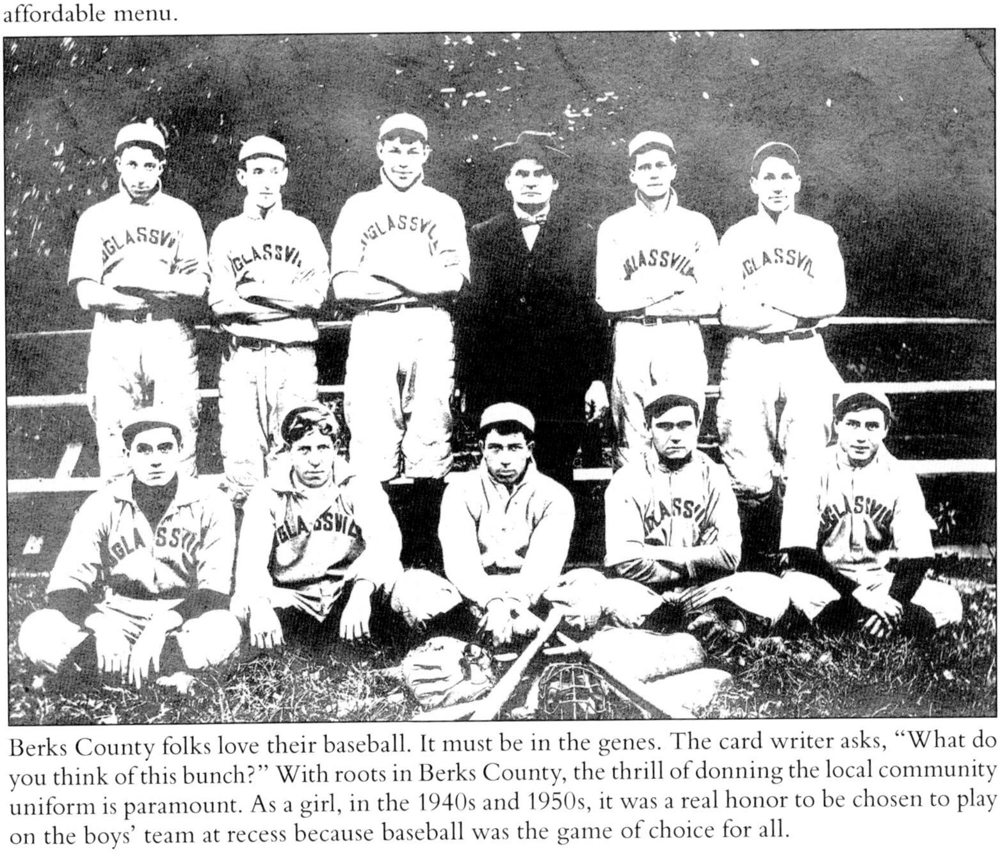
Berks County folks love their baseball. It must be in the genes. The card writer asks, "What do you think of this bunch?" With roots in Berks County, the thrill of donning the local community uniform is paramount. As a girl, in the 1940s and 1950s, it was a real honor to be chosen to play on the boys' team at recess because baseball was the game of choice for all.

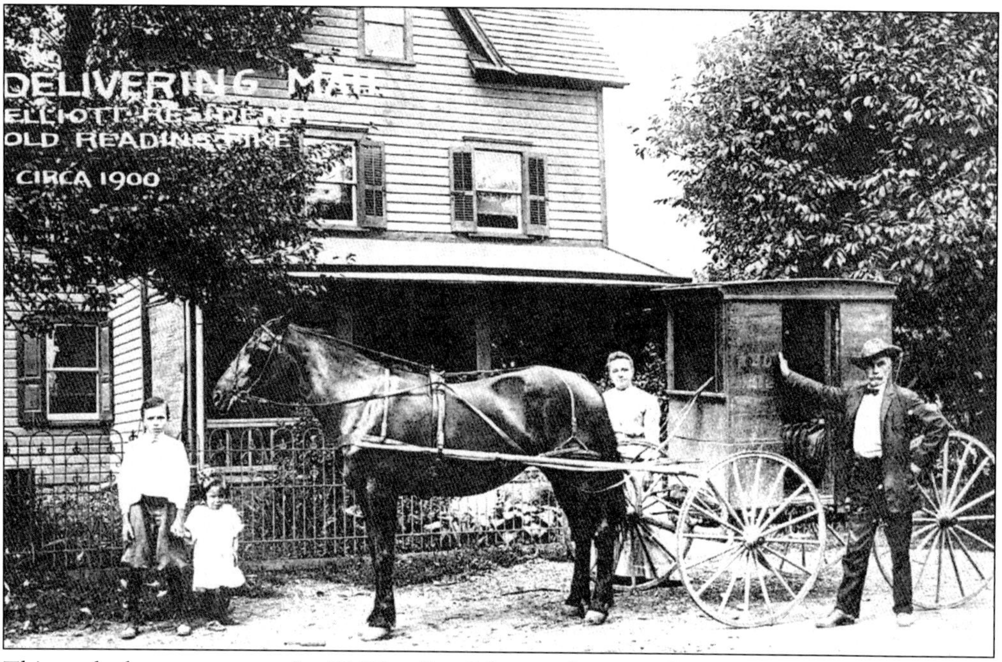

This card takes one east on the Old Reading Pike to where a milk delivery is being made to the Elliott family. One is now in Douglass Township, having left Amity Township.

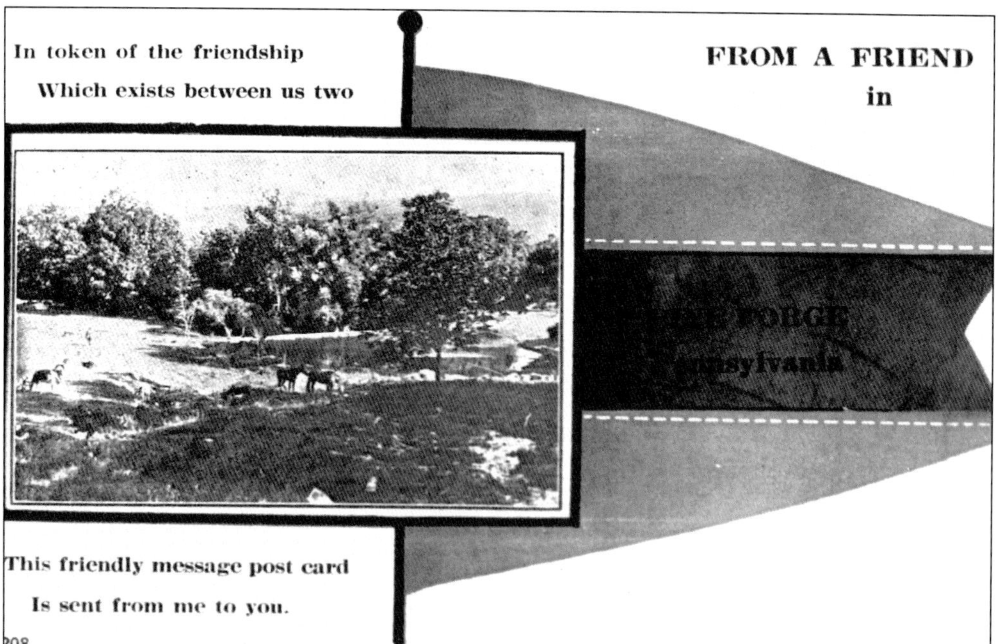

Even though generic, it is nice to have a greeting card from such a small hamlet as Pine Forge. The tour continues across Route 422 and continues into Pine Forge on the current Douglass Drive.

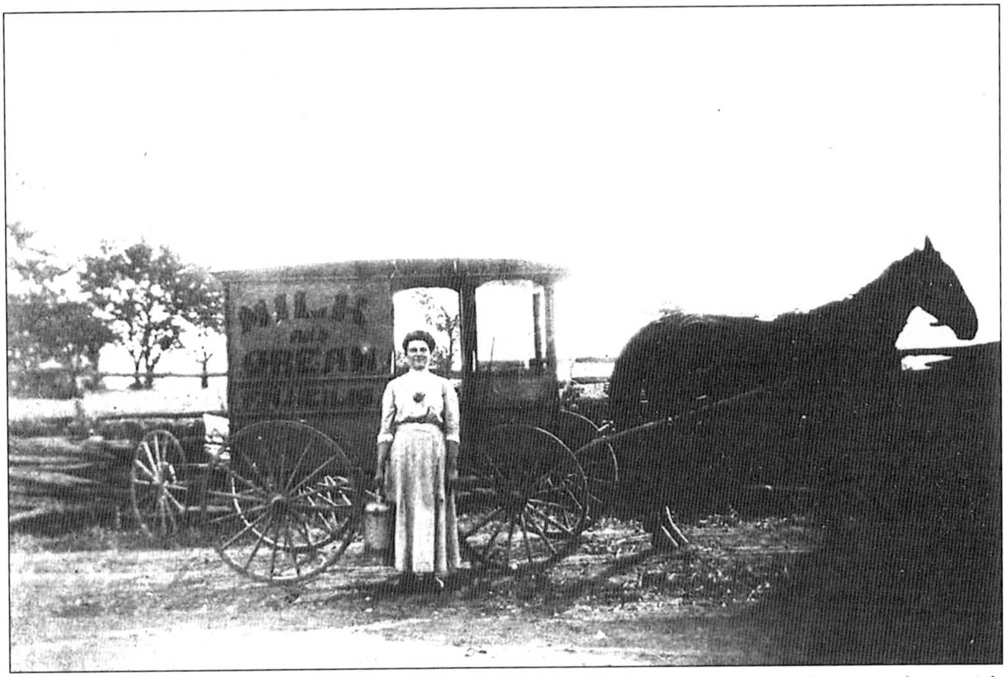

Along the way to Pine Forge is the Francis Heilig farm. His daughter, Hannah, is seen here with a milk can and the horse-drawn dairy wagon belonging to her father. Hannah's mother was Dr. Elizabeth Bertolet Heilig, who was discussed in the Oley chapter.

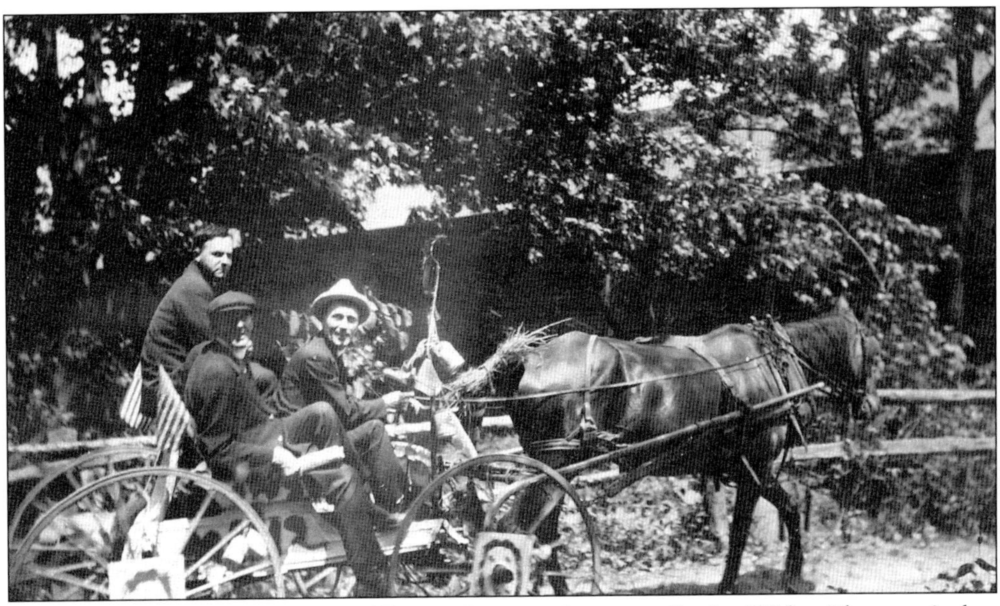

Traveling to Pine Forge are these fellows who are going to see Squire Wisler. They are Arthur Jones, Elmer Heilig, and William Detwiler.

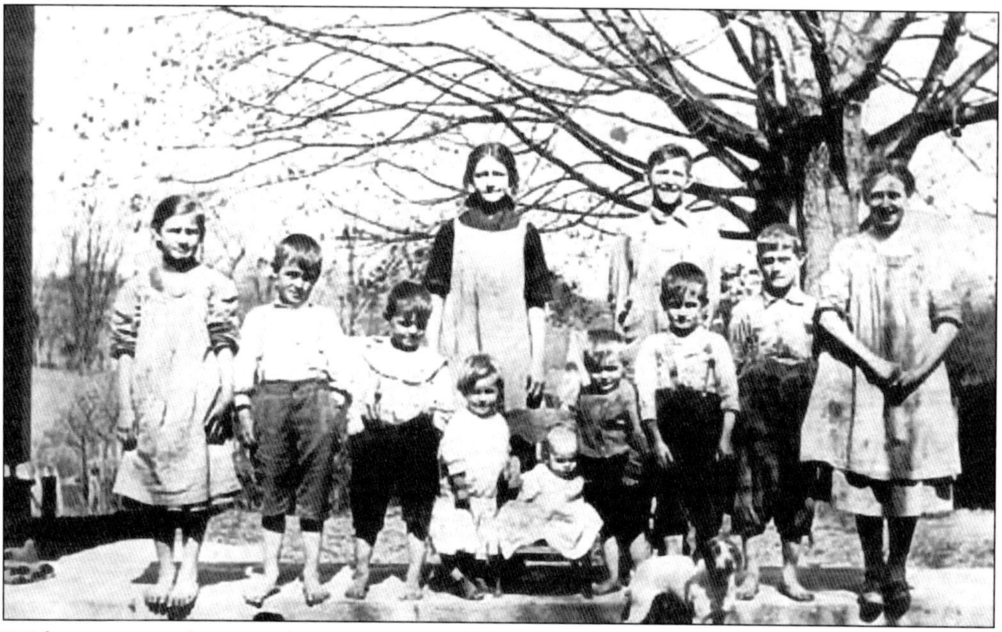

Wisler was a very busy gentleman. He was a schoolteacher for many years, a justice of the peace, a barber, a prize poultry grower, and a farmer. He always said his 11 children were his best crop. This card dates from about 1915.

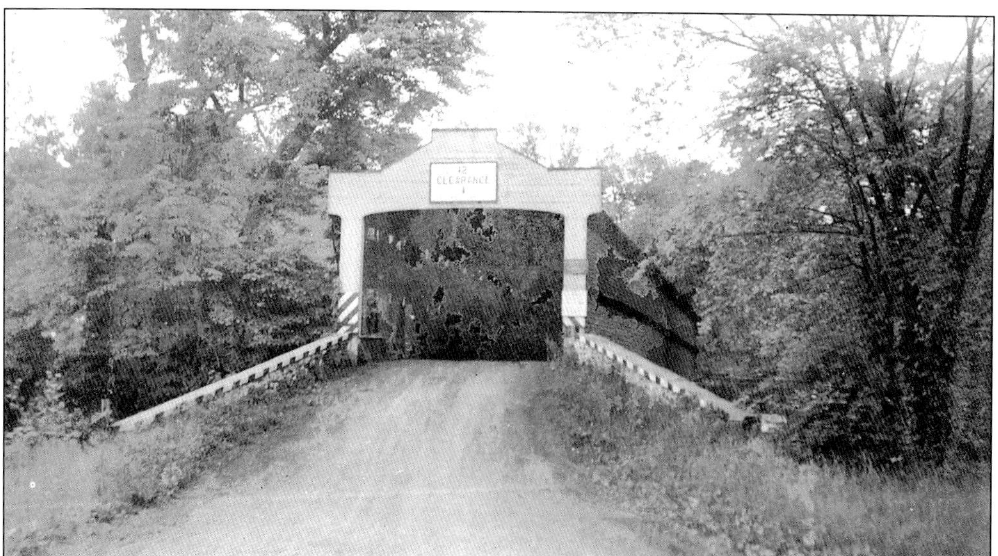

Just below the Wisler farmstead, one crosses the Manatawny Creek through a covered bridge, which is no longer there. This leads to the south end of the former Rutter Estate, now the Pine Forge Academy.

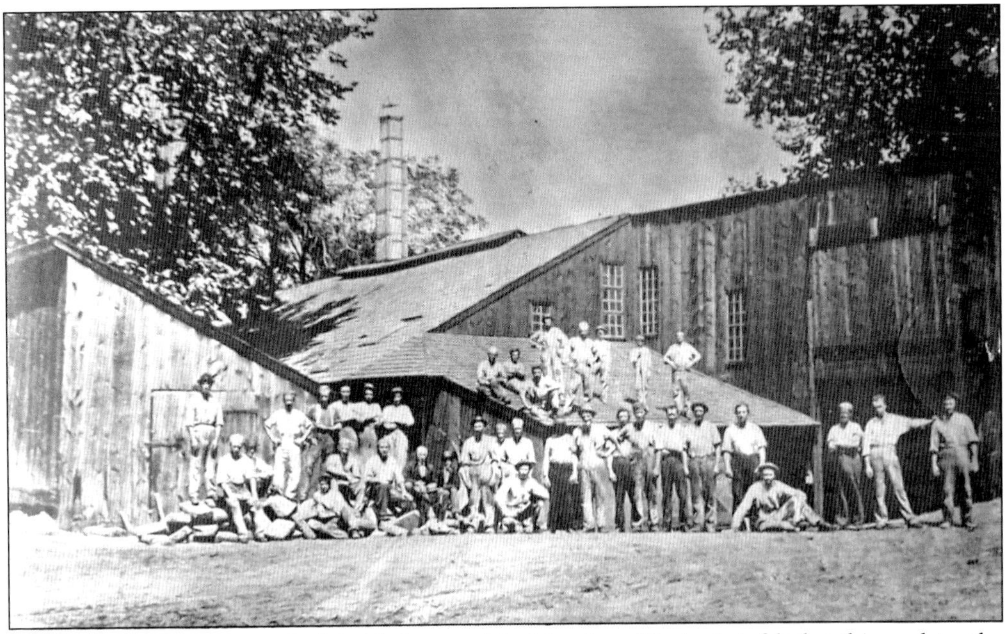

This was taken from a wonderful old picture of the Pine Iron Works. It is felt that this predates the roller mill in later postcards and was situated on the Rutter Estate near where Thomas Rutter had his second early forge. Obviously the mill was a big employer, judging from all these men.

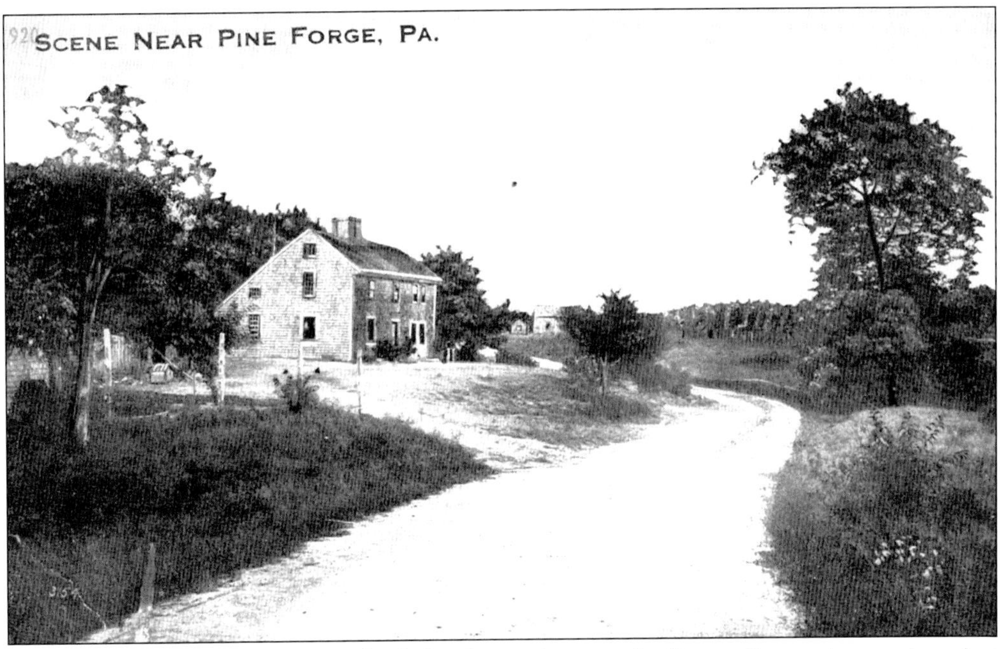

Seen here are some of the homes built for the workers on the Rutter Estate. At one time, just across the covered bridge, a group of early row homes provided housing for the farmer, the cook, the chauffeur, and the child's nurse. These were razed in the 1950s.

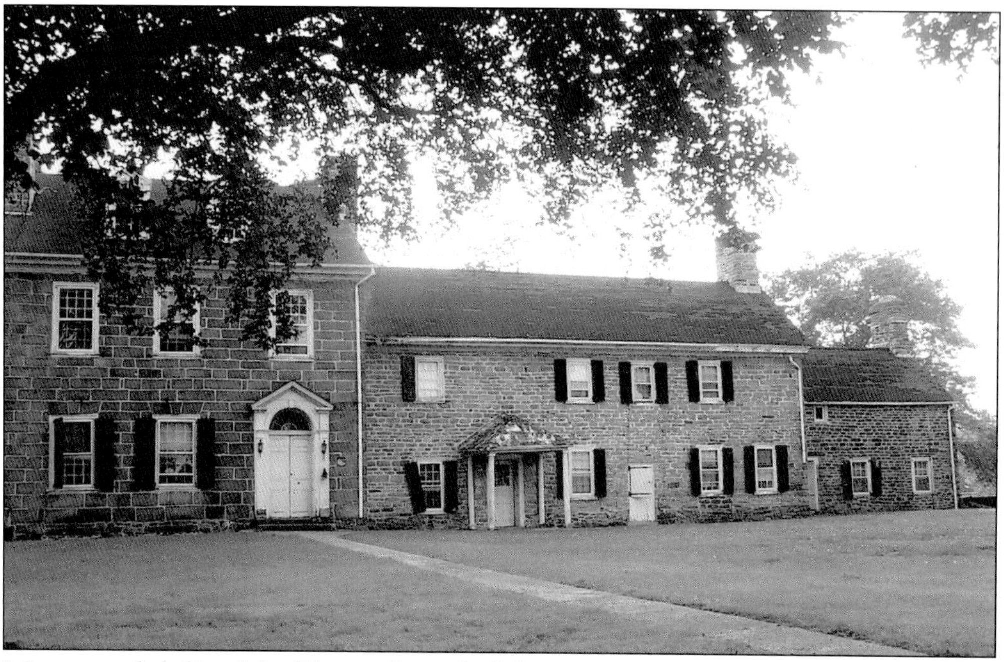

It is commonly believed that Thomas Rutter built his mansion Pine in 1723. The center section is the original portion. Rutter, upon urging from William Penn, left a comfortable life in England to come to Penn's colony to establish an iron forge, the earliest in Pennsylvania. During the Civil War era, the home was a station of the Underground Railroad, housing former slaves overnight as they continued their journey to freedom.

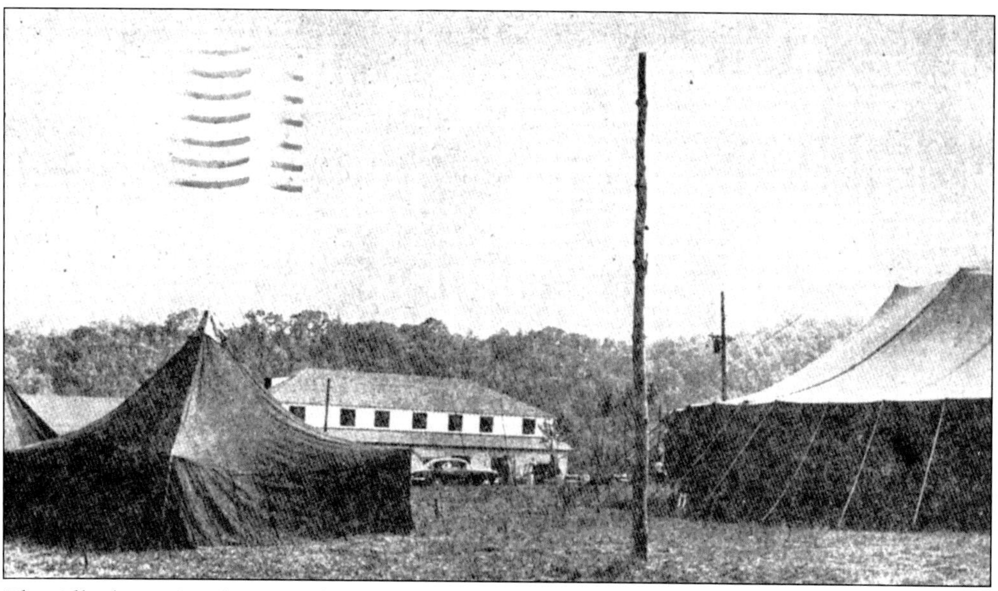

The Allegheny Conference of Seventh Day Adventist Churches acquired the former Rutter property around 1950. They established the Pine Forge Academy as a high school for young people and hold camp meetings, such as pictured on this card, in the summertime.

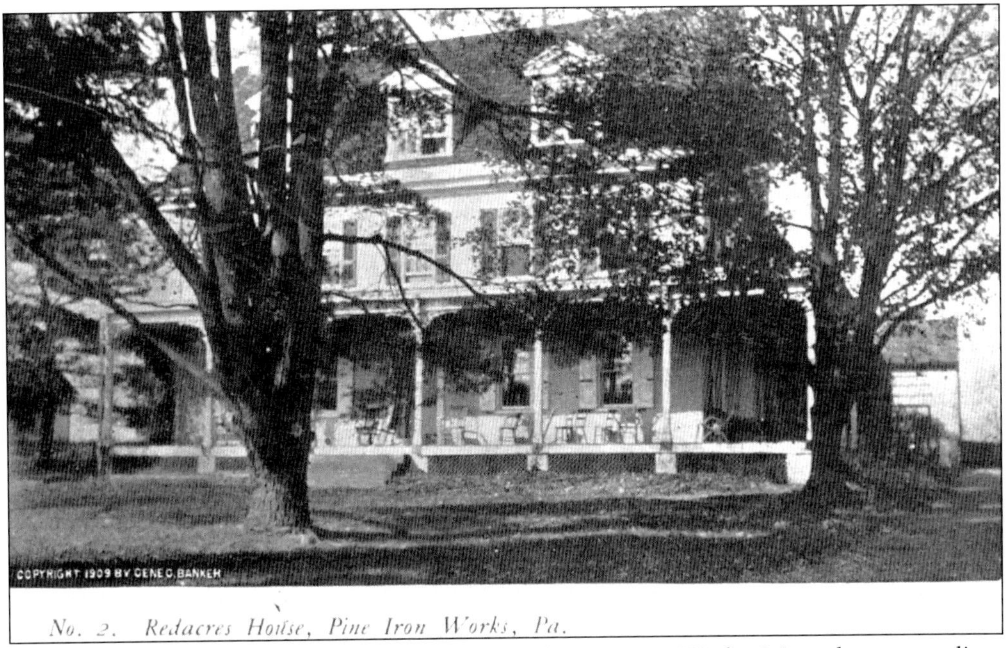

Shown here is Red Acres, Joseph Bailey's home at the Pine Iron Works. It is no longer standing, but it is believed to have stood in the vicinity of the present Pine Forge Academy Administration building. This was across from the Rutter mansion.

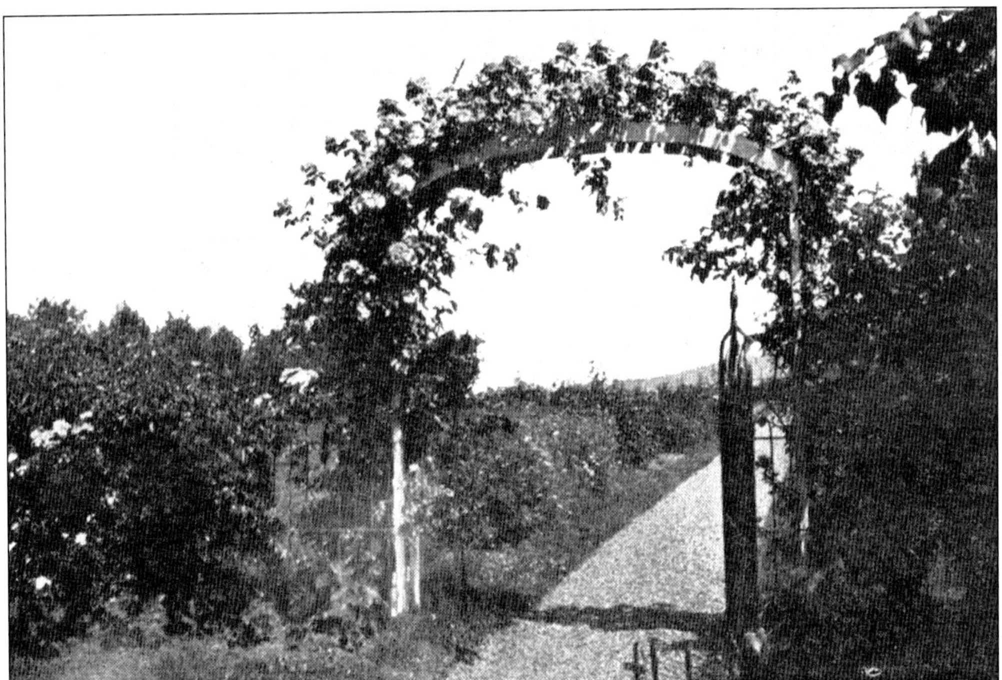

Hill Road, near Red Acres, is pictured. Bailey cared for his workers and their families by paying them on Monday, assuring that the week's wages would not be squandered on hard drink as they might have been if paid at the end of the week.

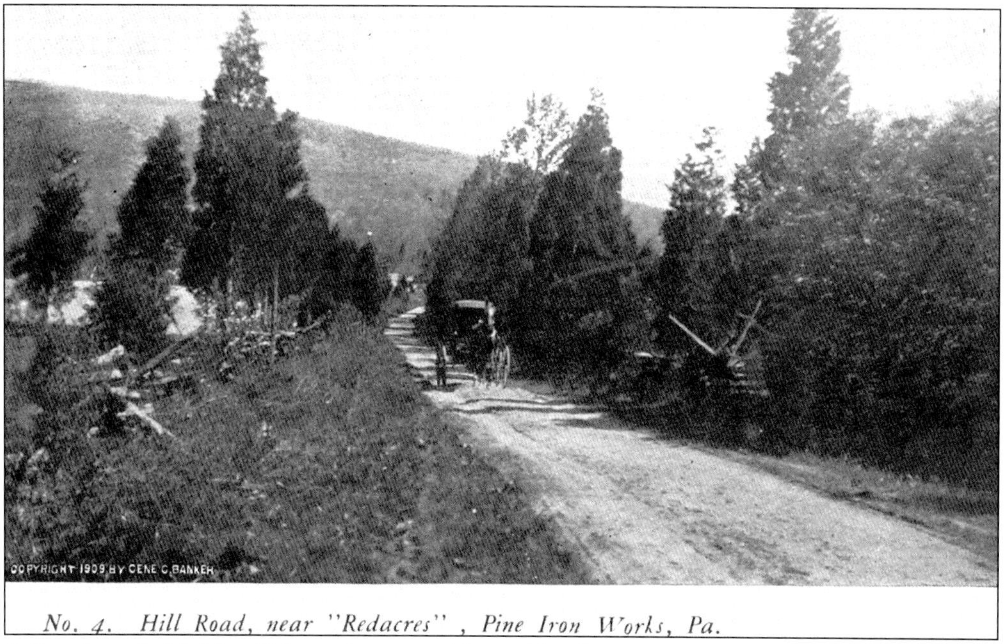

Bailey thought highly of his gardens, as evidenced by this postcard. He prized his workers and their families as well. Each Christmas the adults would be given the *Christian Weekly*, the teenagers would receive the *Youth's Companion*, and the tots would receive *Nursery*.

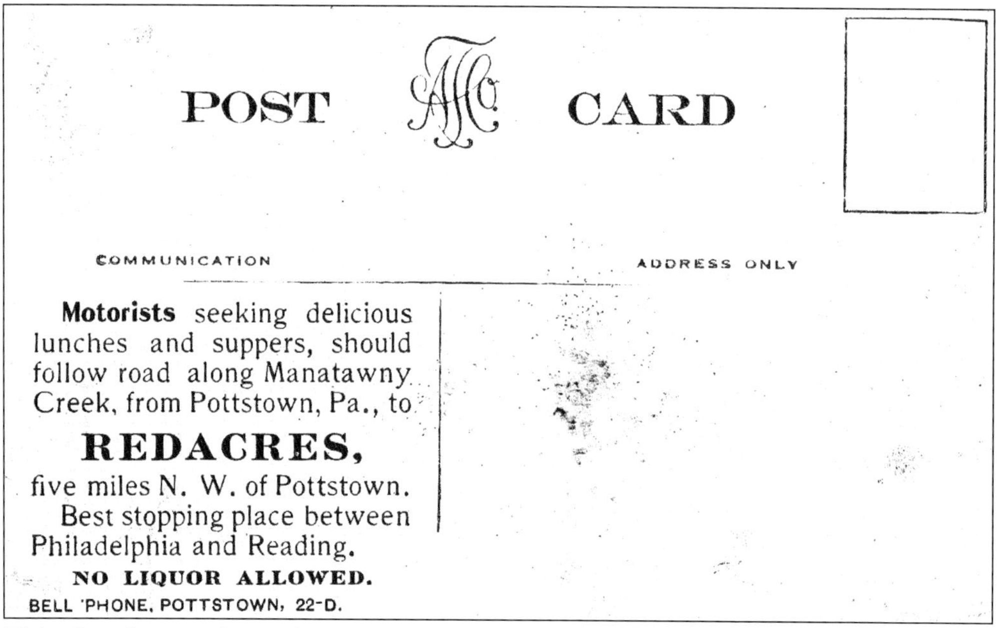

This advertisement for Red Acres further shows Bailey's ingenuity by running a restaurant located at his home. He had the third telephone in the area installed at his iron plant and the seventh one installed at his home. He certainly was a progressive businessman.

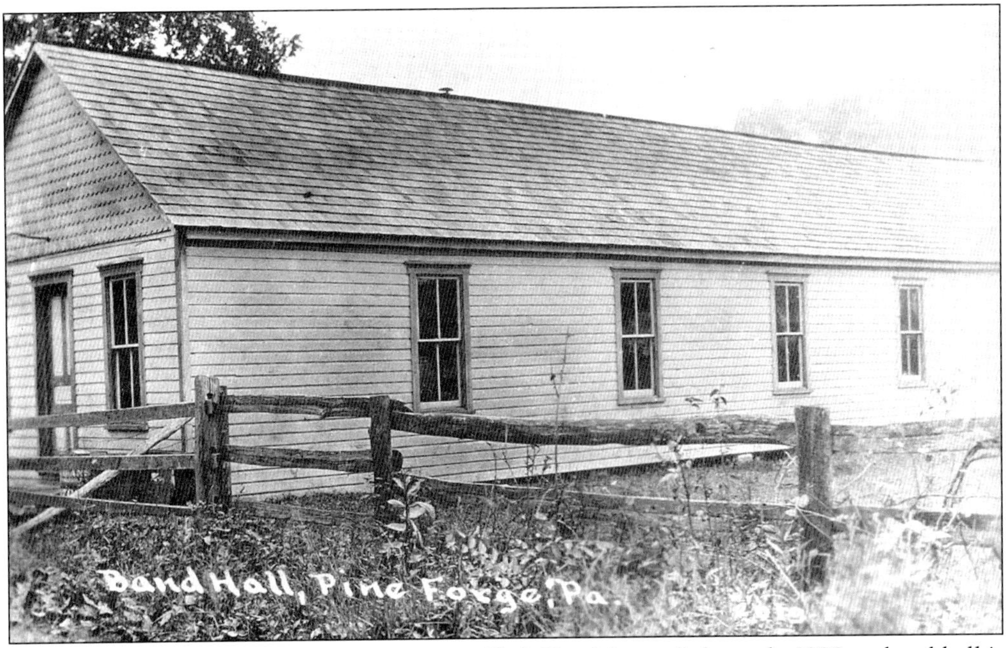

Continuing into the village of Pine Forge, called Glendale until the early 1900s, a band hall is visible on the right nearly across from the new Pine Forge Elementary School. About 1918, a clarinet soloist with the John Philip Sousa Band wrote a march "Old Pine Forge" dedicated to the citizens' band of Pine Forge. This structure burned many years ago.

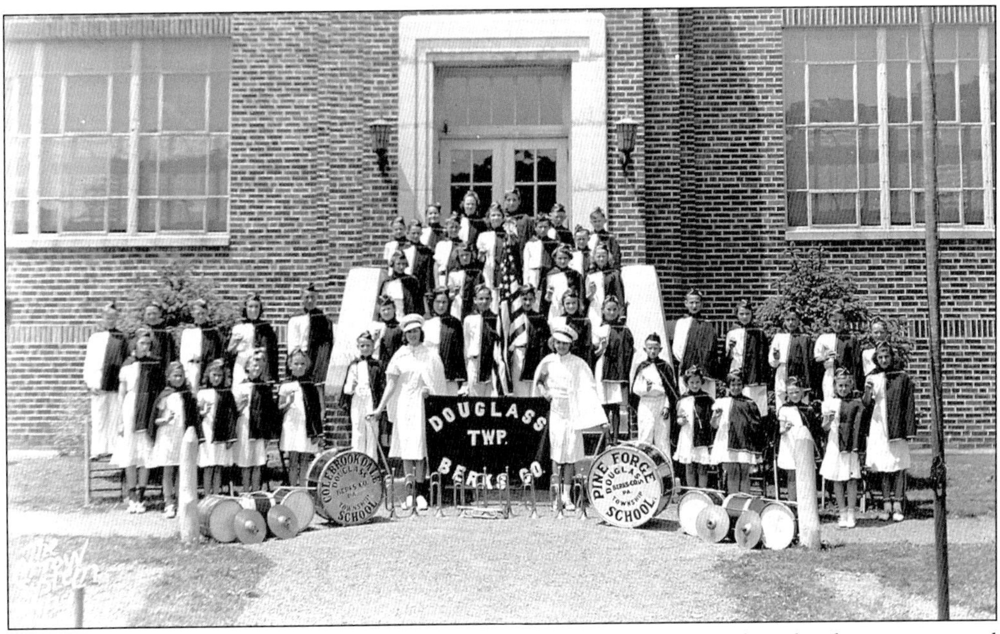

This is a 1939 view of the front of Pine Forge Elementary School. The school was composed of four classrooms, each housing two grades. It became a part of the Boyertown Area Schools in 1952. The marching band pictured here was comprised of the two schools in Douglass Township—Pine Forge and Colebrookdale.

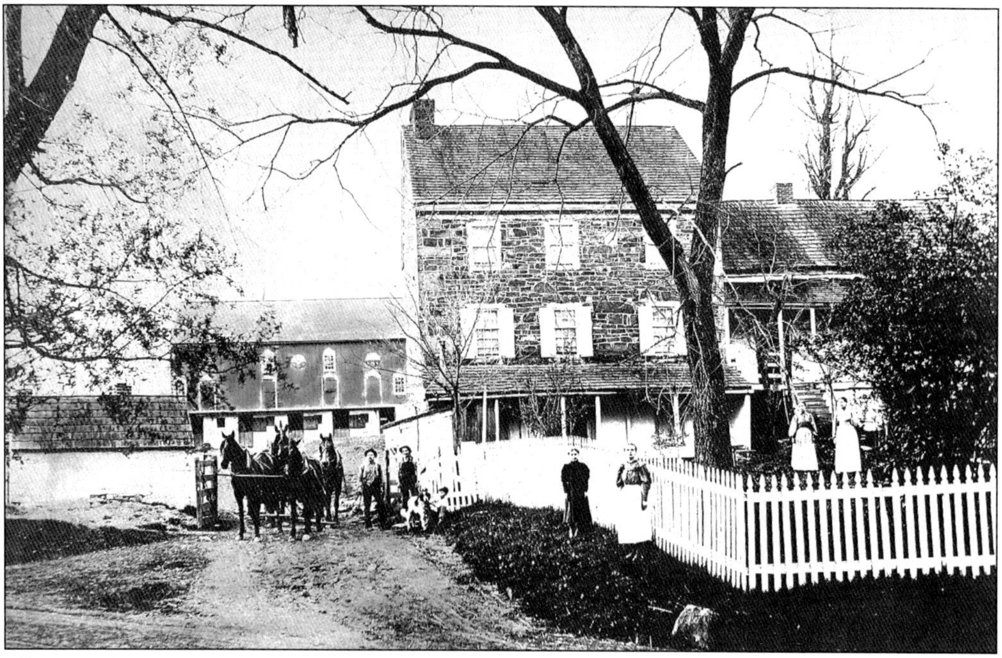

The next few pictures are a study of the evolution of a building. This old photograph from the late 1800s shows the Wisler Family Homestead located at the intersection of Glendale Road and Douglass Drive.

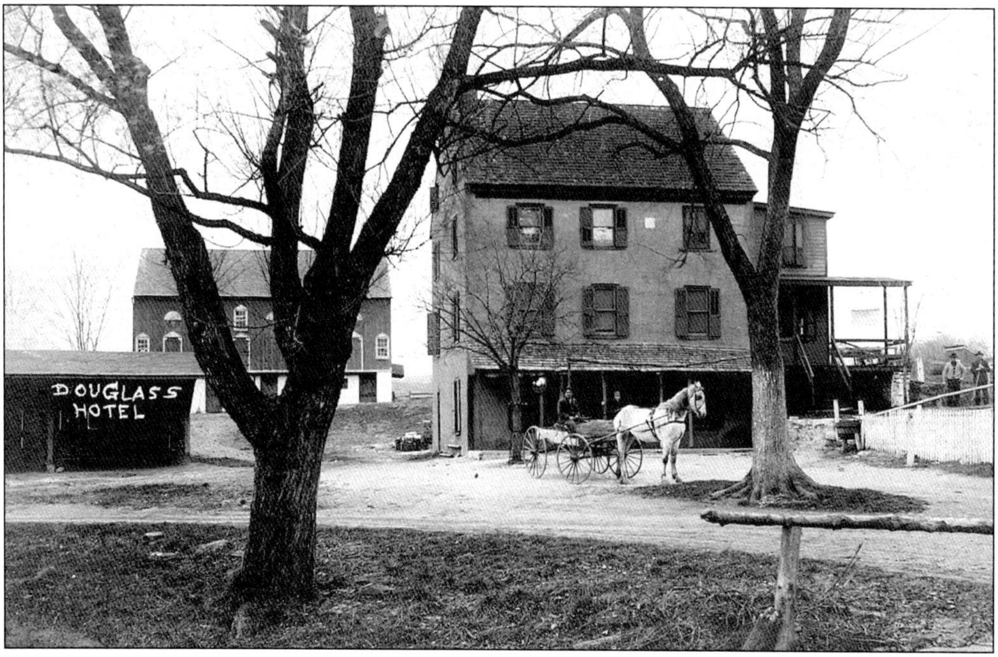

In this picture, prior to 1911, the building has become the Douglass Hotel. It is just across Glendale Road from the elementary school.

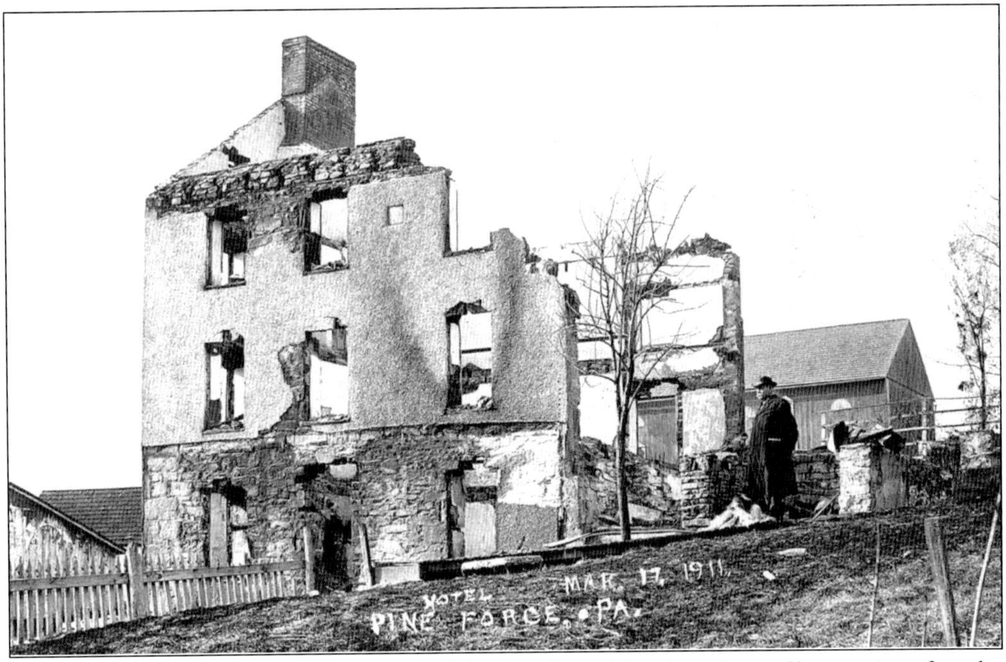

In this extremely rare photo postcard of the hotel, nothing but the walls remains after the devastating fire on March 17, 1911.

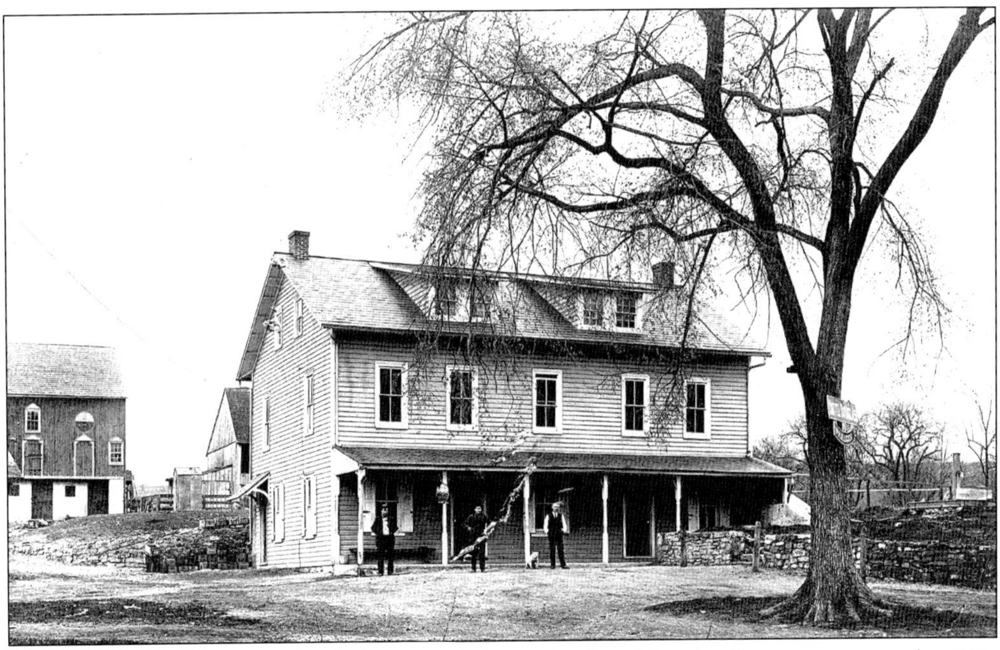

Obviously the hotel was rebuilt, but certainly not in the old style. For many years, the Fritz family ran the hotel business. This building still stands but has become an apartment house. The barn remains as well. It was the barn that remained consistent throughout the period of these pictures, allowing for positive identification.

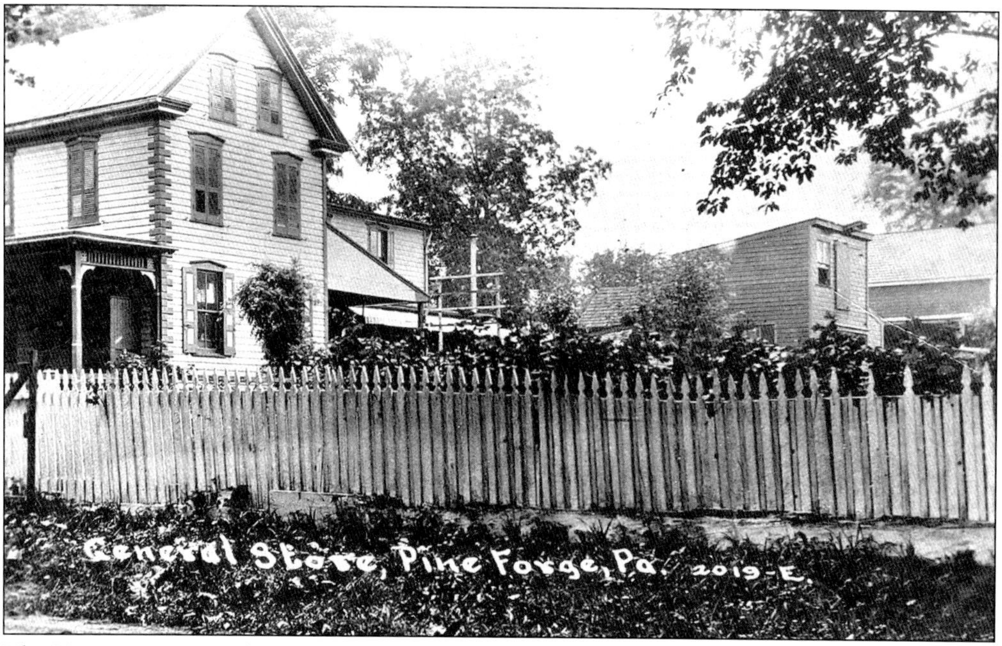

The Pine Forge General Store stood across from the hotel. In the 1950s, this building also served as the post office.

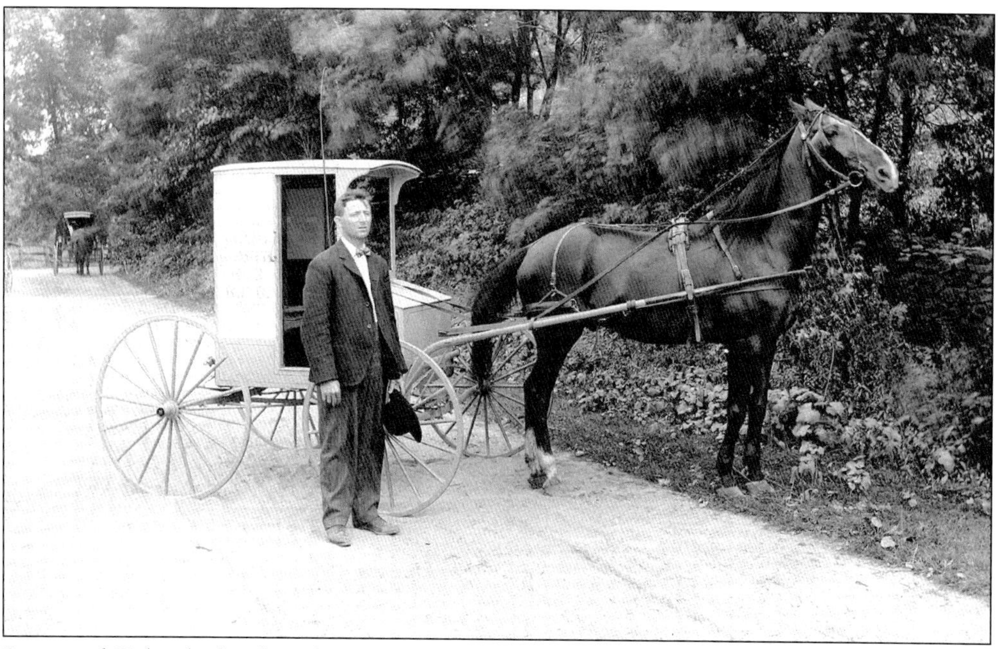

Raymond Kulp, the local mailman, is pictured on his delivery route.

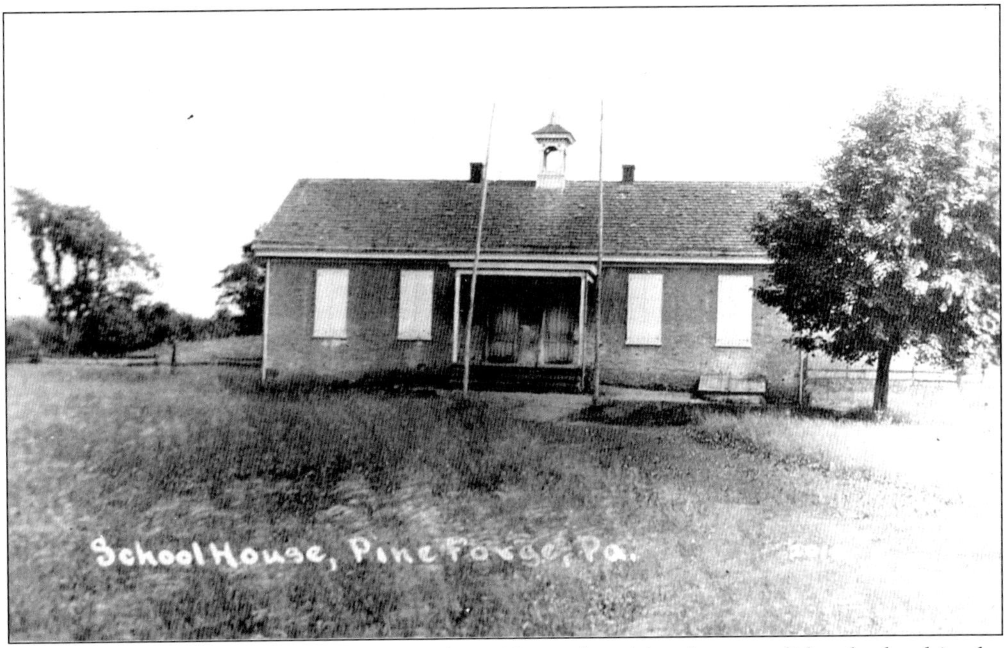

This is the Pine Forge School of the early 1900s, replaced by the consolidated school in the 1930s. This building was modern for its time, having more than one room. William Wisler was a teacher here, having begun his career in the more traditional one-room schoolhouse on Hill School Road in Douglass Township. That earlier school has crumbled to nothing with the years, while this one is now the home of the Pine Forge Sportsman's Club.

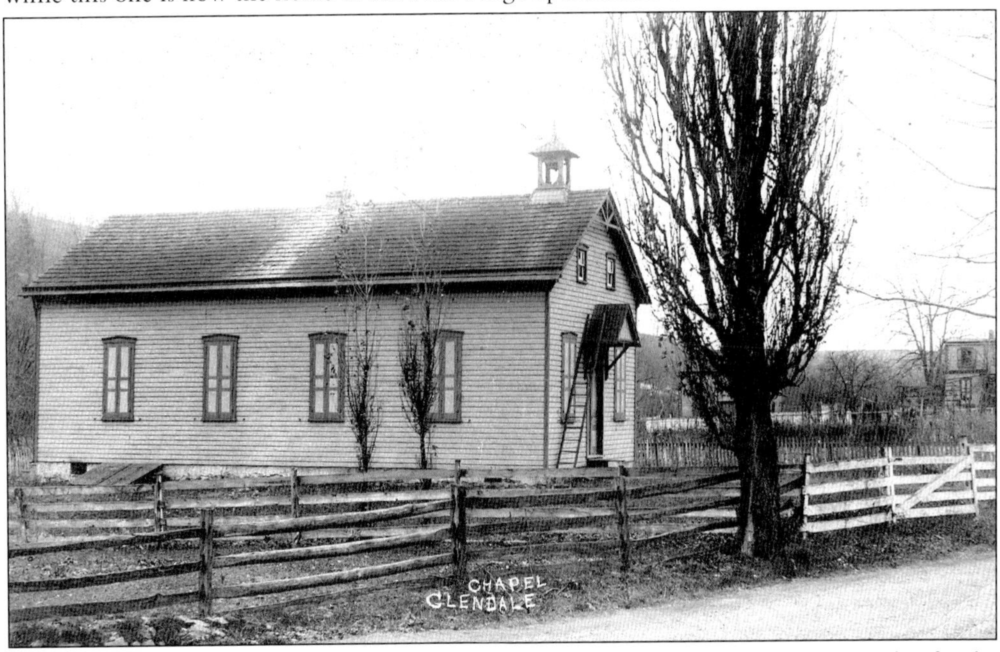

Just up the street on the south side is the Glendale Chapel built in 1887 by Joseph Bailey for the townspeople. They rented it for $1 per year and were required to maintain it and keep it open as a house of worship. The Girl Scouts held their meetings here in the 1950s. It is now home to the Pine Forge Academy Alumni Association.

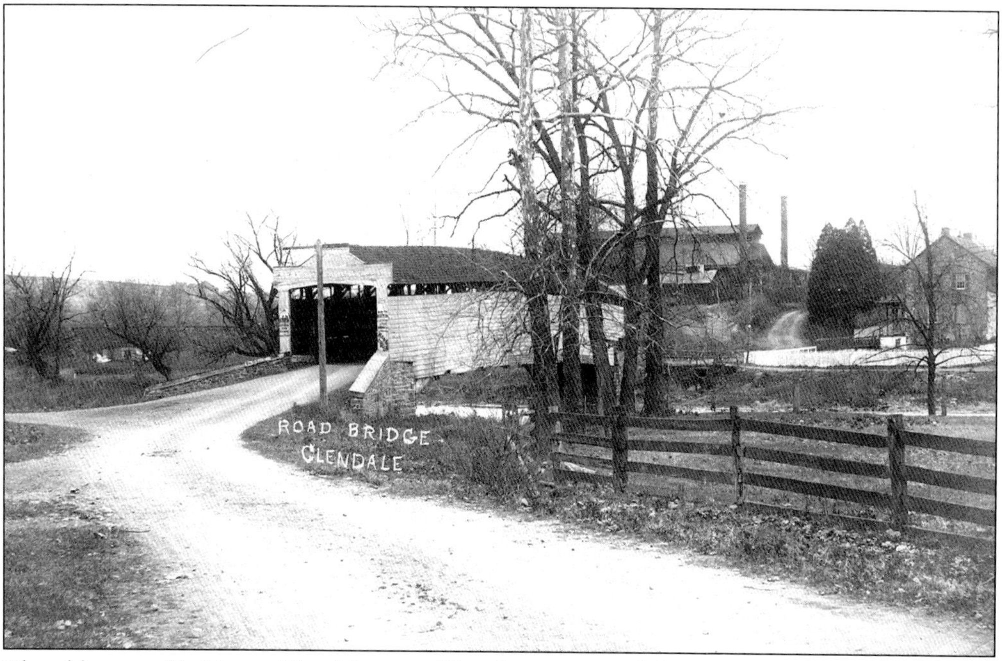

The old covered bridge at Glendale, now Pine Forge, crossed the Manatawny Creek. It carried Manatawny Road, which became Manatawny Street in Pottstown. The Pine Iron Works are seen in the background. This was a very large industry for a very small community, providing employment for many of the village men and others.

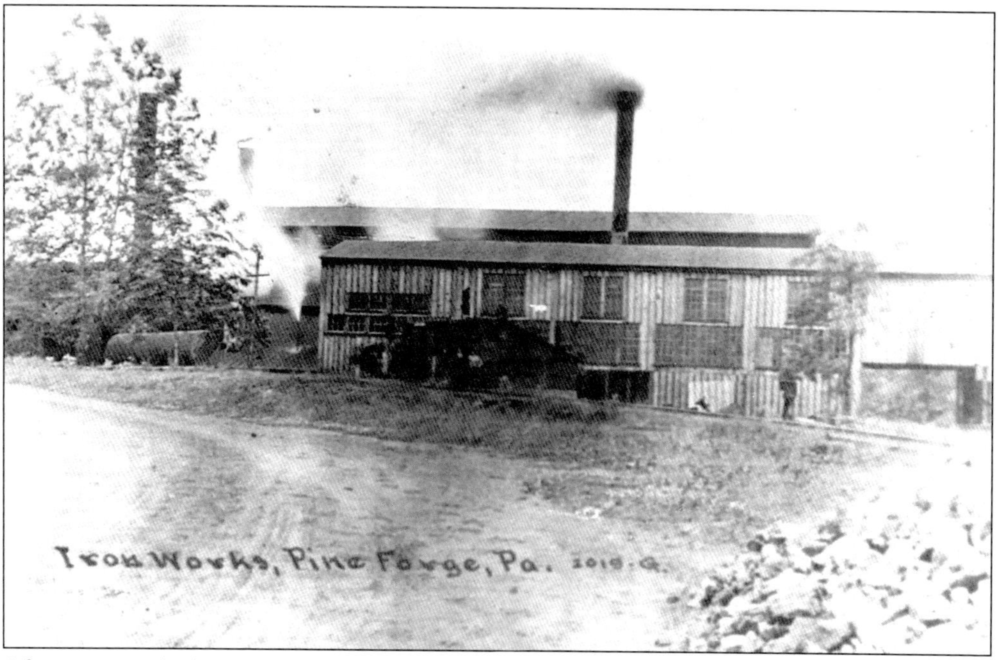

After crossing the bridge, the Pine Iron Works are on the left. For many years, the foundry was known for a very tough steel plate called Extra Locomotive Fire Box Plate. Obviously with the demise of the steam locomotive the need for this plate was lessened. The Stainless Corporation now owns the mill.

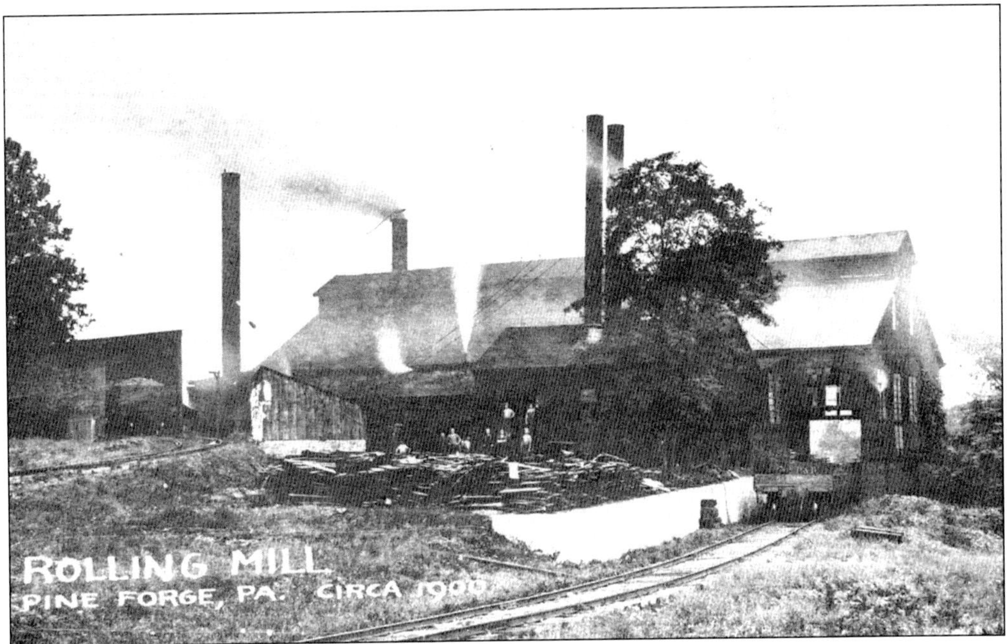

A later picture of the mill shows a railroad car servicing it. The author heard a funny story concerning several young boys from the Pine Forge area who decided it would be fun to loosen the brakes on one of these railroad cars. No damage was done to the property or the boys, but the crashing noise scattered the children to the four winds because they did not want to be blamed for any consequences that might have occurred.

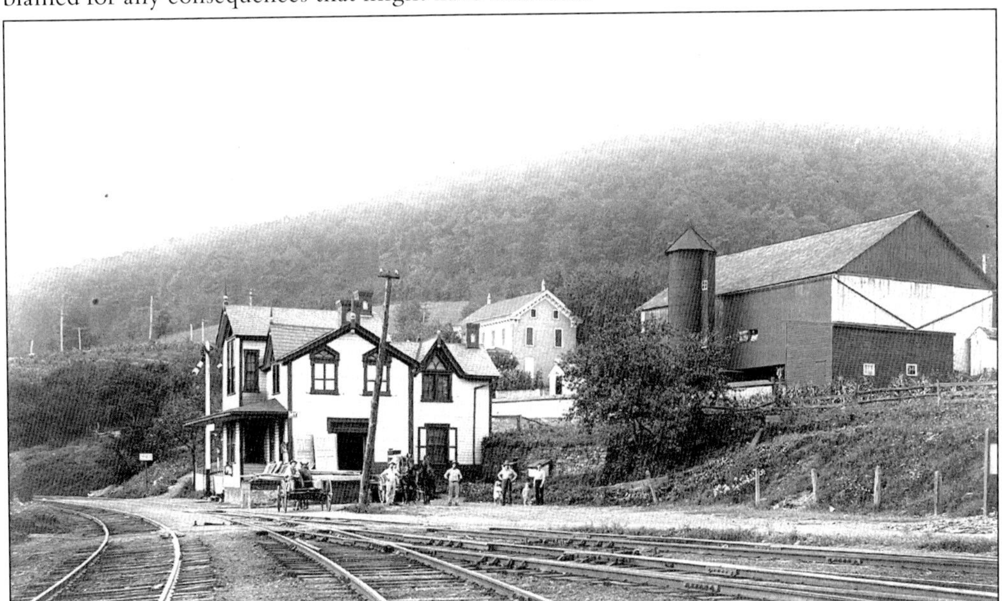

The Pine Forge Railroad Station was near the Pine Iron Works, just off Manatawny Road behind the old Focht dairy farm. It became a part of the Reading Railroad, and this spur connected Pottstown with Boyertown and included stops at Glasgow, Pine Forge, Ironstone, Colebrookdale, Boyertown, New Berlinville, Bechtelsville, and Mt. Pleasant, which is now Barto. This station burned in 1969.

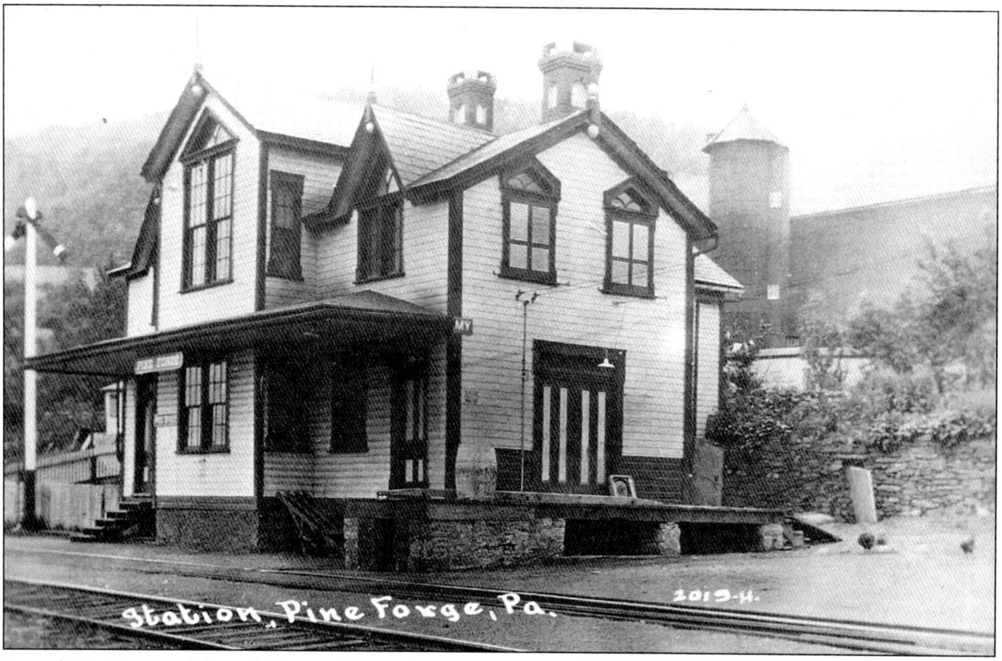

Joseph Bailey petitioned Pennsylvania's Governor Curtin in 1865 to have the railroad built. By 1869, it was completed from Pottstown to Boyertown. Bailey was president of the 13-mile railway until the Reading Railroad absorbed it. All that is left is the track, memories, and a once-a-week train, which runs to maintain the rail rights. This is a wonderful close-up view of the station, also pictured on the cover of this book.

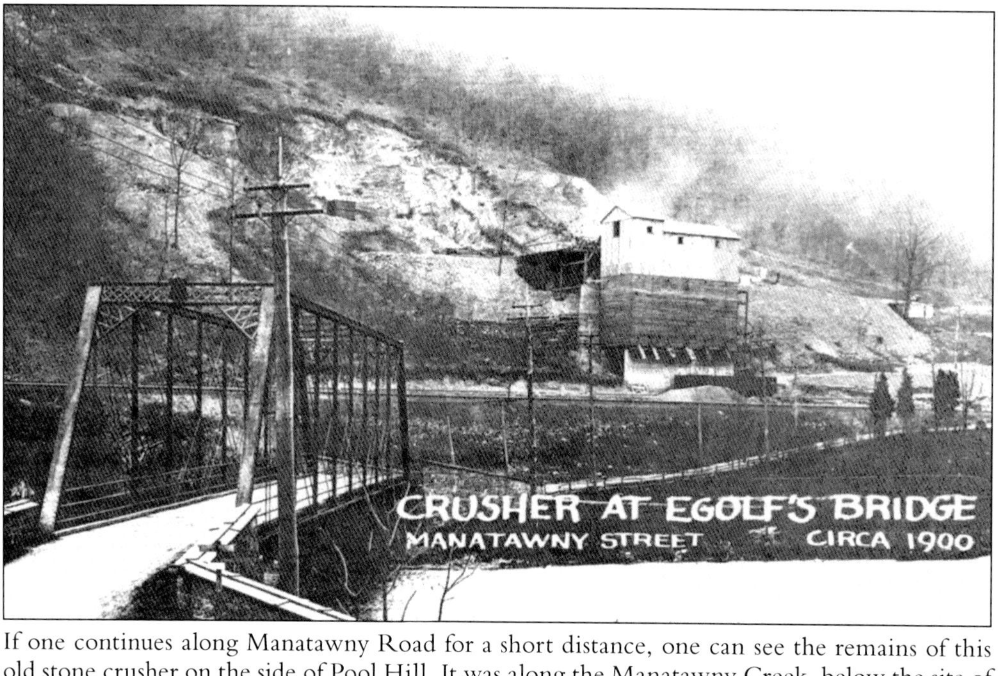

If one continues along Manatawny Road for a short distance, one can see the remains of this old stone crusher on the side of Pool Hill. It was along the Manatawny Creek, below the site of this picture, that Thomas Rutter built his first bloomery-type forge in 1716. Bloomery iron ore smelting was a labor-intensive, primitive process replaced by blast furnaces.

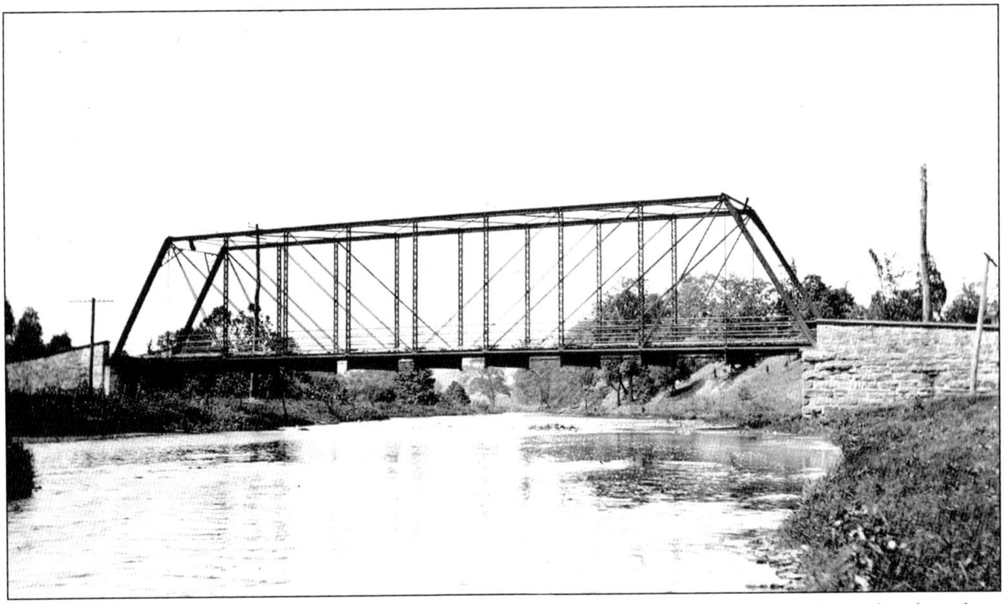

Within a short distance of the site of Rutter's first endeavor at wrenching iron from the abundant ore in the area is a bridge crossing the Manatawny Creek leading into Pottstown.

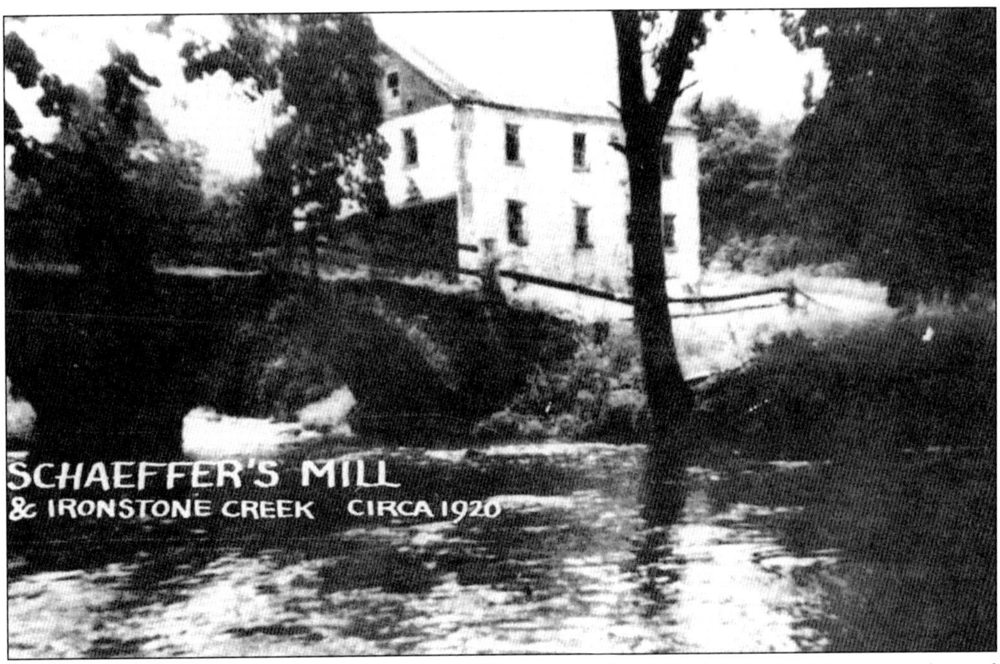

Returning to Pine Forge, one turns right while coming through the covered bridge and travel along the Ironstone Creek. The confluence of the Manatawny and Ironstone Creeks is just before the bend in the road. Perhaps not quite as impressive as some rivers joining, it is still interesting to see. In this picture is Schaeffer's Mill along the Ironstone.

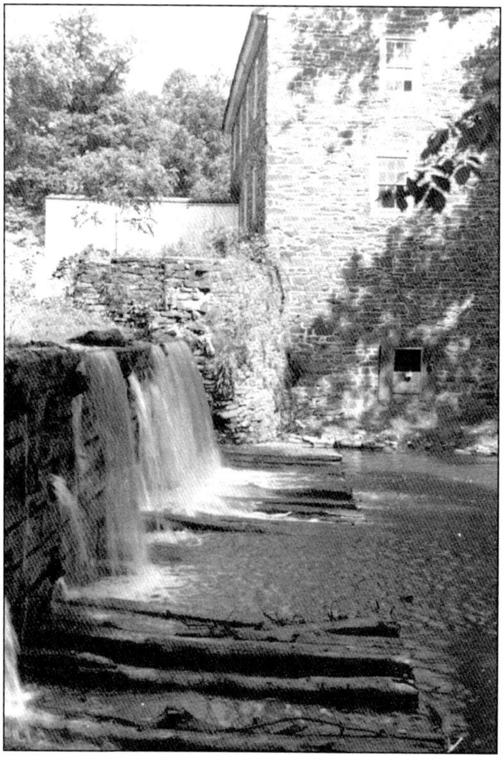

Along Grist Mill Road is another old mill belonging to the Bongazone Family in the mid-1900s. The building is still standing.

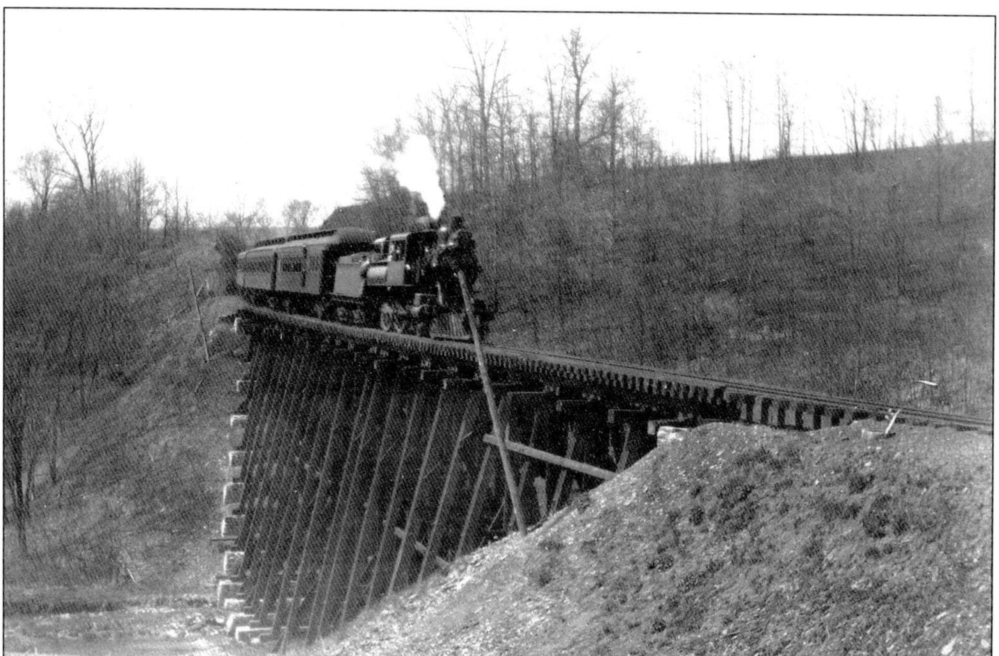

Crossing the Ironstone Creek, this train to Boyertown negotiates a high-trestle bridge. The author remembers scrambling to get off the trestle when the once-a-week train came through in about 1952. It was scary just to walk on it, but even scarier when the toot-toot of the train was heard.

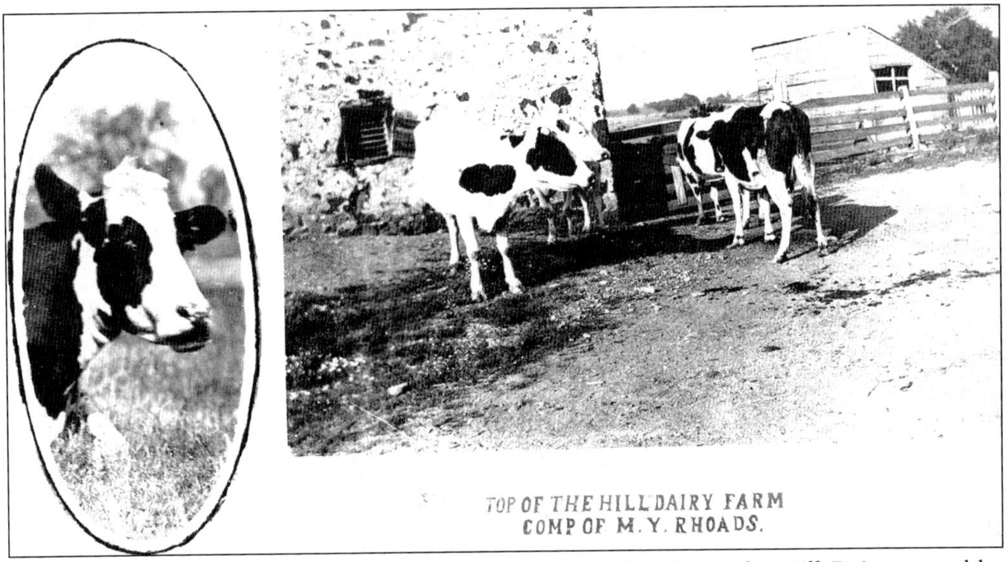

At the top of the hill on the way from Pine Forge to Little Oley is the Hill Dairy owned by Melvin Rhoads, a well-known historian of the area.

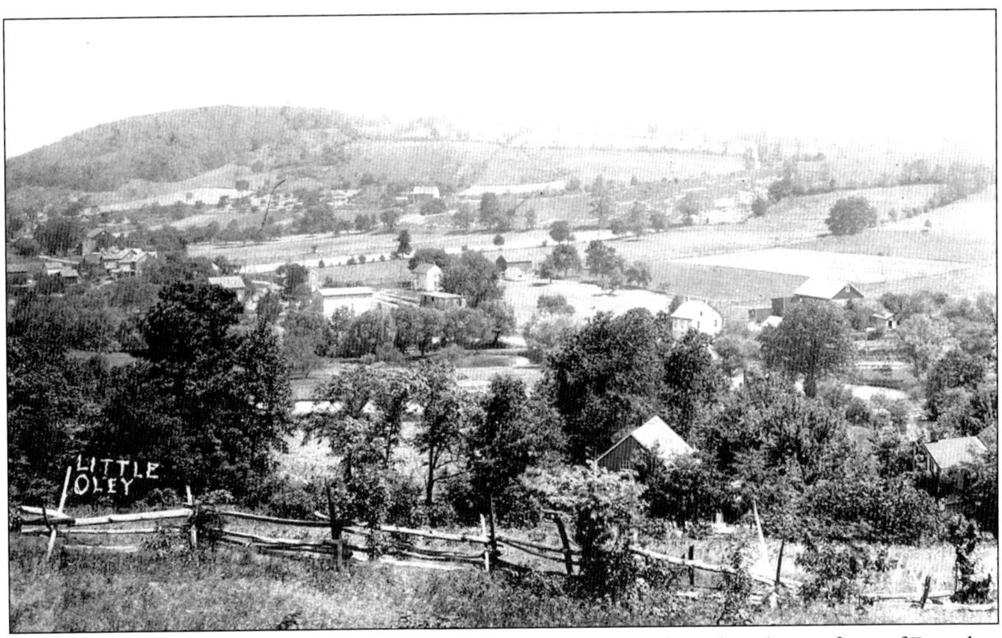

This is the verdant scene approaching Little Oley. Little Oley is still within the confines of Douglass Township. In the mid-20th century, Douglass Township had two consolidated elementary schools. The Colebrookdale School in Little Oley was a sister school to the Pine Forge School, and each year, on field day, they competed in physical games, including a baseball game.

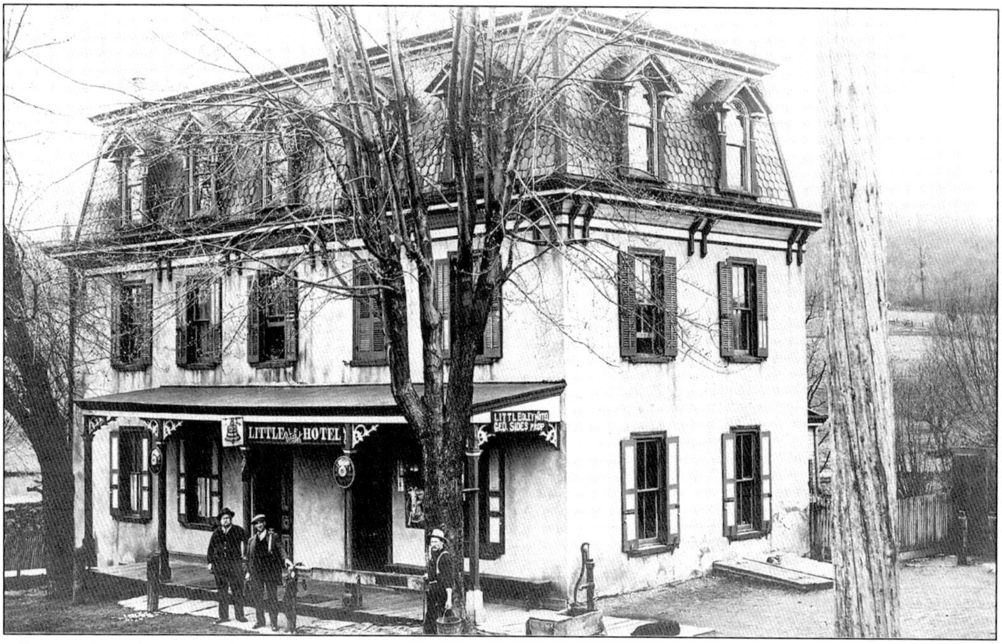

The Little Oley Hotel stands on Farmington Avenue and is now called the Little Oley Tavern. It is easily recognized today. This was a favorite watering hole for the locals throughout the 20th century.

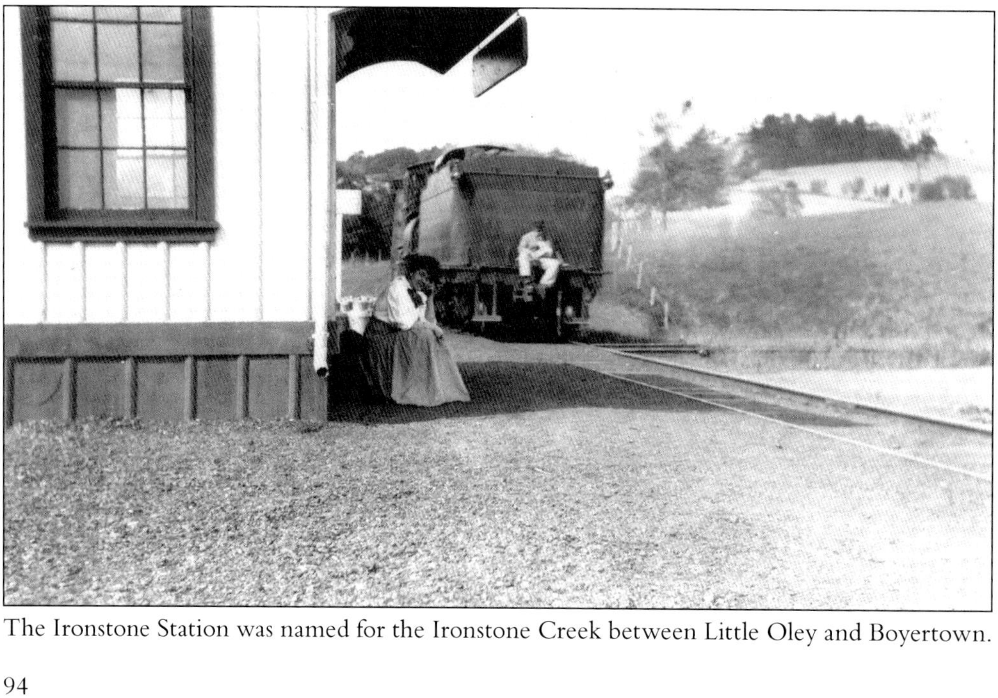

The Ironstone Station was named for the Ironstone Creek between Little Oley and Boyertown.

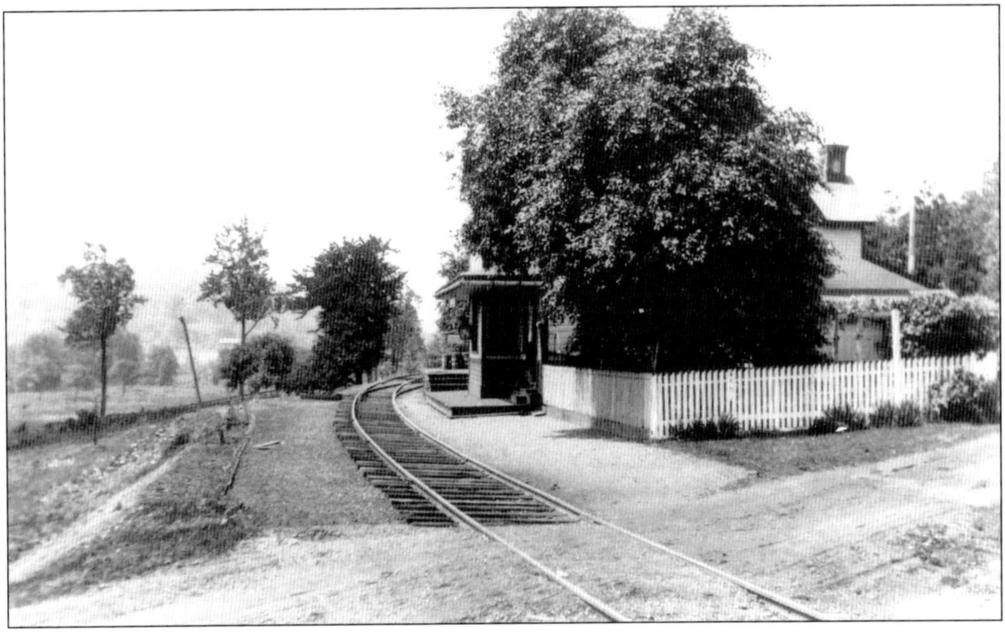

The Colebrookdale Station was another of the local stops on Bailey's line to Barto. Later this, too, became a part of the Reading Railroad.

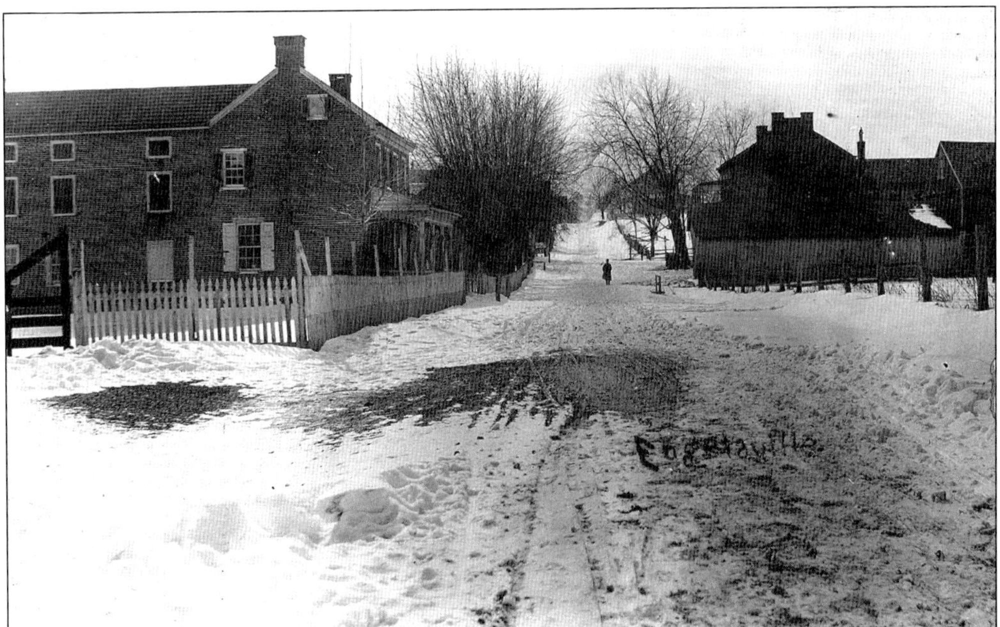

Near to the villages of Pine Forge and Little Oley is the village of Englesville, which sits nearly on the border of Berks and Montgomery Counties. Shown here is the early crossroads.

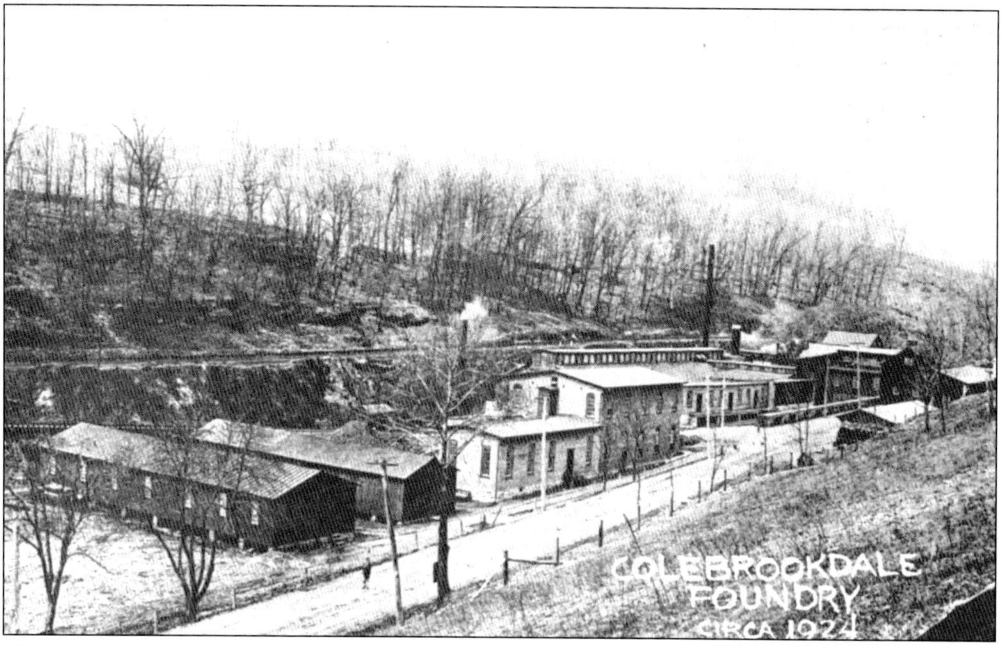

Here is an early view of the Colebrookdale Foundry. An uncle related that during the early and even to the mid-20th century the speaking of Pennsylvania Dutch was a real plus to ensure employment in this industry, as he found out on his return from service in World War II.

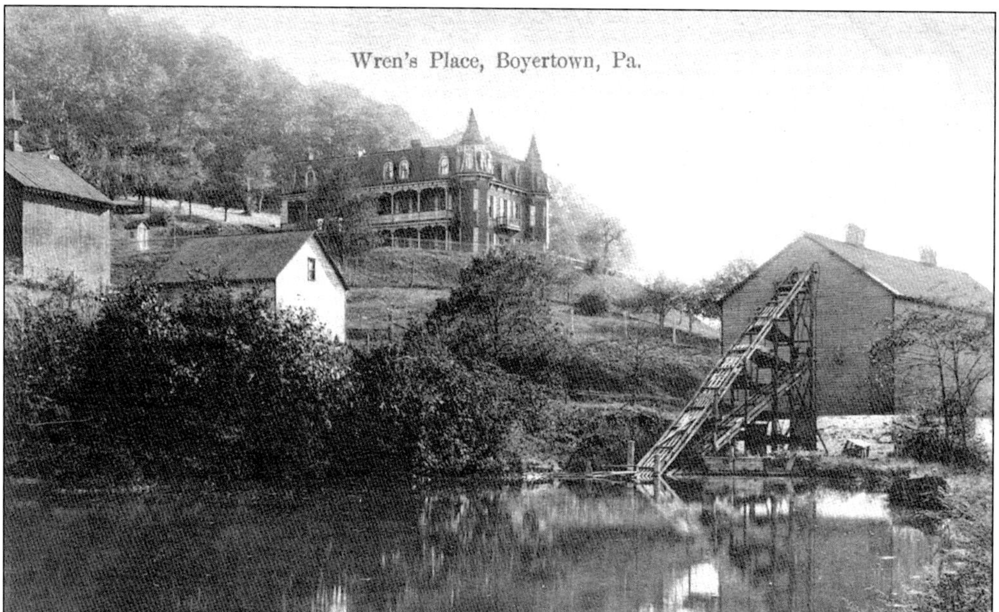

This lovely mansion known as Wren's Place still stands above the valley. Gone, however, is the equipment in the lower part of the picture that was used to harvest ice from the pond. Ice harvesting and storage was an important industry prior to electric refrigeration.

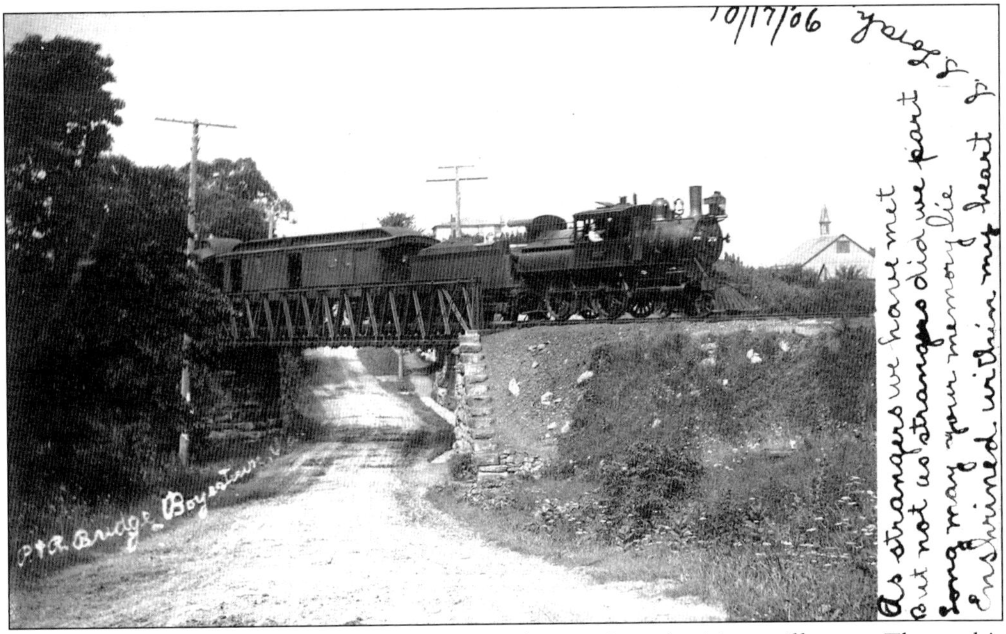

The railroad bridge still spans the roadway on the way into the Morysville area. The card is dated 1906. The author of this card was quite a poet. It sounds like romance was on his mind. One can read those thoughts on the margin of the card.

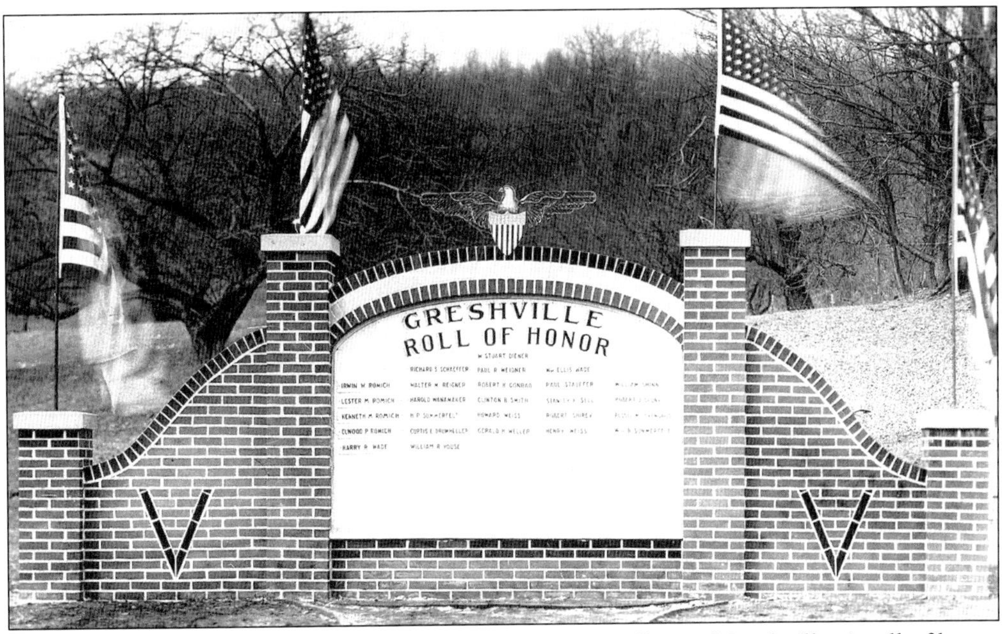

Just a short turn from the route to Boyertown is the tiny village of Greshville. A roll of honor shows the World War II veterans names of 26 people who served their country proudly during that era.

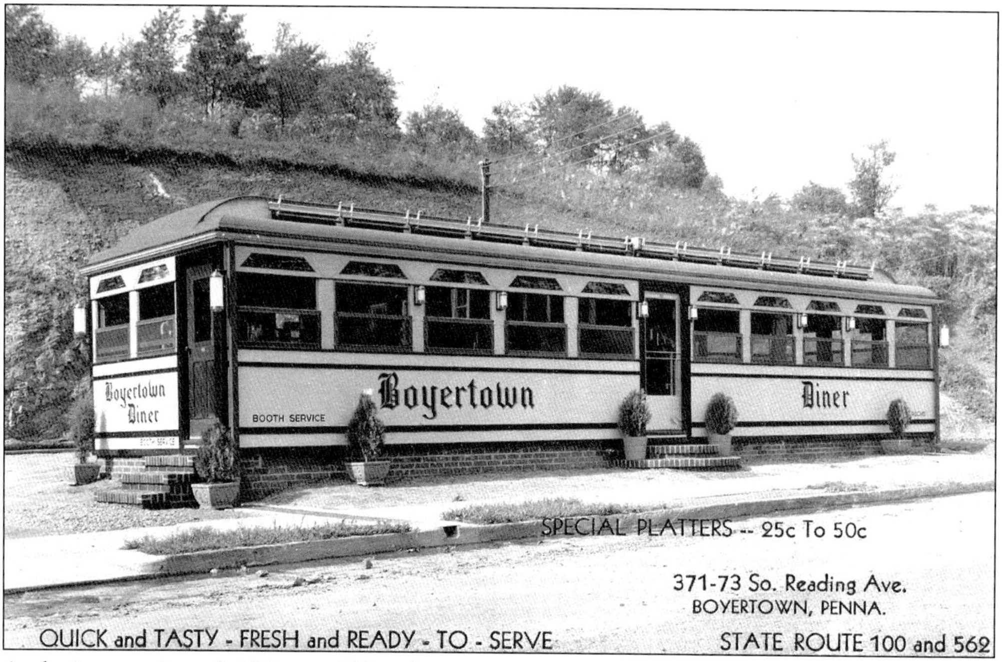

At the intersection of old Route 100 and Route 562 stood the Boyertown Diner. Please note the special platters of 25¢ to 50¢. What a bargain! This is a magnificent example of an old-time dining car. It appears that it just came from the railroad, which is where entrepreneurs got the idea.

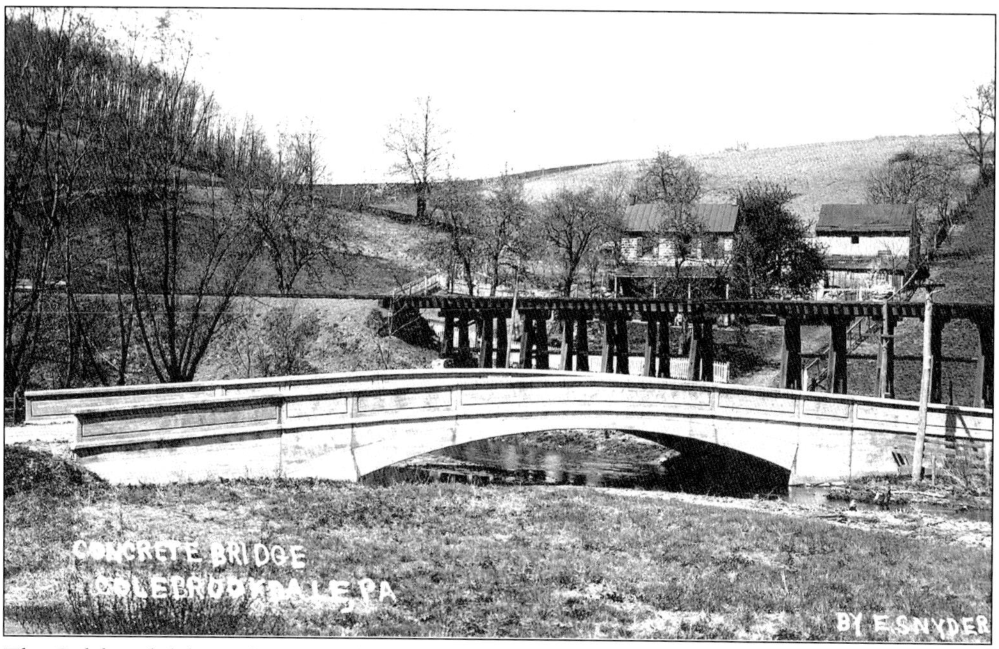

The Colebrookdale Bridge is seen here. It appears quite modern in contrast to the many covered bridges pictured earlier.

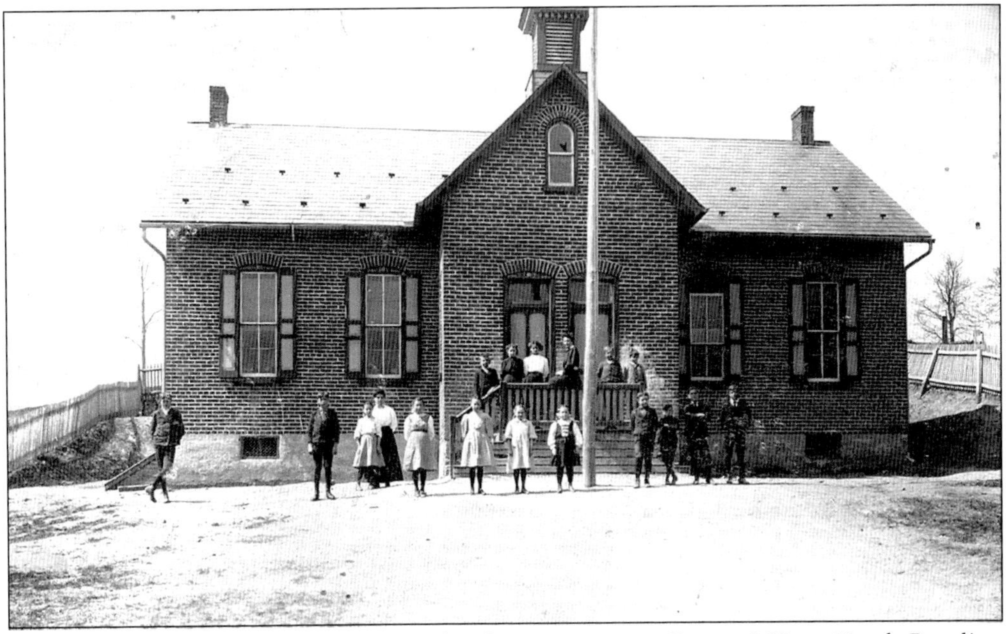

Morysville lies just outside the borough of Boyertown on Route 562 or North Reading Avenue. Annie Dengler sent this card in 1906 to her uncle. It is thought that she taught at this no-longer-existing school while her sister Amy Dengler taught for many years at the Pine Forge Consolidated School. Amy, long past retirement age when she left teaching, was presented a new car by the PTA for her many years of service to the community.

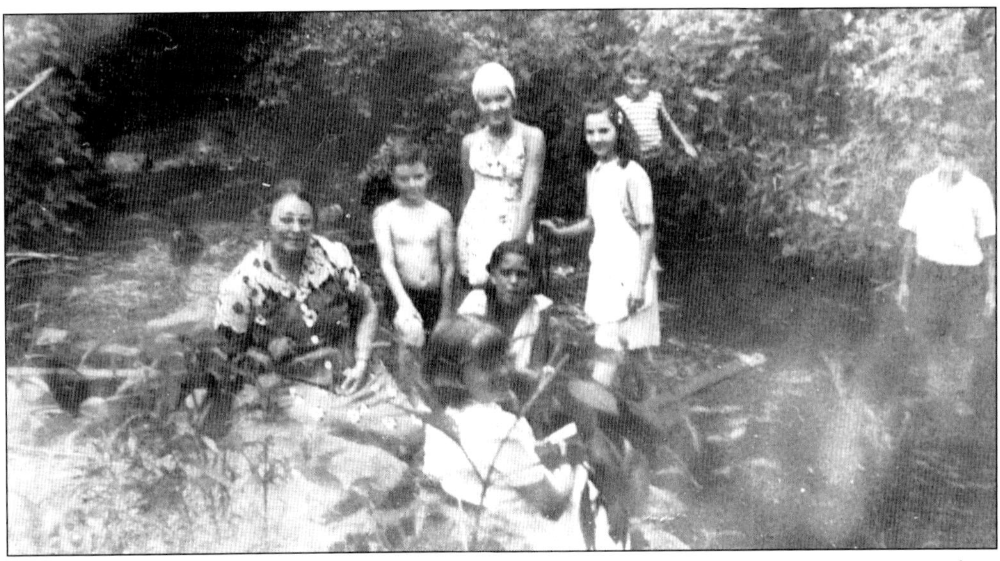

Each year the Denglers entertained the fourth-grade class from Pine Forge with a picnic at their home near Little Oley along the Ironstone Creek. Seen here is a class of 1948 fourth-grade graduates. With two grades to a room in that school, these young people would be moving to the "big side" of the school, into the fifth grade. Shown here is Amy Dengler with some of her students.

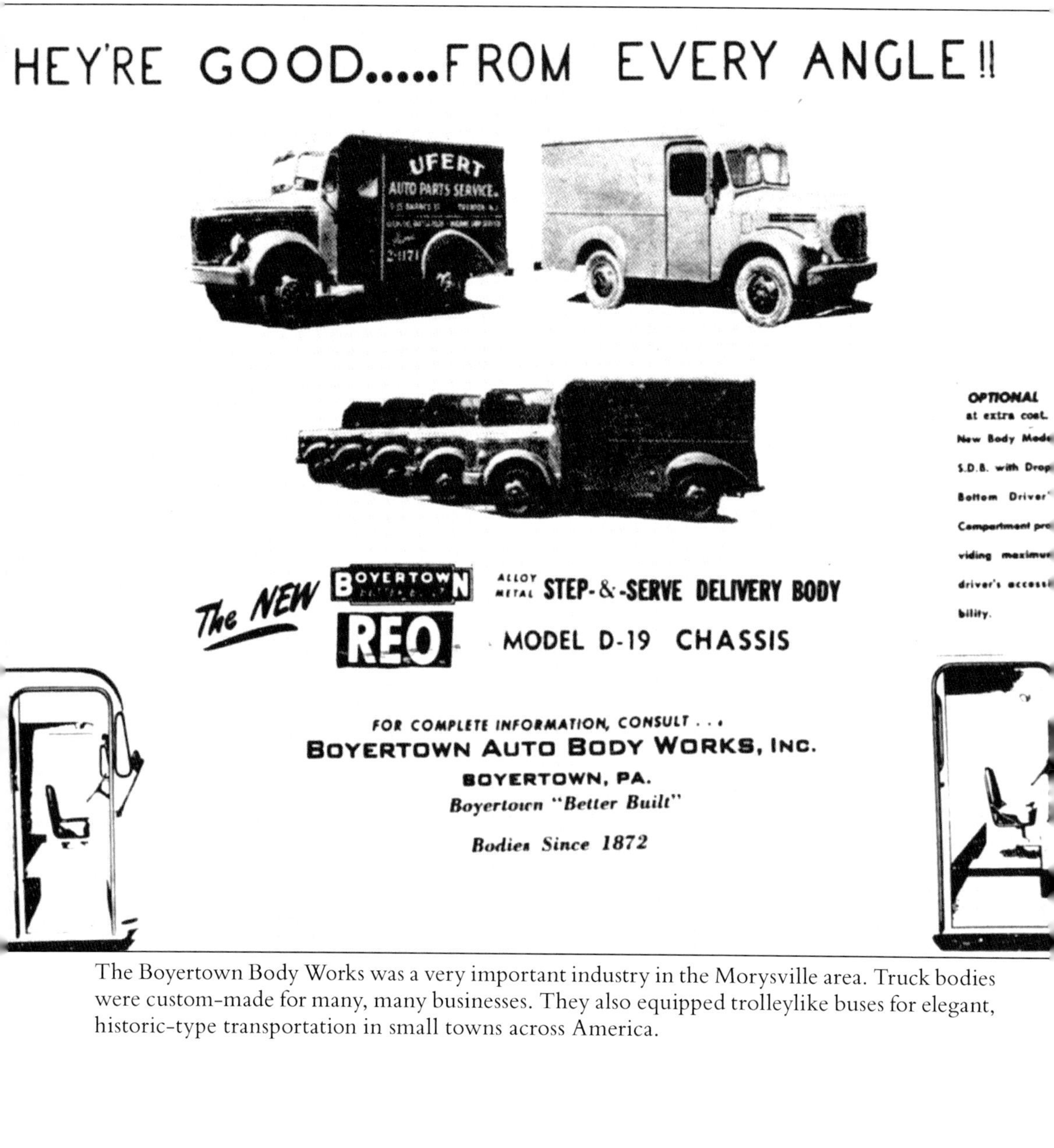

The Boyertown Body Works was a very important industry in the Morysville area. Truck bodies were custom-made for many, many businesses. They also equipped trolleylike buses for elegant, historic-type transportation in small towns across America.

Four

BOYERTOWN, GABELSVILLE, SHANESVILLE, AND PLEASANTVILLE

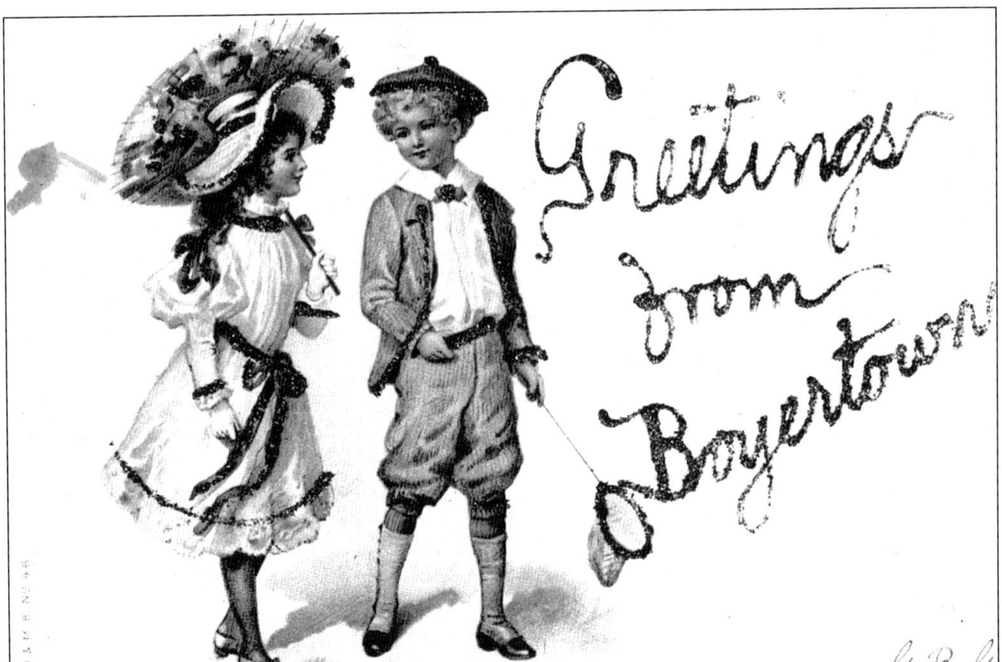

Greetings from Boyertown are extended on this old postcard dating before 1907. Boyertown is the largest town in southeastern Berks County and was a very important center of commerce and manufacturing in that area.

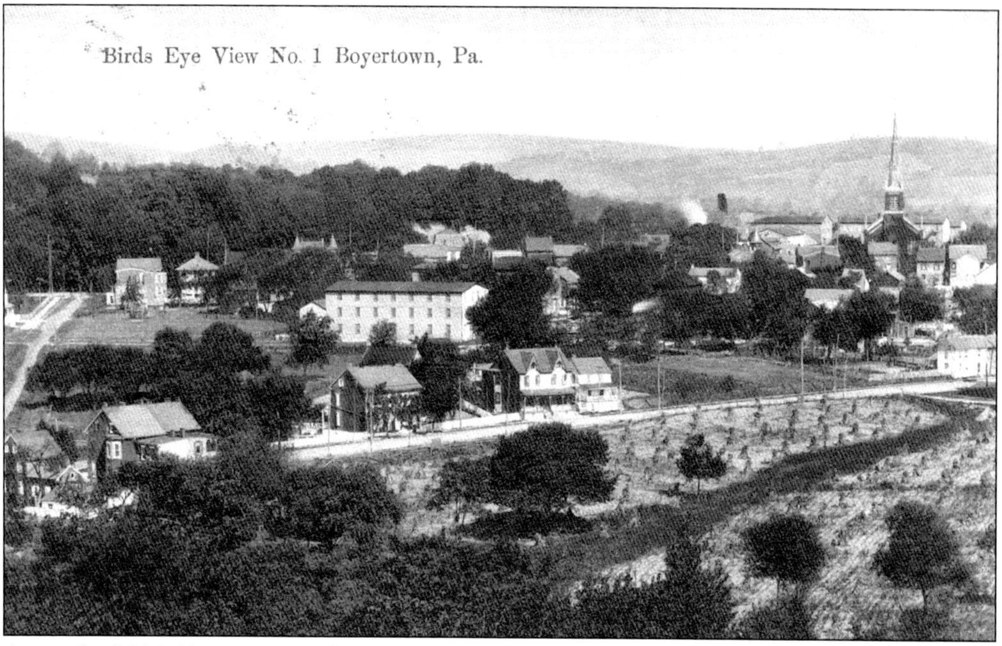

A wonderful bird's-eye view of Boyertown is pictured in this early series card.

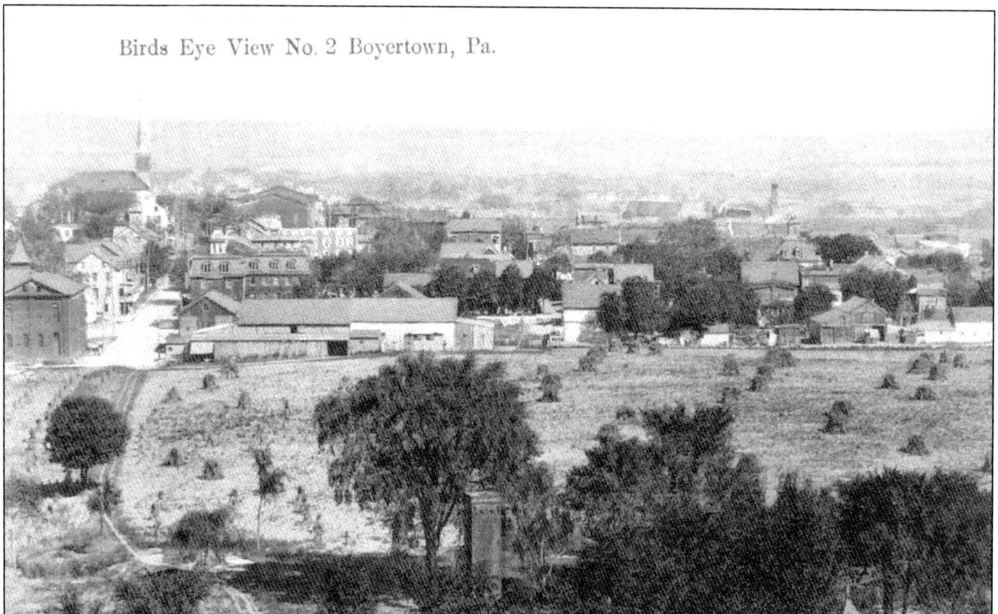

The town is seen from a different perspective in the second of the series.

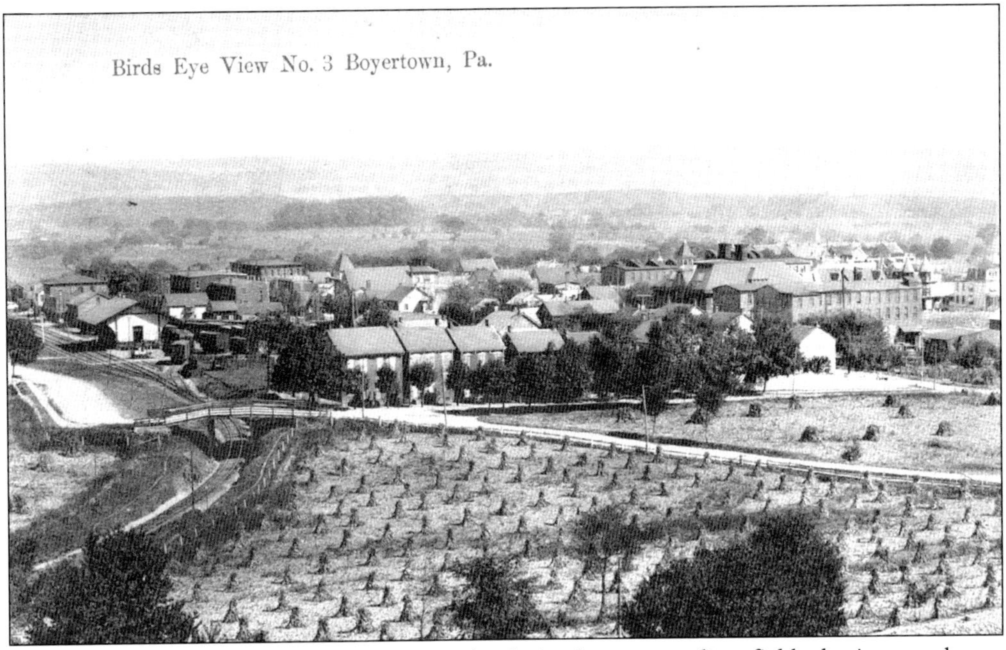

Scene three shows even more of the corn shocks in the surrounding fields, letting one know that surely these cards were taken in the fall of the year.

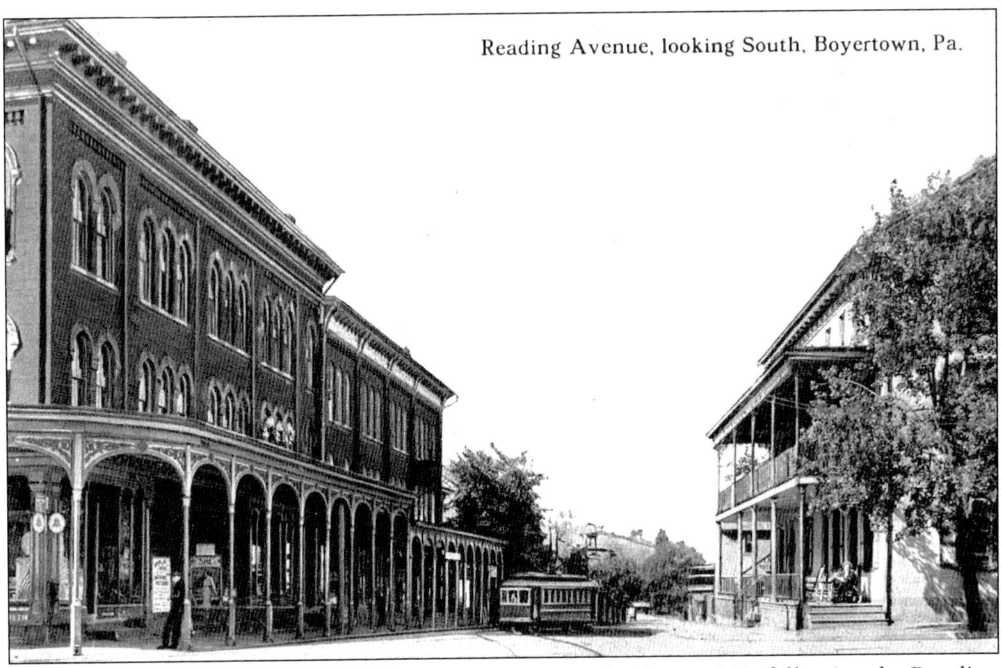

One enters Boyertown on South Reading Avenue, now also Route 562, following the Reading Trolley Line whose car can be seen in the distance.

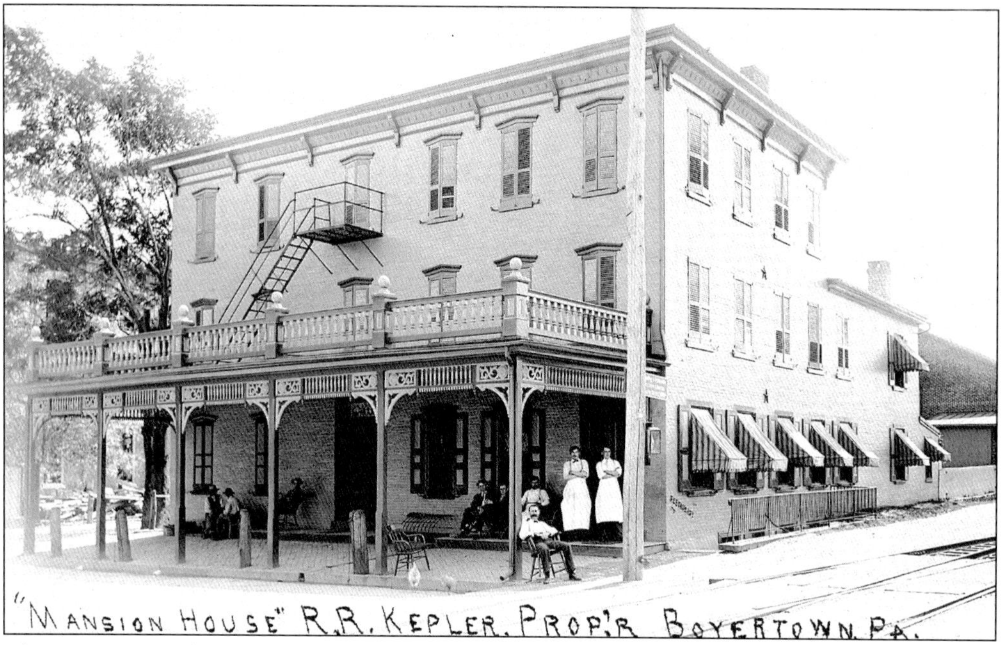

This view passes the Mansion House where R. R. Kepler was the proprietor at the time of this real-photo postcard.

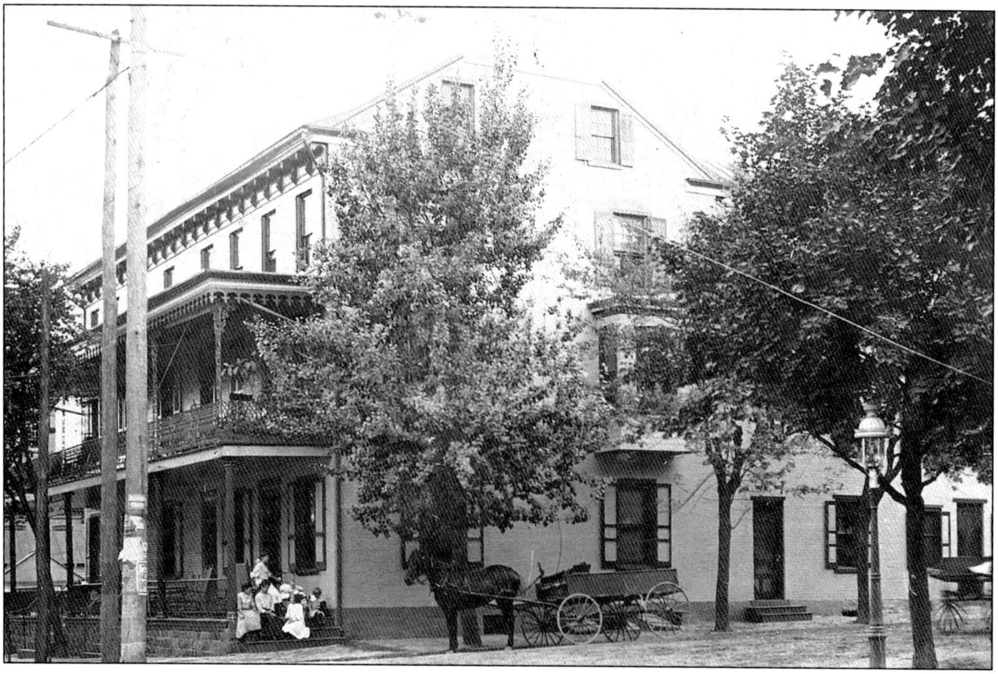
Continuing north along South Reading Avenue, the Union House is pictured here in 1907. It was built in 1855.

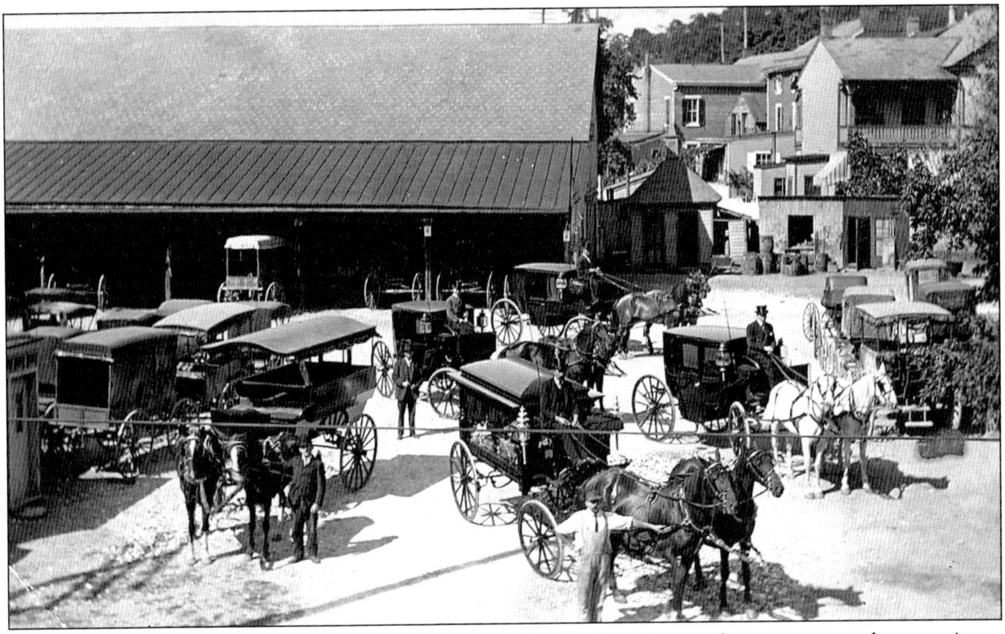

Behind the Union House, now the Boyertowne Inn, there is much room to park a carriage. The Union House was a very important meeting place for the residents of Boyertown. The first formal election of officials was held here following the incorporation of Boyertown in 1866. The Union Hotel was owned by Frederick Graff at that time.

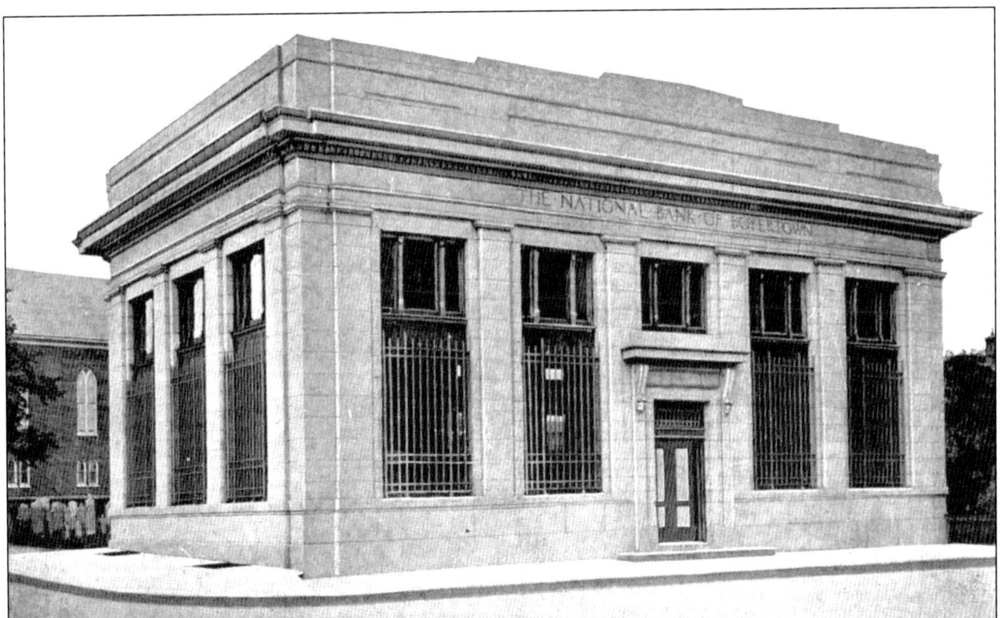

Just across Philadelphia Avenue on the northwest corner of the intersection is the National Bank of Boyertown, pictured here about 1915. A long-lasting, conservative institution, it lives on today as National Penn Bank and, with additions, utilizes the old bank in its operations.

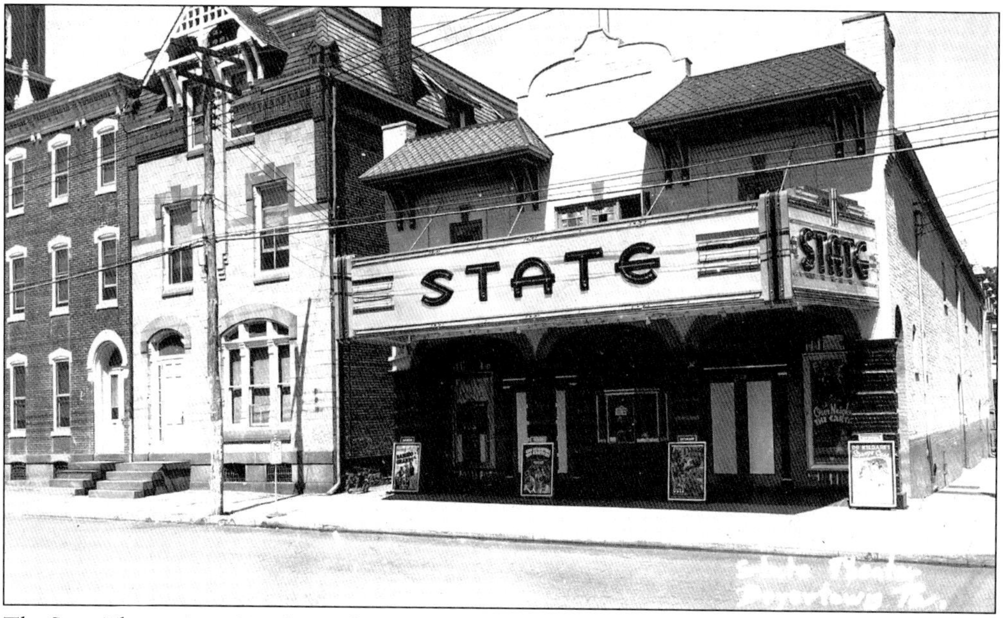

The State Theater is on North Reading Avenue. Of art deco design, it continues to show second-run films at greatly reduced prices. It is a great old theater, and going there is a real treat. It is certainly one of the few single movie houses to have survived the advent of the multiscreen theaters.

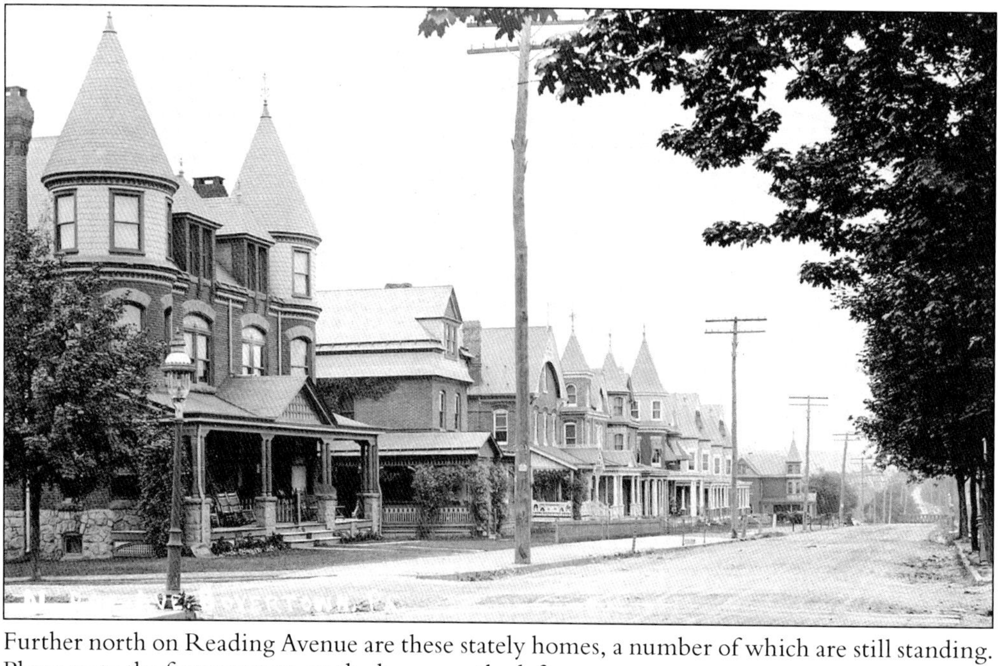

Further north on Reading Avenue are these stately homes, a number of which are still standing. Please note the fancy turrets on the home on the left.

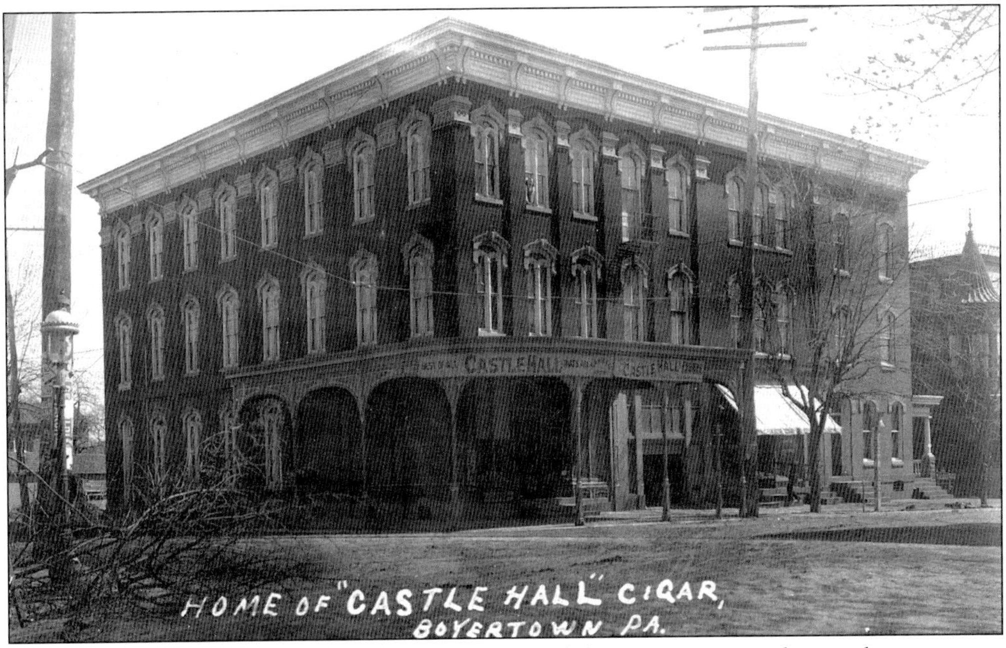

Going back to the corner of Reading and Philadelphia Avenues, on the northeast corner, is the home of Castle Hall Cigars, shown here in 1908. Cigar making was an art, and its industry in Boyertown produced not only Castle Hall cigars but Henrietta, Cinco, Erb, and El Producto brands, thus employing many people of the area. This building is being utilized today by other businesses.

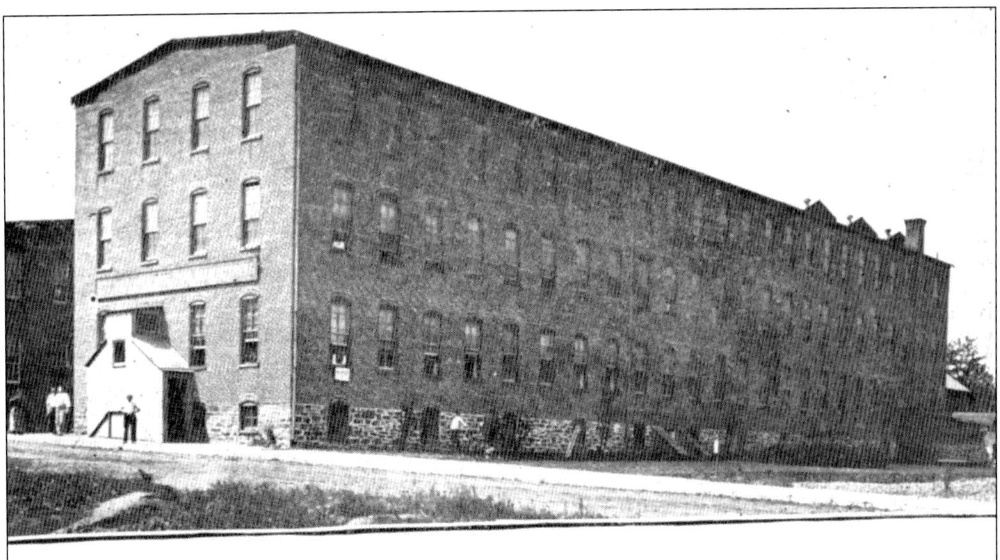

OTTO EISENLOHR'S CIGAR FACTORY, BOYERTOWN, PA.

Otto Eisenlohr's factory was capable of producing 100,000 cigars per day. Here is one of his factory's buildings. Eisenlohr began his business in 1864 at Fifth and Walnut Streets.

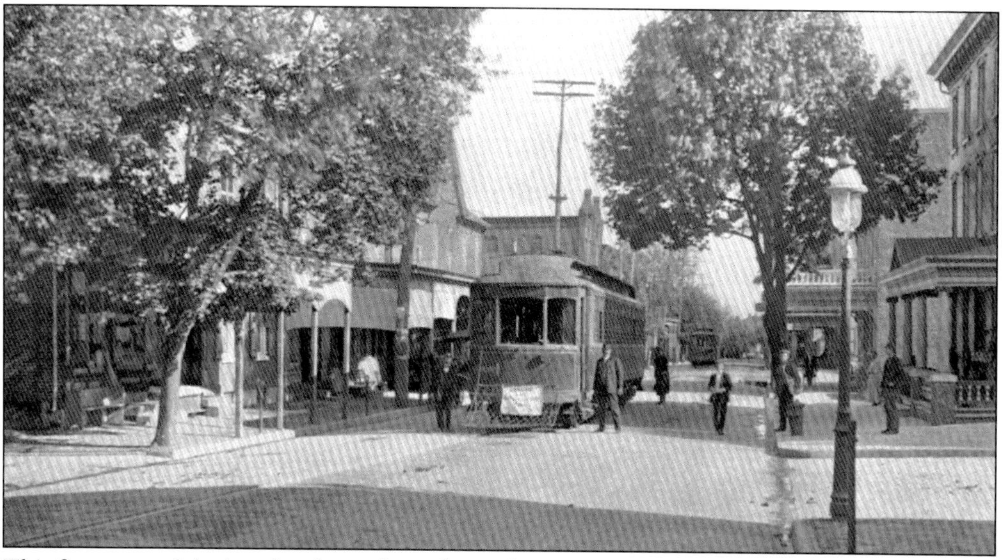

This famous card depicts the place where the trolley from Reading and the one from Pottstown would meet. There one would change cars to continue to one's destination, as it has been said that the cars could not legally use one another's lines.

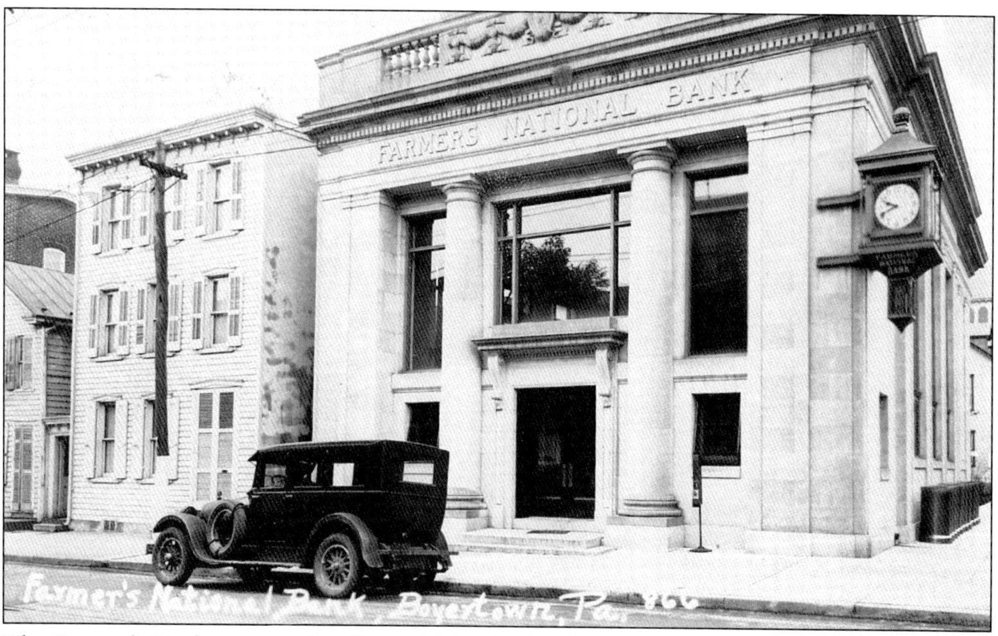

The Farmer's Bank was another financial institution in Boyertown. This card is from about 1922, judging by the vehicle shown in front of it. The bank has changed names a few times over the years, but the building is still being used as a bank. The building on the left has been razed for a drive-up window.

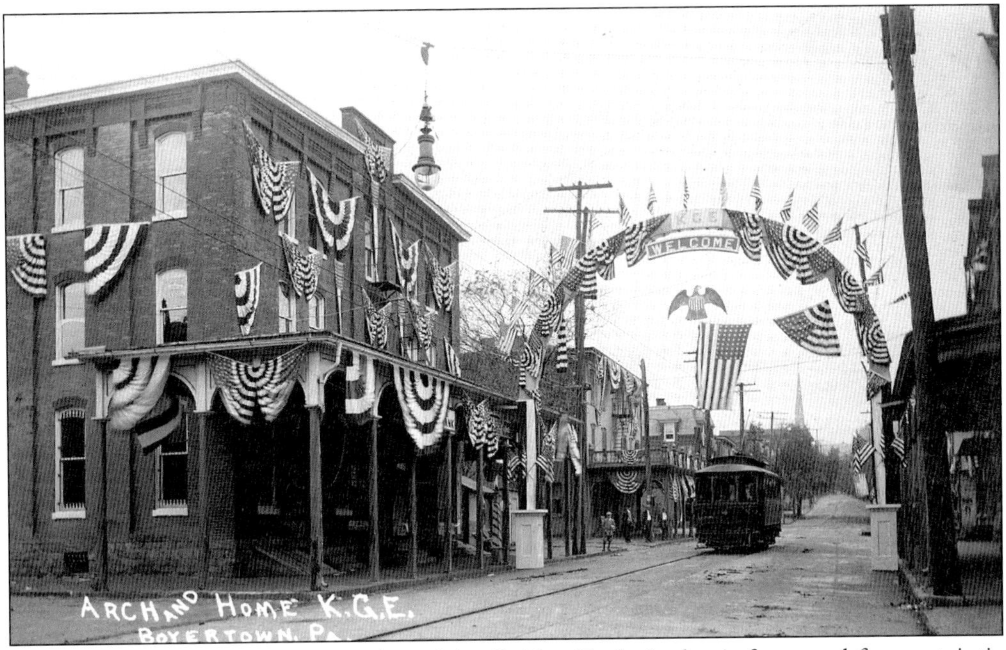

Here is another parade. The Knights of the Golden Eagle Lodge is festooned for a patriotic holiday. The trolley car lends a nice photographic touch to the picture.

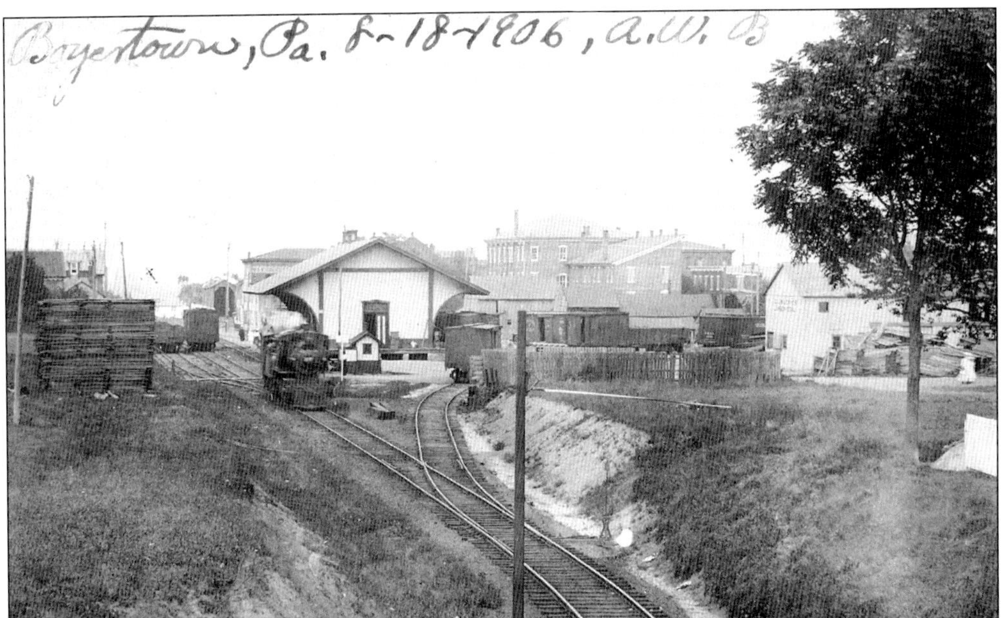

The Boyertown railroad depot is found on this card. The writer of the card very kindly identified the time period as 1906. A great old steam locomotive is puffing its way down the track.

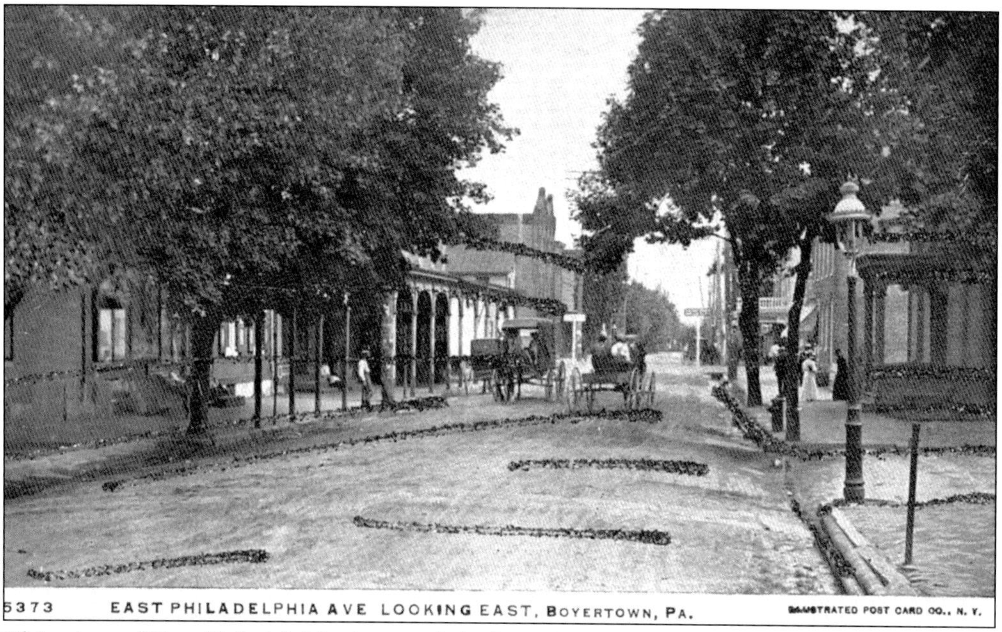

This view of East Philadelphia Avenue is before 1907. No trolley tracks are apparent here, revealing that it is a very early card. The only street congestion appears to be two horses and wagons. The trolley transfer service came into existence in 1908.

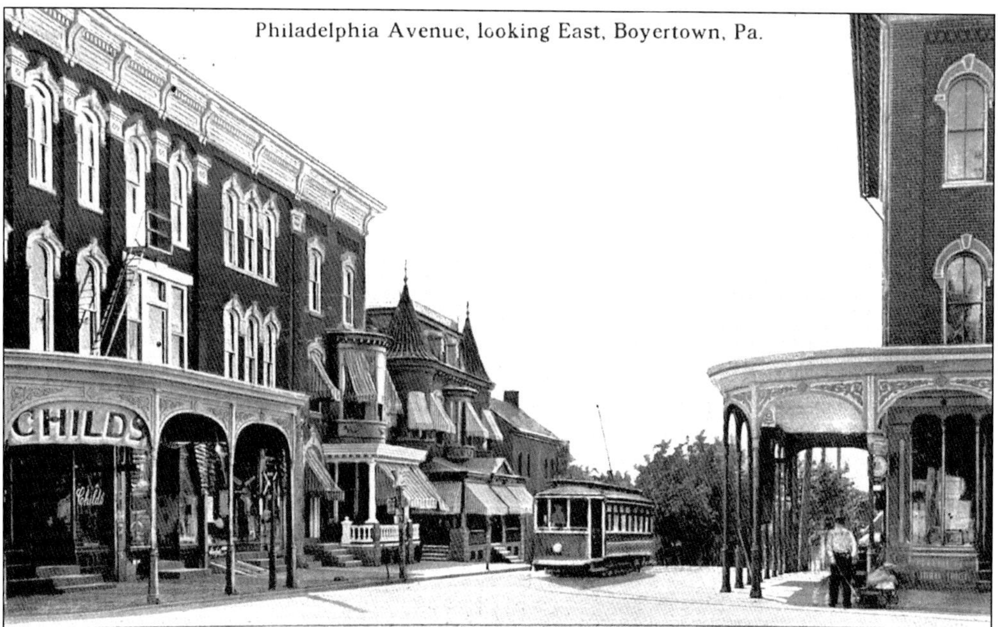

Graeff's Drug Store was in this location in 1914. This card is also a good advertisement for the Child's Store. Graeff sent this card as a promotion for his establishment.

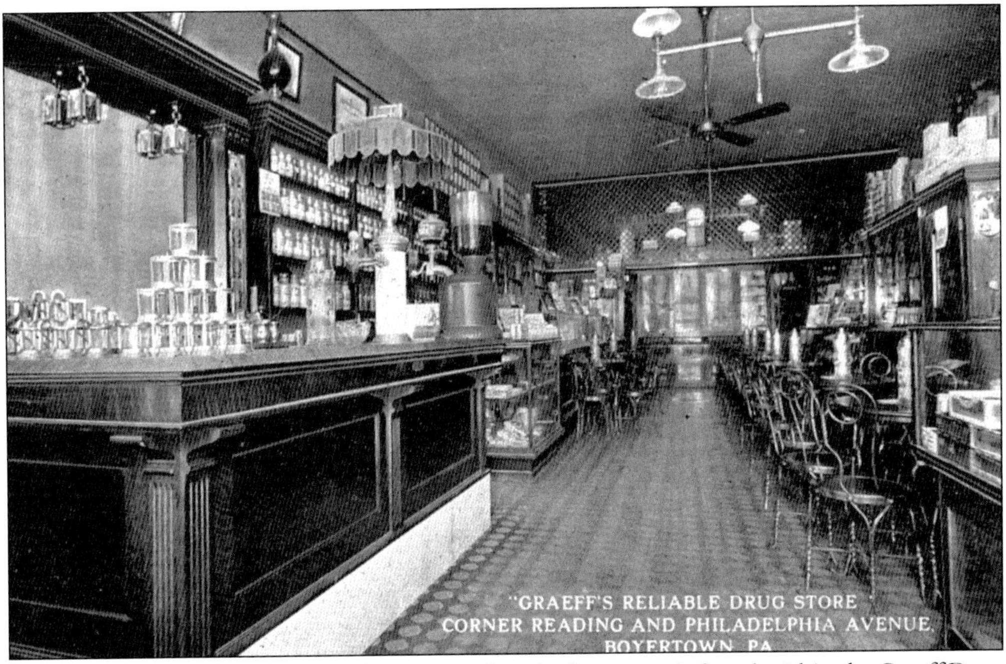

The magnificent interior of one of Boyertown's early drugstores is found within the Graeff Drug Store. In addition to the drugs and sundries, an ice-cream concoction or soda fountain delight could be obtained here. Sit-down dining was also offered on the great ice-cream parlor furniture.

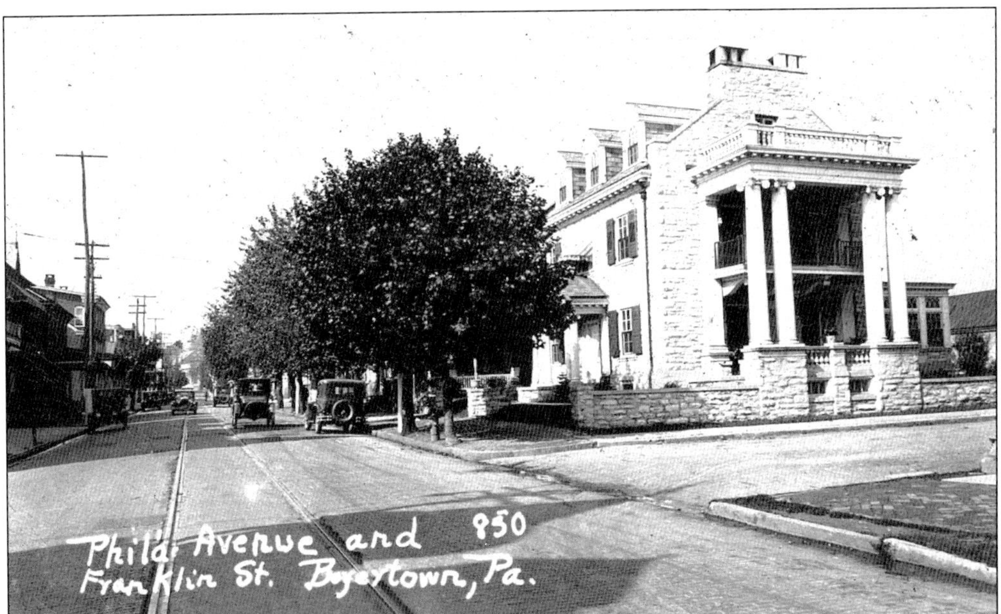

A 1920s view of Philadelphia Avenue at Franklin Street is seen here. This lovely home is still standing on the corner.

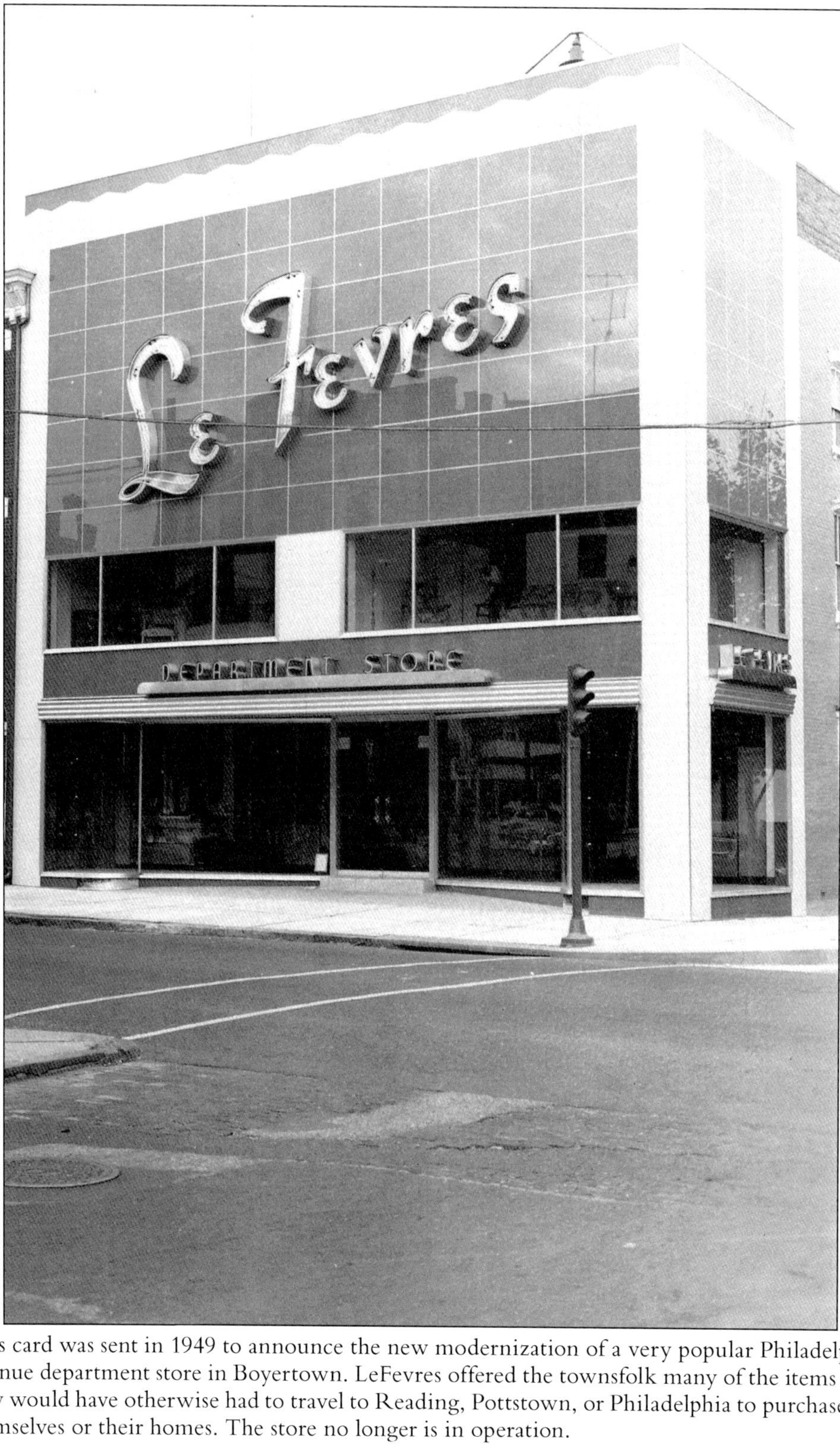

This card was sent in 1949 to announce the new modernization of a very popular Philadelphia Avenue department store in Boyertown. LeFevres offered the townsfolk many of the items that they would have otherwise had to travel to Reading, Pottstown, or Philadelphia to purchase for themselves or their homes. The store no longer is in operation.

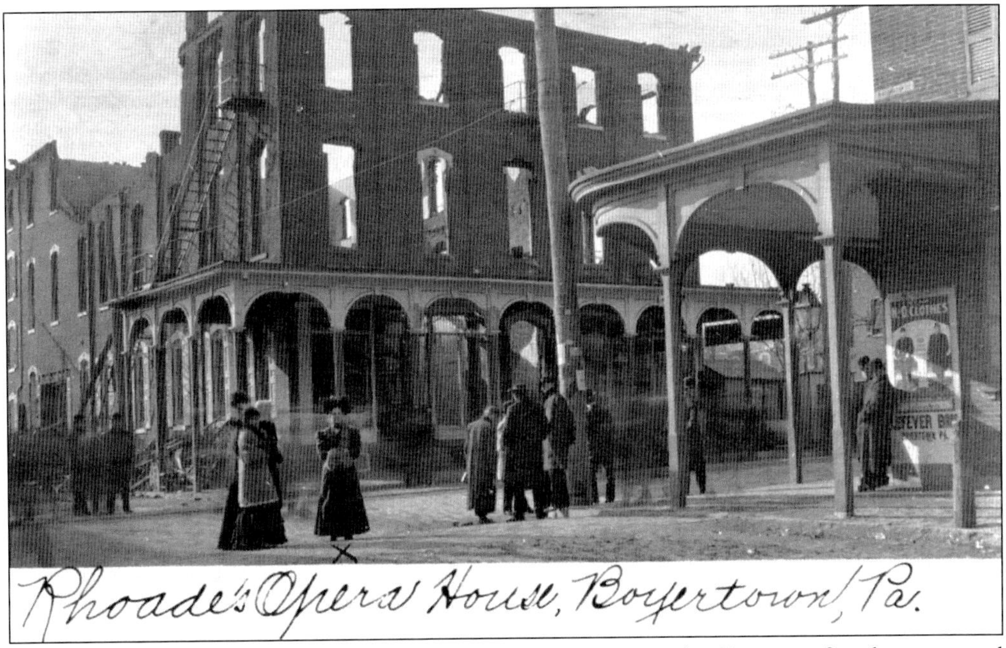

No visit to Boyertown would be complete without mentioning the disastrous fire that occurred at the Rhoade's Opera House on January 13, 1908. The opera house was located on East Philadelphia Avenue at Washington Street. The writer of this card pointed out her cousin who obviously was spared.

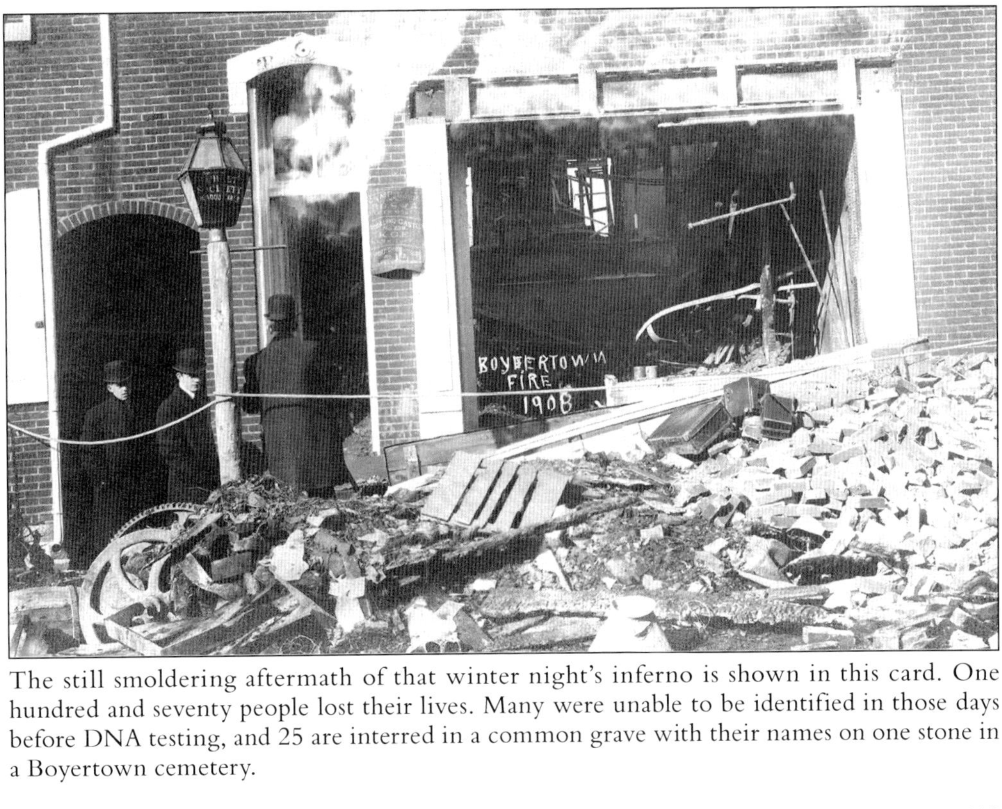

The still smoldering aftermath of that winter night's inferno is shown in this card. One hundred and seventy people lost their lives. Many were unable to be identified in those days before DNA testing, and 25 are interred in a common grave with their names on one stone in a Boyertown cemetery.

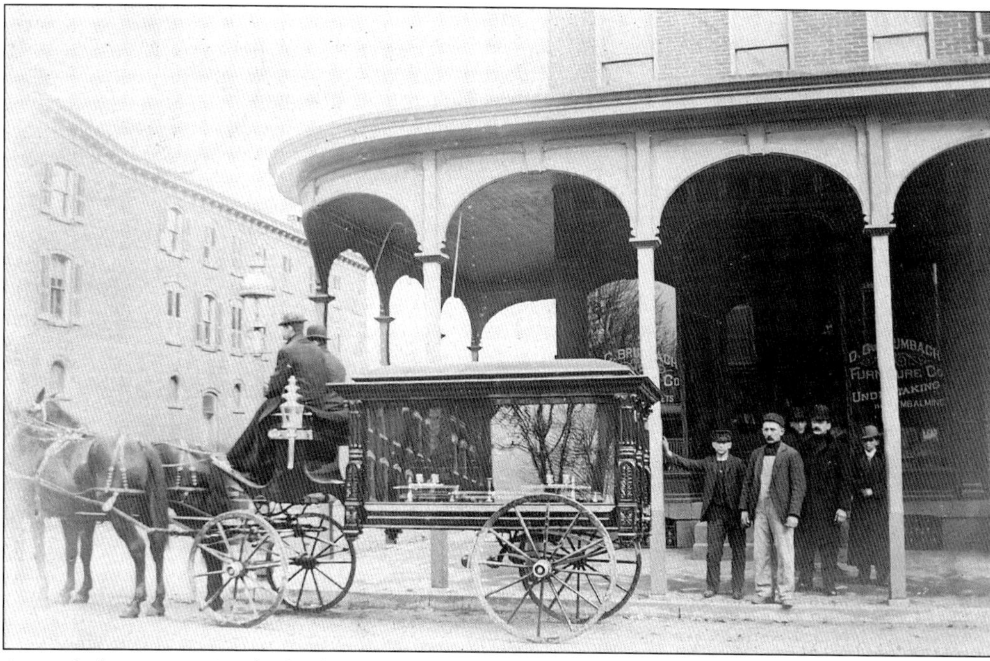

An early hearse carries the body of an unfortunate opera house attendee. Hardly a Boyertown family was spared grief by the loss of a member or friend. This unforgettable tragedy, so long ago, was instrumental in the passage of laws insuring the outward opening of all doors on public buildings. Had this law been present then, it is very likely that many more theatergoers would have survived the tragedy.

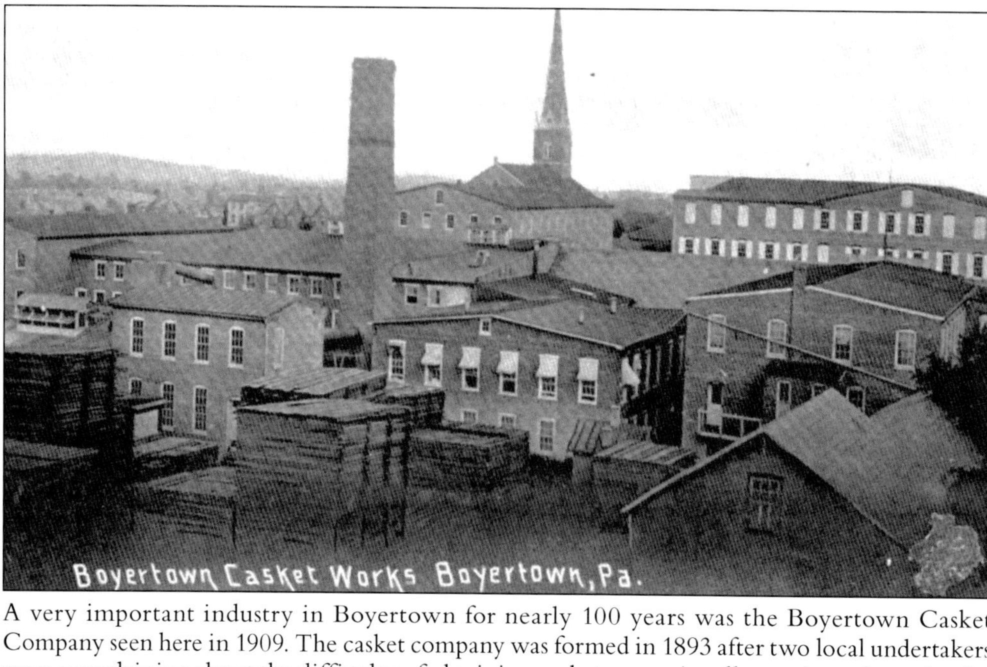

A very important industry in Boyertown for nearly 100 years was the Boyertown Casket Company seen here in 1909. The casket company was formed in 1893 after two local undertakers were complaining about the difficulty of obtaining caskets, occasionally causing a funeral to be postponed. The casket company is no longer a presence in Boyertown; the location has become the site of a beautiful home for the elderly.

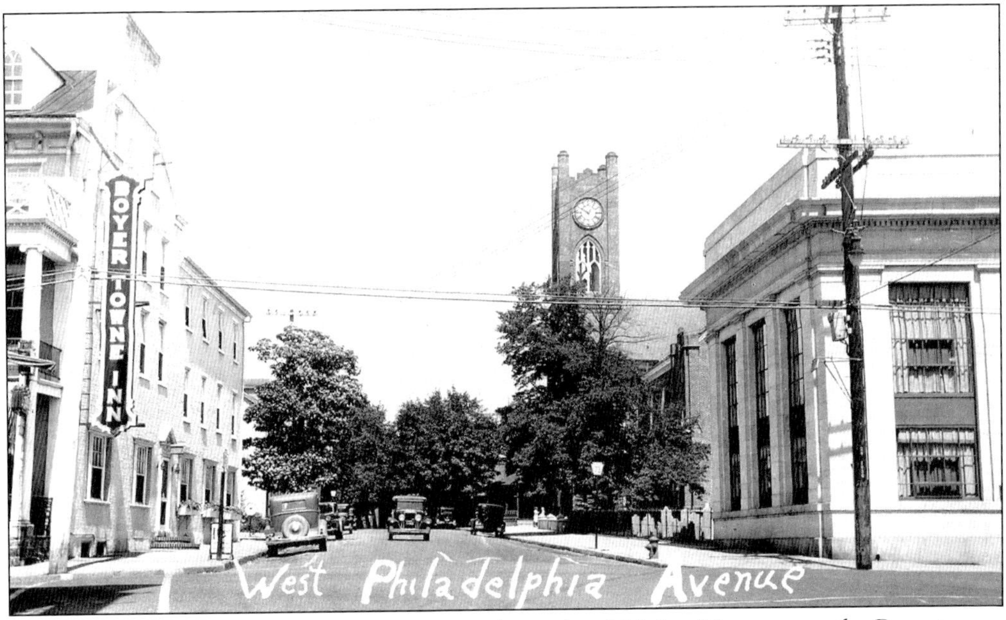

Going west on Philadelphia Avenue one sees the updated Union House, now the Boyertowne Inn. The National Bank remains on the corner, and the Good Shepherd Reformed Church is seen on the right.

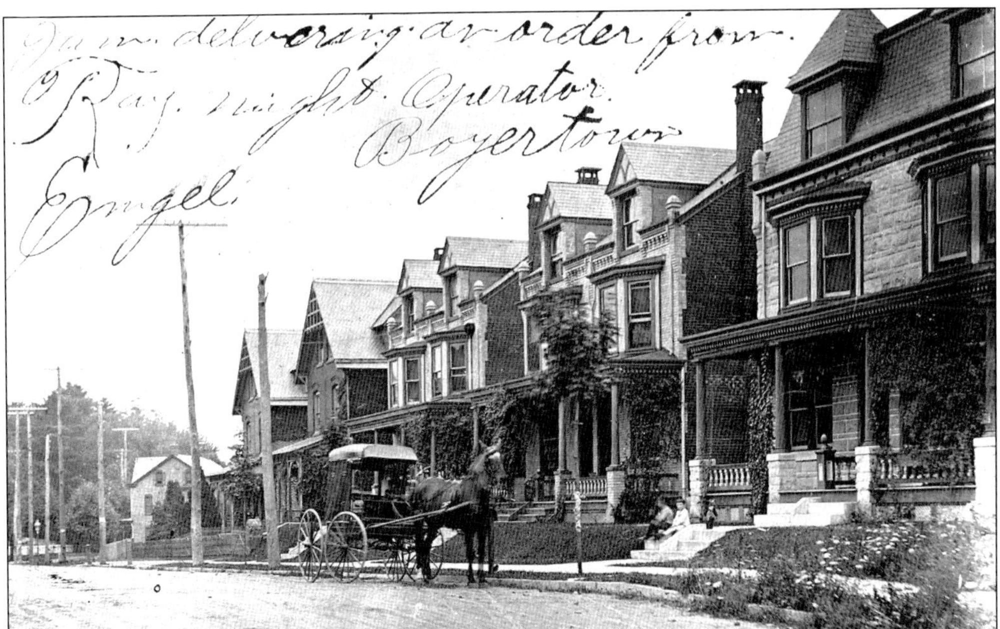

The author of this 1906 postcard proudly announced that he was delivering an order from Ray, the night operator. Telegram, money order, or another type of order is left to the imagination. It is, however, a good view of the homes along west Philadelphia Avenue at that earlier time.

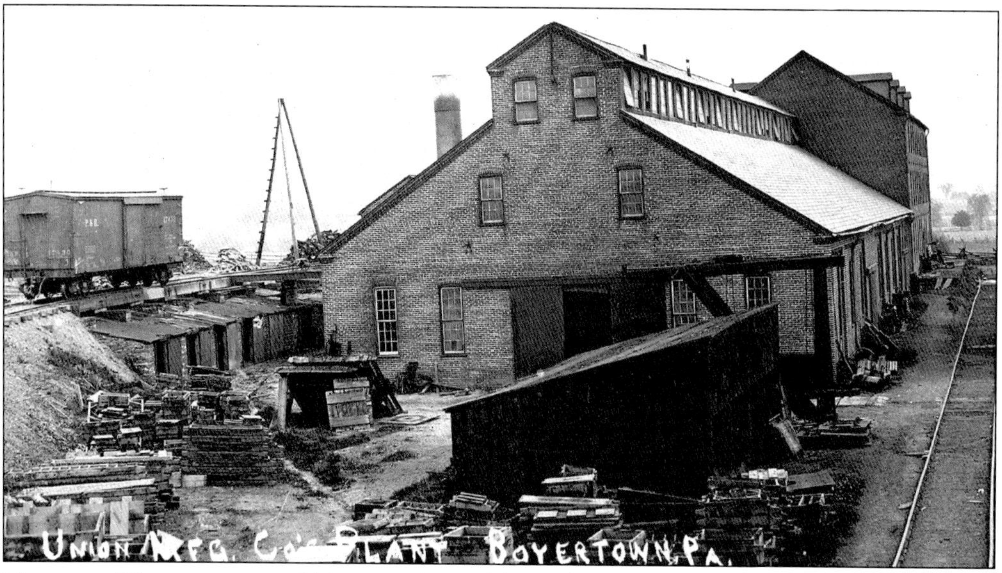

No tour of Boyertown would be complete without showing another industry that employed many of the town's residents. This is an early real-photo postcard of the Union Manufacturing Company at Sixth and Washington Streets. Begun in 1855, stoves and later furnaces were made here. An advertisement from the 1950s shows the production of novelty items and Pennsylvania Dutch souvenirs at this location.

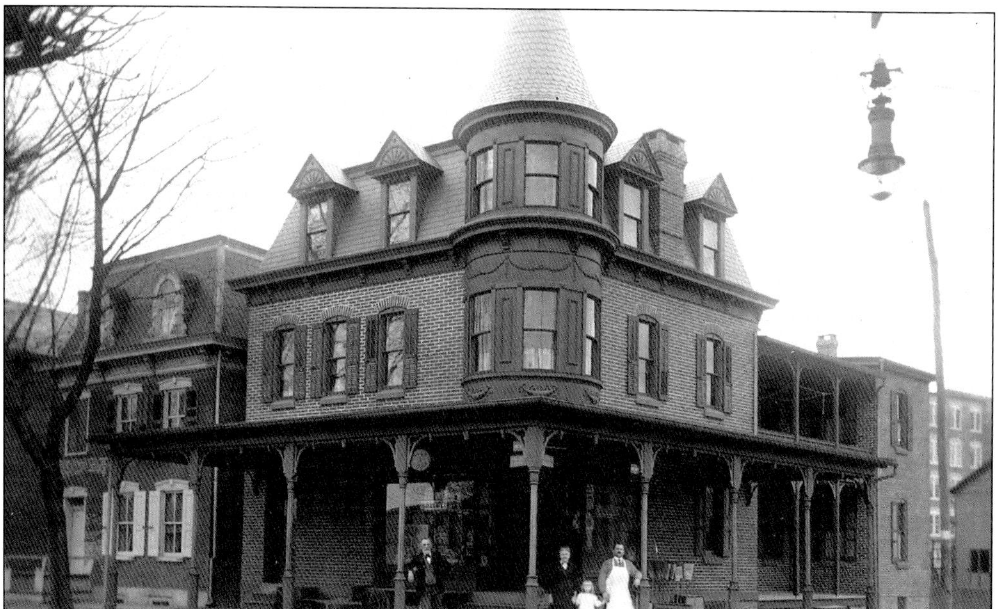

Leidy's Store was an important and thriving general store in the early 1900s era. It is assumed that Leidy, with his butcher's apron, is posed with his family or a few customers in front of his store on Philadelphia Avenue.

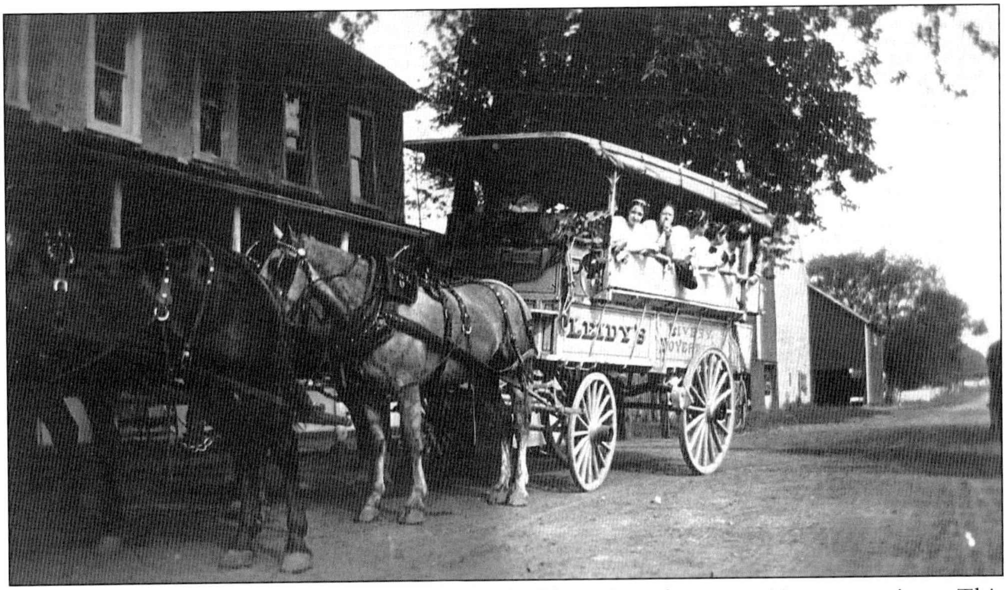

Leidy also provided a livery service. This would be likened to a bus or taxi in current times. This four-horse rig is pictured in front of the New Hanover Square Hotel in Montgomery County, just a few miles east of Boyertown.

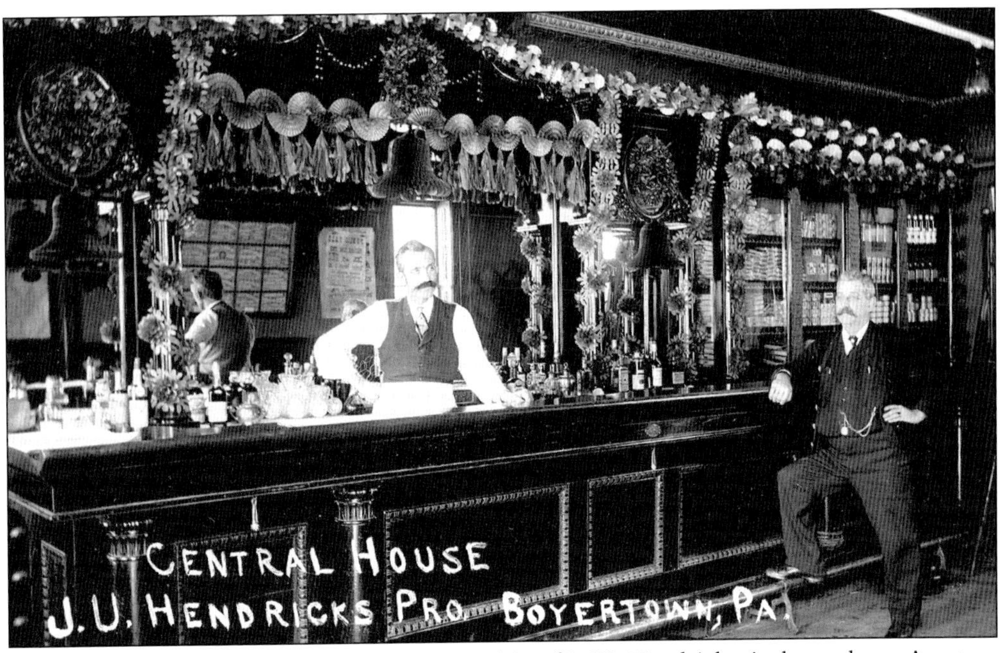

The Central House Bar, under the proprietorship of J. W. Hendricks, is shown here. A patron seems to be awaiting service at the holiday-decorated bar. The Central House was found at Philadelphia Avenue and Boyer Street.

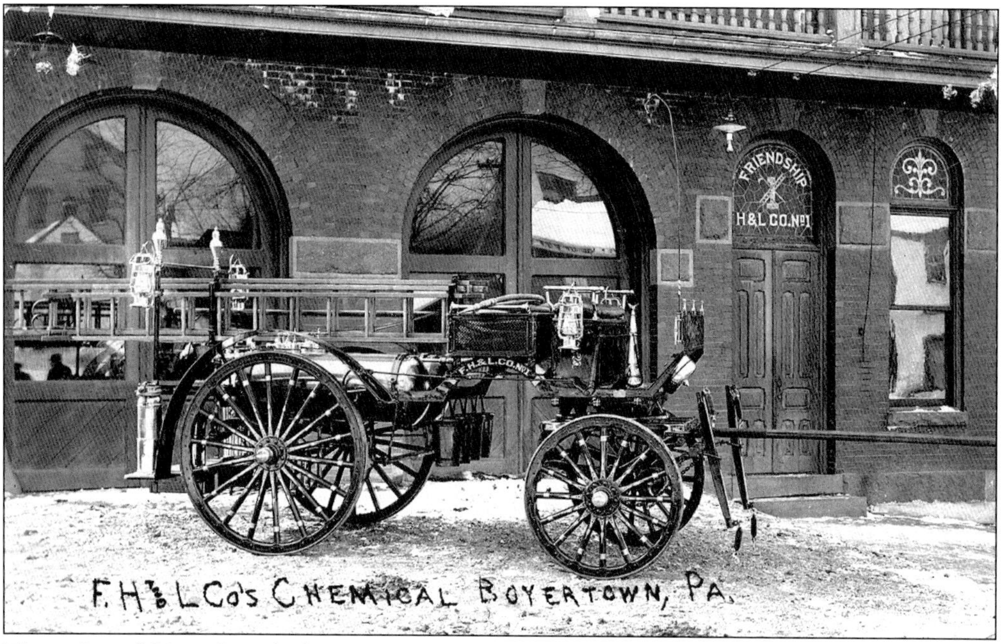

The writer of this early real-photo postcard identified this Friendship Hook and Ladder Chemical Engine as Friendship's first engine dating from 1888. In addition, this is also a nice view of the building housing the fire company, as well as this early piece of fire apparatus.

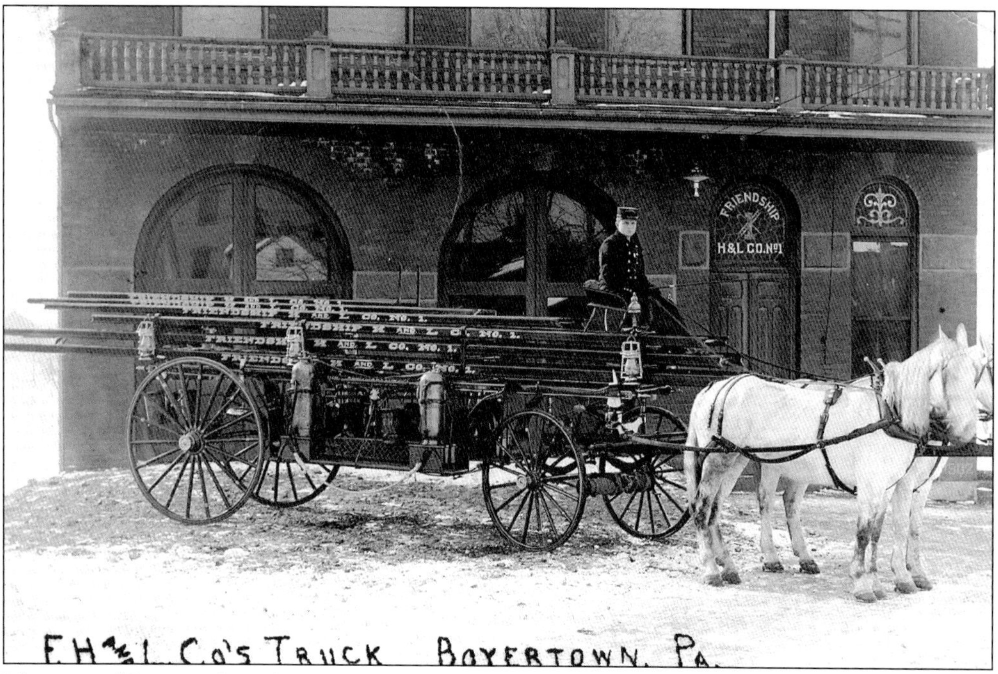

The Friendship Hook and Ladder Fire Company's ladder truck from 1910 is shown here with its team and driver.

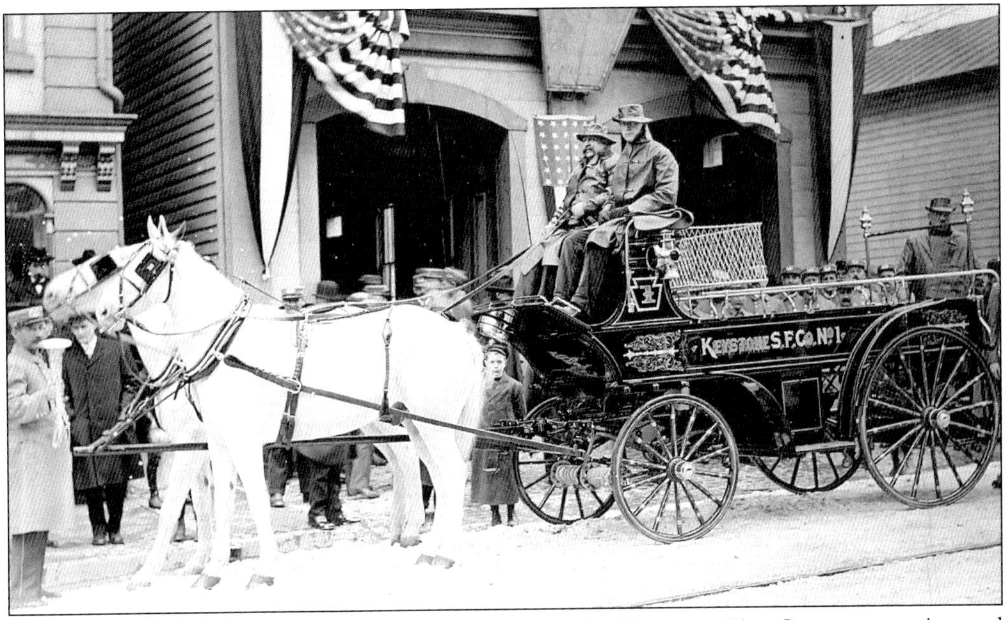

Not to be outdone by the Friendship Fire Company, the Keystone Fire Company engine and crew are pictured here in front of their building.

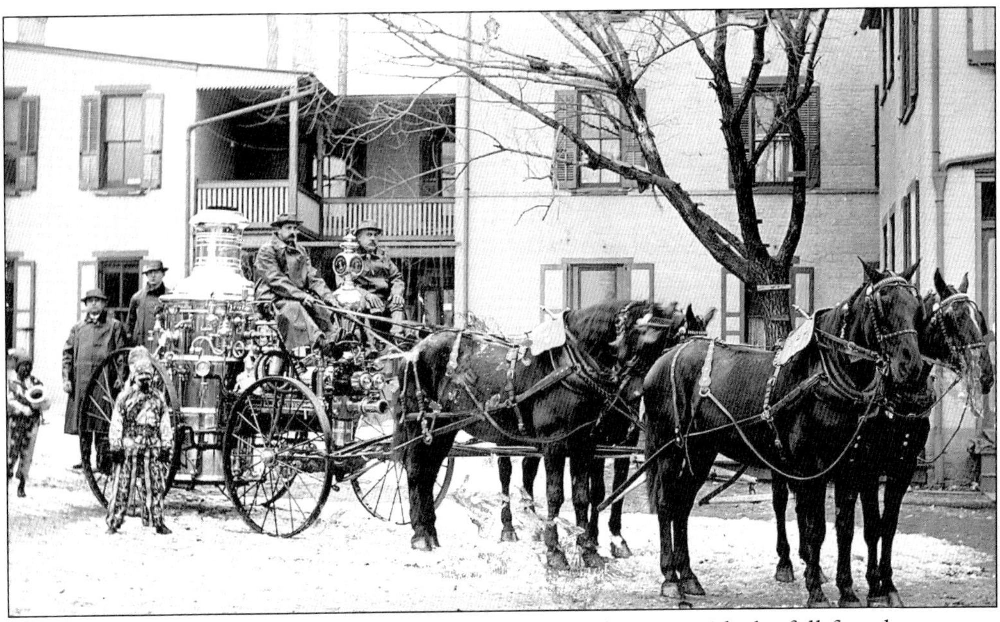

Another view of the Keystone Fire Company's engine shows it with the full four-horse team necessary for a rapid response to the community's needs. The Keystone Fire Company is still a viable part of the community, providing fire protection for the community with much more modern equipment.

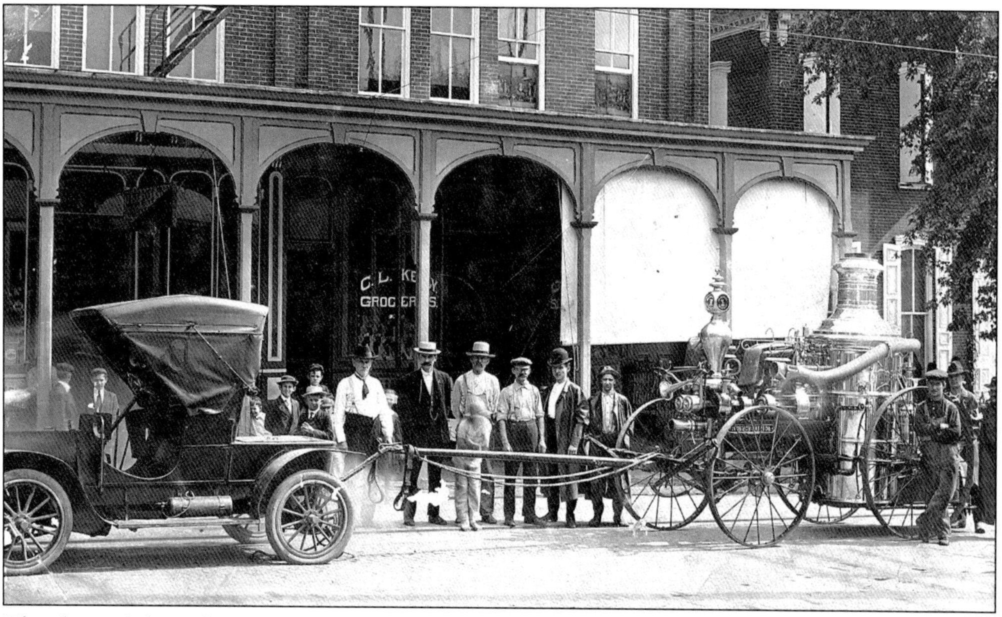

The doctor's horseless carriage is shown hitched to the Keystone Fire Company's engine. It is doubtful this is anything more than a joke on the doctor, who probably just got his first automobile. A grocery store is seen in the background.

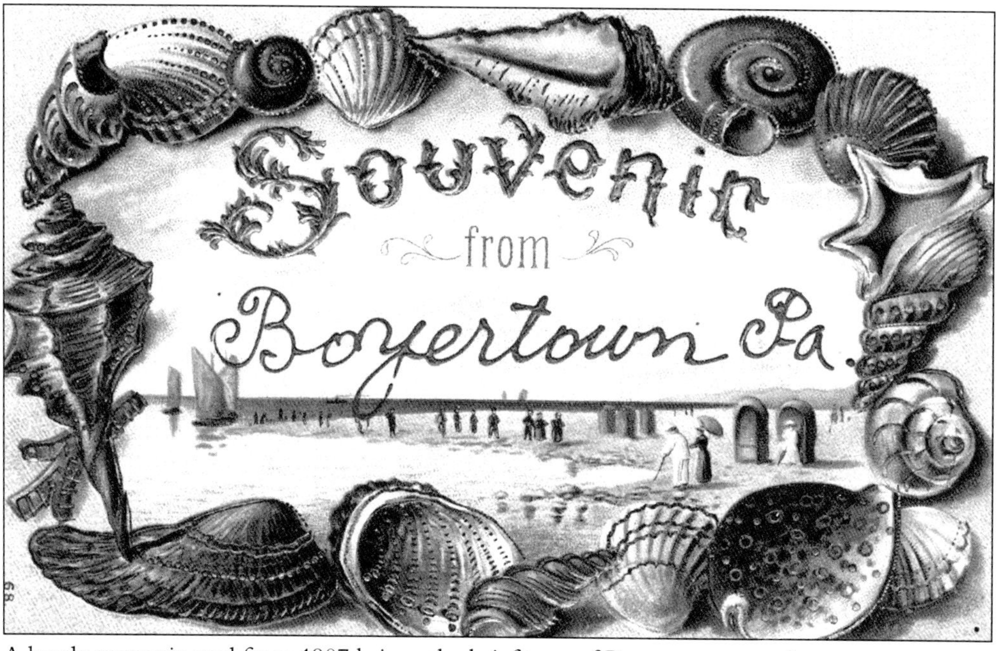

A lovely souvenir card from 1907 brings the brief tour of Boyertown to a close.

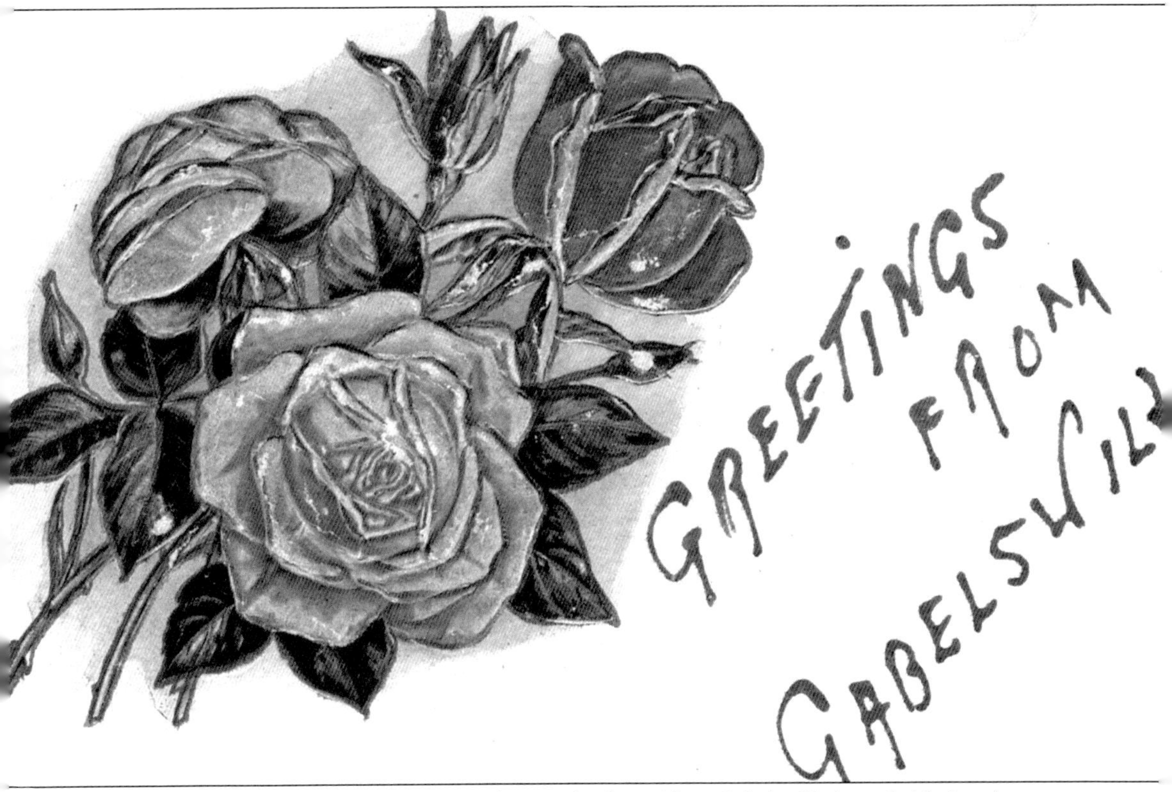

A nice welcome awaits in Gabelsville on the way back to Oley. Gabelsville is probably best known today for its great baseball field that lies next to the highway. The Boyertown area is a mecca for American Legion baseball players who are quite famous for their annual tournaments there.

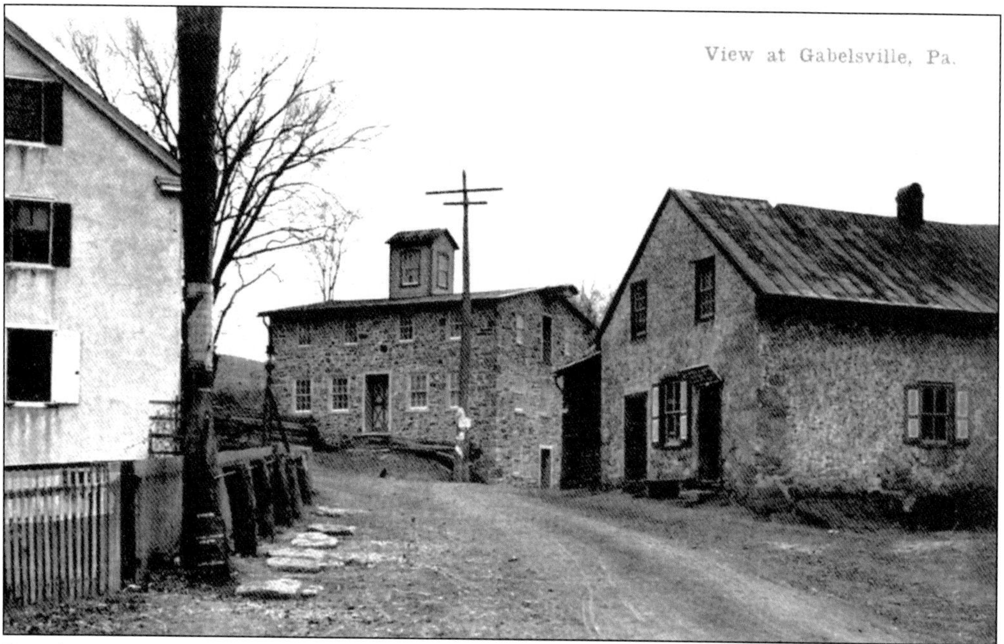

Seen here is a very early view of Gabelsville just off the present Route 73 north of Boyertown. Very early buildings are visualized in this crossroads picture. They are still standing.

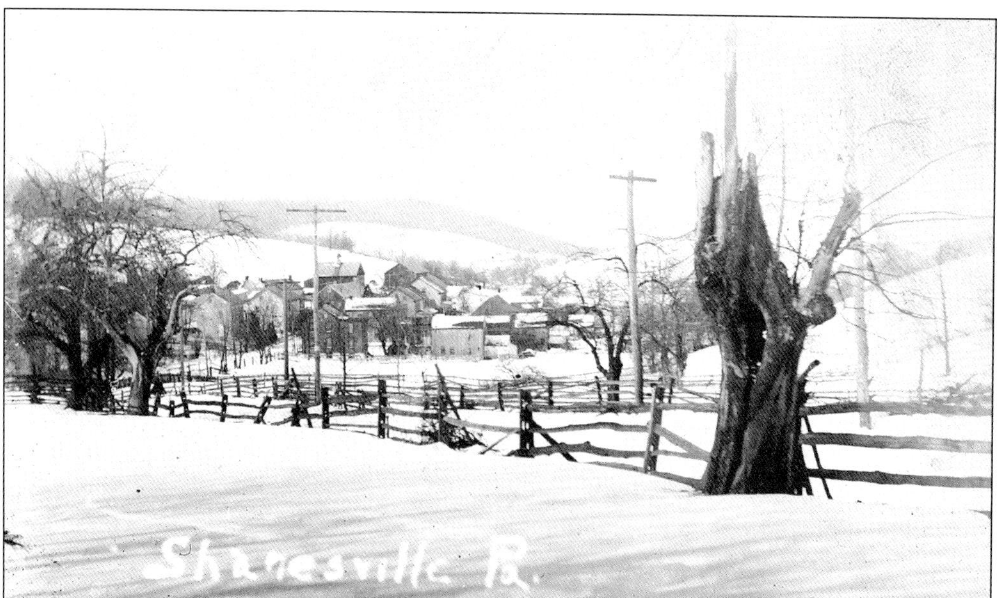

In the distance, on a snowy day, is the village of Shanesville along present Route 73. The broken-down tree, possibly an elm from the blight that scoured the area in the early 1900s, stands as mute evidence of times gone by.

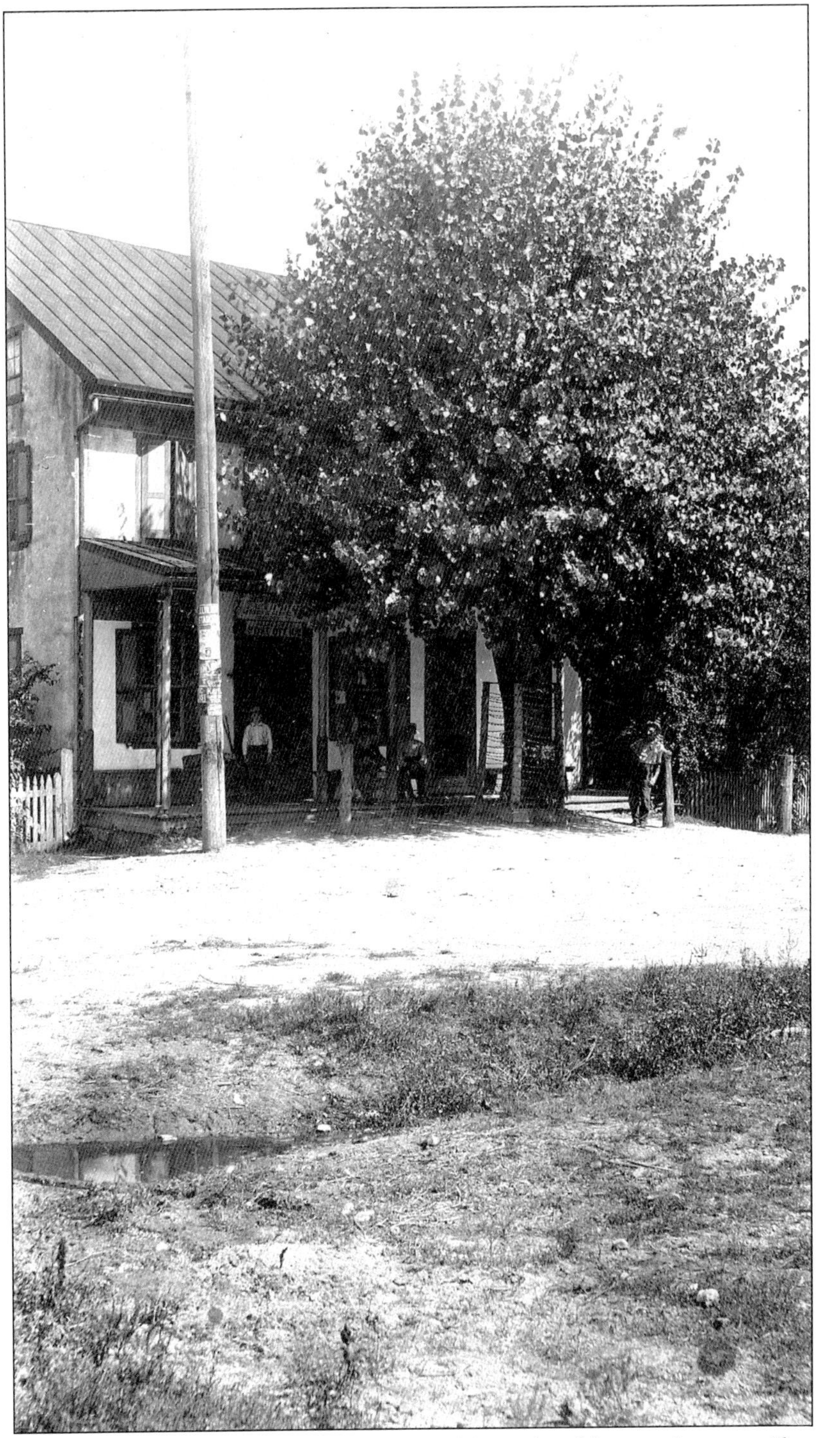

Although the tree in full leaf hides much of the building, the old general store at Shanesville is pictured here in this early card. No village would be complete without its general store, not only for its goods and services but also for the socialization with other residents in the area. News of births, deaths, illness, marriages, politics, and local and regional happenings were shared.

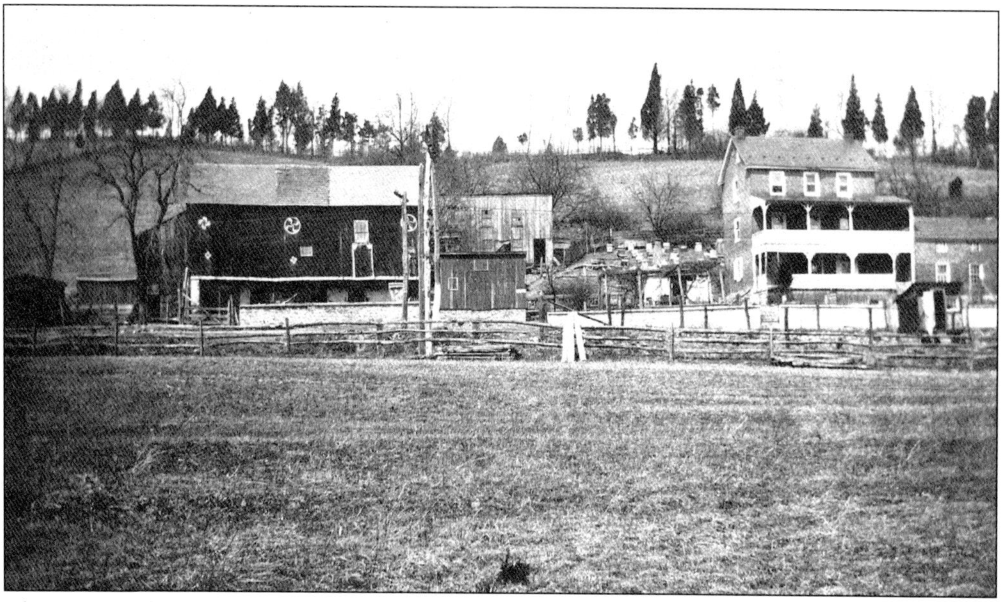

This is one of many farms that are located in the Shanesville area. Note the hex signs on the barn, an old Pennsylvania Dutch custom used to ward off the evil spirits. Many people use them today merely as decoration, but in days gone by, they served with real meaning to their owners. They believed that bad storms, lightning, blighted crops, and human illness could be averted with the use of the hex sign.

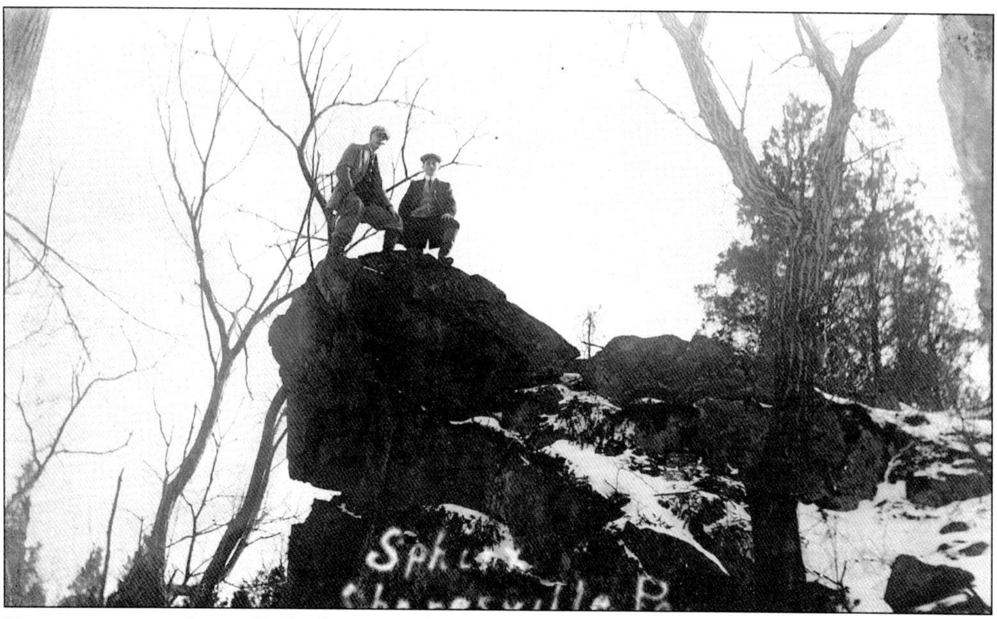

Two young men have climbed a natural outcropping of rocks near Shanesville. The profiled stones are aptly named the Sphinx.

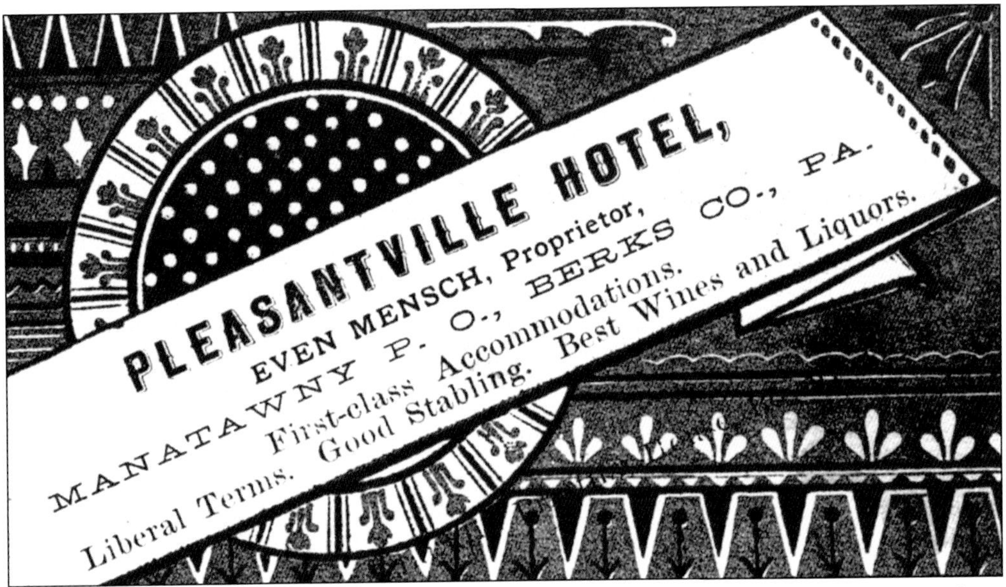

Over the years many have stopped for food and lodging at the Pleasantville Hotel, with its mailing address of Manatawny.

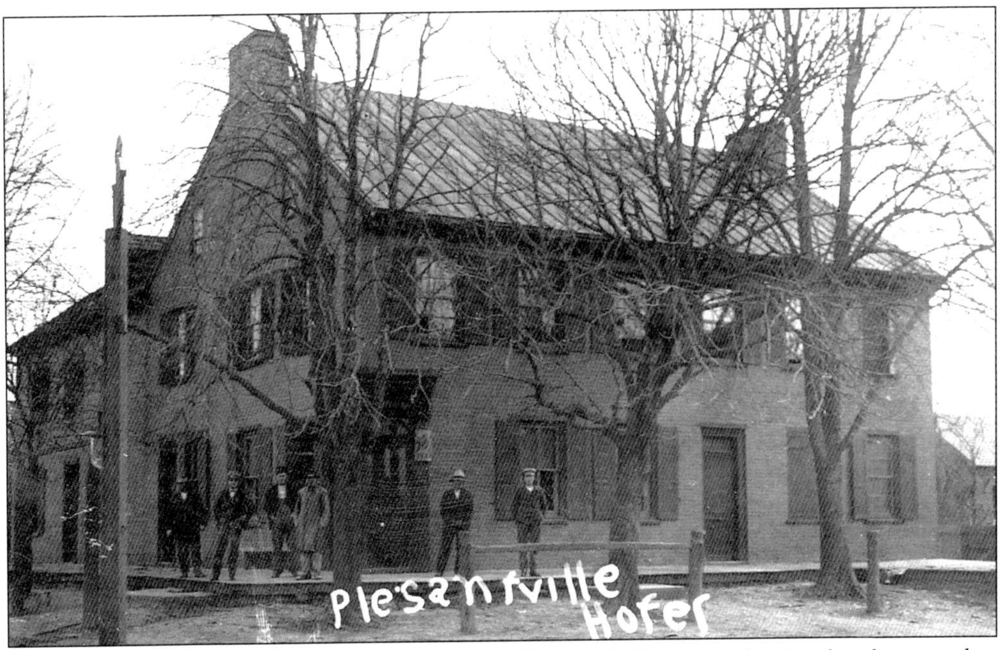

Seen here is a very early picture of the Pleasantville Hotel. One must forgive the photographer for his spelling. Perhaps the food and drink were just too good. It is still a great place to dine. The outside has been changed over the years, but one can still catch a glimpse of the earlier building along the roofline.

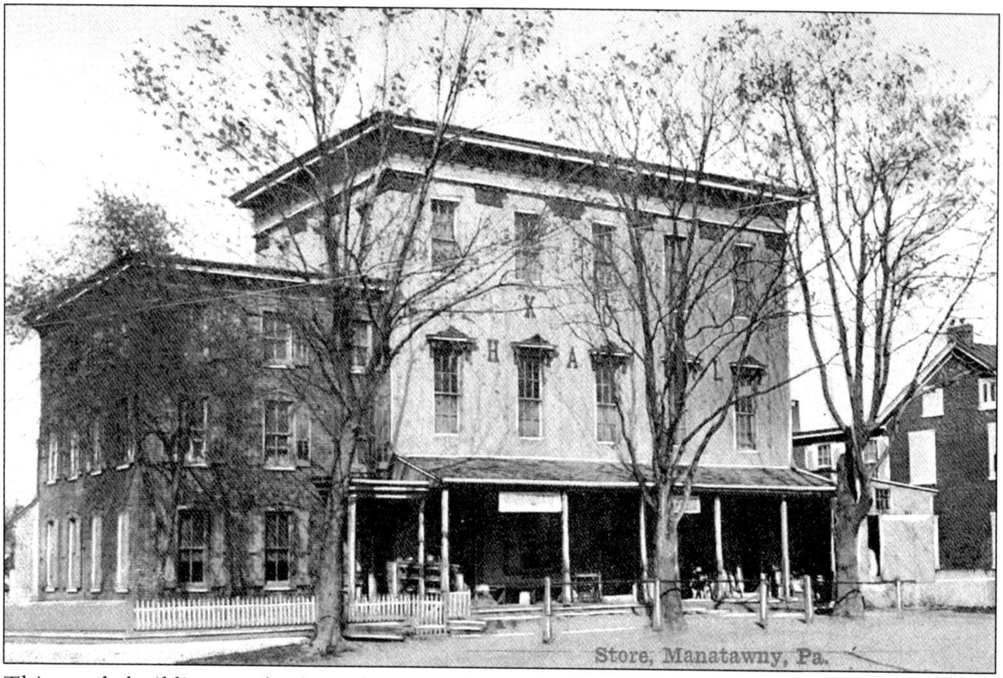

This stately building was built as a lodge with a general store shown operating on the first floor. It still stands along Route 73 about halfway between Boyertown and Oley. At this early date, the village was still known as Manatawny. Currently the village draws many visitors to it for its several businesses, including a delicious chocolate factory where, in the author's humble opinion, they make the best confections in the world.

Manatawny Temple, No. 33, L. G. E.

Manatawny, Pa. March 14, 1918.

Respected Companion:——

You are hereby notified of the death of Charles F., husband of Companion Odella Clouser. Funeral Tuesday, March 19, at 9.30 A. M. from the residence of his parents at Griesemersville. Interment at Oley Churches.

Note that you are assessed 30 cents as funeral tax.

A Boom Session

will be held on Saturday evening, April 6. Enclosed find application card.

Bring an applicant, also lunch basket. "Whoop-it-up-Campaign."

Yours fraternally,

Lydia Y. Hafer, G. of R. Elsie Freeman, N.T.

Here is a card sent to members of the Manatawny Temple. As was the custom in farming and other communities, the deceased was laid out in a private residence, this time at the home of his parents. It seems somewhat humorous to discuss a funeral in one paragraph and then a "whoop-it-up" campaign in the next.

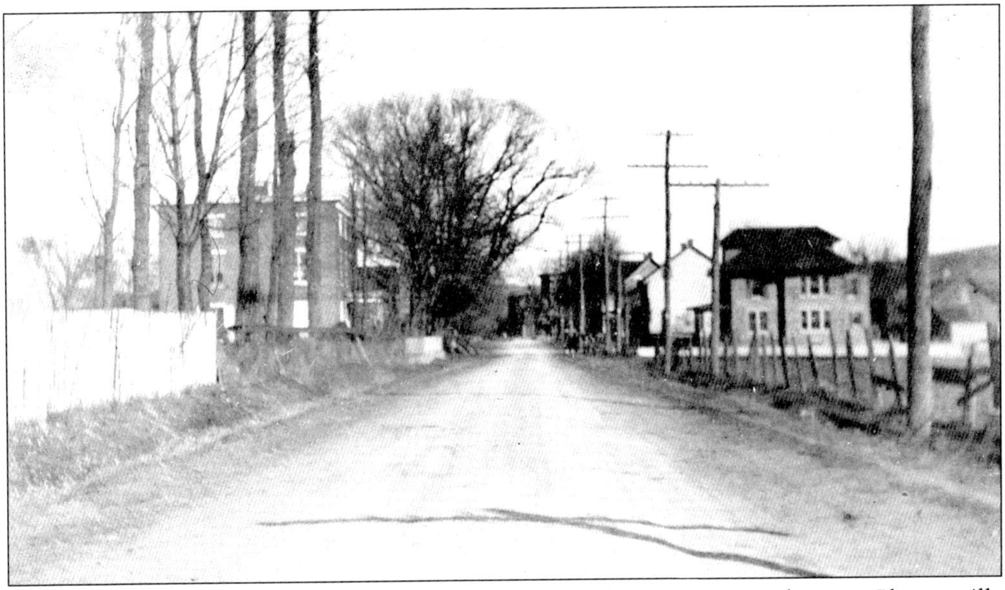

Covered Bridge Road is seen here leading to Pleasantville. In the distance is the store. Pleasantville will be the last stop on the way back to Oley. Although there is not a postcard depicting it, be sure to drive past the Griesemersville Hotel, now a store, on the return to Oley by way of Oley Turnpike Road. The Griesemers were a very early family to take up residency in the Oley Valley.

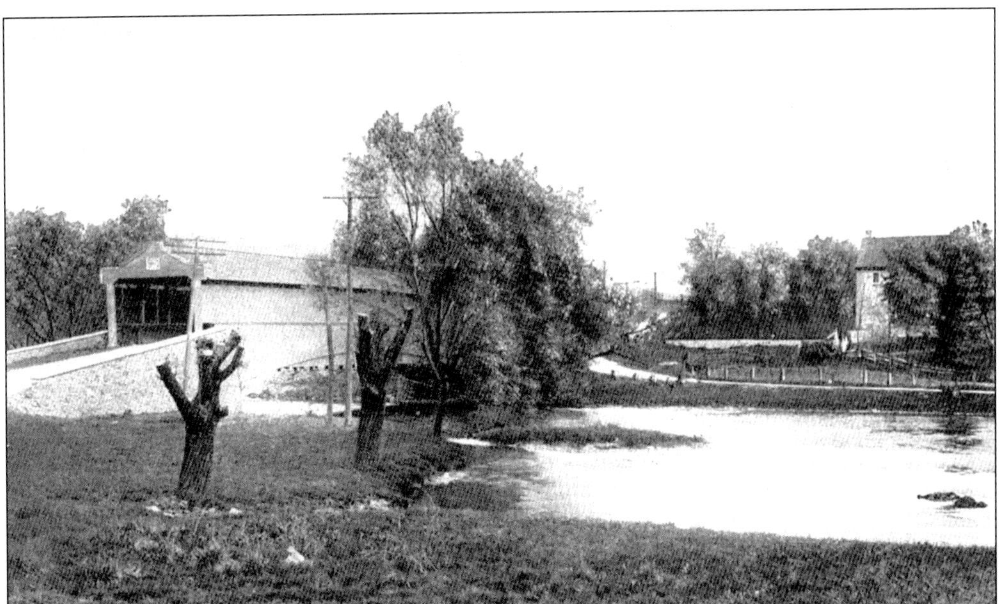

This is a picturesque scene of the covered bridge at Pleasantville. Although not the original, a covered bridge still spans the Manatawny Creek at this point.